Citizens, Participation and Media in Central and Eastern European Nations

Central and Eastern European (CEE) countries have faced significant political, economic, social and technological transformations over the last four decades. Democratic processes, after relative stabilization, have begun to tremble again around polarizing values, populist leaders or nationalistic ideologies. Online communication, especially social media platforms, play a vital role in shaping how citizens interact with the state, political actors, media and other citizens.

This book focuses on some of the challenges democratic institutions in CEE countries face in transforming and sustaining civil society and captures how the digital media environments mitigate or exacerbate those challenges. The chapters in this book focus on the role that online platforms play in shaping satisfaction with democracy in the CEE region, the interactions between journalists and political actors, the strategic media coverage of elections, affective polarization and political antagonism, and discursive attempts to discourage young people from civic engagement. The first section of the book looks at CEE countries from a comparative perspective, and the second section examines specific case studies within different CEE countries such as Albania and Kosovo, Czechia and Hungary, Poland and Ukraine.

This volume will be a key resource for scholars and researchers of communication studies, politics, media studies, sociology and CEE studies. The chapters in this book were originally published in the *Journal of Information, Technology & Politics*.

Karolina Koc-Michalska is Professor at Audencia Business School and Affiliated Researcher at CEVIPOF Sciences Po Paris, France, and University of Silesia, Poland. She studies the strategies of political actors in the online environment and citizens' political engagement. She employs a comparative approach focusing on the United States and European countries.

Darren Lilleker is Professor of Political Communication at Bournemouth University, United Kingdom; co-editor of the *Journal of Visual Political Communication*; and Director of the Centre for Comparative Politics and Media Research.

Christian Baden is Associate Professor at the Department of Communication and Journalism at the Hebrew University of Jerusalem. His research focuses on the collaborative construction of meaning in dynamic, political public debates, with specific emphasis on the modeling and measurement of textual discourse.

Damian Guzek is an associate professor in digital media and communication at the University of Silesia in Katowice. His research is driven by questions related to media consumption and digital media, religions and politics.

Márton Bene (Ph.D.) is a senior research fellow at the Centre for Social Sciences, Hungarian Academy of Sciences Centre of Excellence, and an assistant professor at the Faculty of Law, Eötvös Loránd University (ELTE), Hungary. His research interests are in political communication, social media and politics, and political behavior.

Larissa Doroshenko is Postdoctoral Teaching Associate at Northeastern University, United States. Her research interests are centered on the effects of new media on political campaigning, with a particular focus on "the dark side" of the Internet: populism, nationalism and disinformation campaigns.

Miloš Gregor is an assistant professor at the Department of Political Science, Faculty of Social Studies, Masaryk University, Czech Republic. He is dealing with topics such as political communication and marketing, propaganda, disinformation and fake news.

Marko M. Scoric is Associate Professor at the Department of Media and Communication, City University of Hong Kong, where he leads the Political Communication and Culture Research Cluster and acts as the Ph.D. Program Coordinator. His research interests are focused on new media and social change, with a particular emphasis on the civic and political implications of digital technologies. He holds a Ph.D. in communication from the University of Michigan and a B.Sc. in psychology from the University College London.

Citizens, Participation and Media in Central and Eastern European Nations

Edited by
Karolina Koc-Michalska, Darren Lilleker, Christian Baden,
Damian Guzek, Márton Bene, Larissa Doroshenko,
Miloš Gregor and Marko M. Scoric

NEW YORK AND LONDON

First published 2025
by Routledge
605 Third Avenue, New York, NY 10158

and by Routledge
4 Park Square, Milton Park, Abingdon, Oxon OX14 4RN

Routledge is an imprint of the Taylor & Francis Group, an informa business

Chapters 1 and 3–8 © 2024 Taylor & Francis
Chapter 6 © 2023 Alena Macková, Martina Novotná, Lucie Čejková, and Lenka Hrbková. Originally published as Open Access.
Chapter 9 © 2023 Lennart Maschmeyer, Alexei Abrahams, Peter Pomerantsev, and Volodymyr Yermolenko. Originally published as Open Access.
Introduction © 2025 Karolina Koc-Michalska, Darren Lilleker, Christian Baden, Damian Guzek, Márton Bene, Larissa Doroshenko, Miloš Gregor & Marko M. Scoric.

With the exception of Chapters 6 and 9, no part of this book may be reprinted or reproduced or utilised in any form or by any electronic, mechanical, or other means, now known or hereafter invented, including photocopying and recording, or in any information storage or retrieval system, without permission in writing from the publishers. For details on the rights for Chapters 6 and 9, please see the chapters' Open Access footnotes.

Trademark notice: Product or corporate names may be trademarks or registered trademarks, and are used only for identification and explanation without intent to infringe.

British Library Cataloguing in Publication Data
A catalogue record for this book is available from the British Library

ISBN13: 978-1-032-85231-7 (hbk)
ISBN13: 978-1-032-85232-4 (pbk)
ISBN13: 978-1-003-51720-7 (ebk)

DOI: 10.4324/9781003517207

Typeset in Minion Pro
by Newgen Publishing UK

Publisher's Note
The publisher accepts responsibility for any inconsistencies that may have arisen during the conversion of this book from journal articles to book chapters, namely the inclusion of journal terminology.

Disclaimer
Every effort has been made to contact copyright holders for their permission to reprint material in this book. The publishers would be grateful to hear from any copyright holder who is not here acknowledged and will undertake to rectify any errors or omissions in future editions of this book.

Contents

Citation Information vii
Notes on Contributors ix

Introduction: *Citizens, Participation and Media in Central and Eastern European Nations* 1
Karolina Koc-Michalska, Darren Lilleker, Christian Baden, Damian Guzek, Márton Bene,
Larissa Doroshenko, Miloš Gregor, and Marko M. Scoric

PART I
Central and Eastern Europe in a comparative perspective

1 Social media, quality of democracy, and citizen satisfaction with democracy in Central
  and Eastern Europe 9
  Matthew Placek

2 Patterns of negative campaigning during the 2019 European election: Political parties'
  Facebook posts and users' sharing behaviour across twelve countries 26
  *Paweł Baranowski, Simon Kruschinski, Uta Russmann, Jörg Haßler, Melanie Magin,
  Márton Bene, Andrea Ceron, Daniel Jackson, and Darren Lilleker*

3 One conflict, two public spheres, three national debates: Comparing the value conflict over
  judicial independence in Europe across print and social media 43
  Stefan Wallaschek, Kavyanjali Kaushik, and Monika Eigmüller

PART II
Country case studies

4 Interactive election campaigns on social media? Flow of political information among
  journalists and politicians as an element of the communication strategy of political actors 61
  Kinga Adamczewska

5 The audience logic in election news reporting on Facebook: What drives audience engagement
  in transitional democracies of Albania and Kosovo? 76
  Lindita Camaj, Erlis Çela, and Gjylie Rexha

6 One way or another? Discussion disagreement and attitudinal homogeneity on social
  networking sites as pathways to polarization in Czechia 92
  Alena Macková, Martina Novotná, Lucie Čejková, and Lenka Hrbková

7 Soros's soldiers, slackers, and pioneers with no expertise? Discursive exclusion
  of environmental youth activists from the digital public sphere in Hungary and Czechia   107
  Lenka Vochocová, Jana Rosenfeldová, Anna Vancsó, and Annamária Neag

8 Like, share, comment, and repeat: Far-right messages, emotions, and amplification
  in social media   122
  Larissa Doroshenko and Fangjing Tu

9 Donetsk don't tell: 'Hybrid war' in Ukraine and the limits of social media influence operations   139
  Lennart Maschmeyer, Alexei Abrahams, Peter Pomerantsev, and Volodymyr Yermolenko

   Index   155

Citation Information

The following chapters in this book were originally published in various issues and volumes of the *Journal of Information, Technology & Politics*. When citing this material, please use the original page numbering for each article, as follows:

Chapter 1
Social media, quality of democracy, and citizen satisfaction with democracy in central and eastern Europe
Matthew Placek
Journal of Information, Technology & Politics, volume 24 issue 1 (2024), pp. 6–22

Chapter 2
Patterns of Negative Campaigning during the 2019 European Election: Political Parties' Facebook Posts and Users' Sharing Behaviour across Twelve Countries
Paweł Baranowski, Simon Kruschinski, Uta Russmann, Jörg Haßler, Melanie Magin, Bene Márton, Andrea Ceron, Daniel Jackson, and Darren Lilleker
Journal of Information, Technology & Politics, volume 20 issue 4 (2023), pp. 375–392

Chapter 3
One conflict, two public spheres, three national debates: comparing the value conflict over judicial independence in Europe across print and social media
Stefan Wallaschek, Kavyanjali Kaushik, and Monika Eigmüller
Journal of Information, Technology & Politics, volume 21 issue 3 (2024), pp. 288–302

Chapter 4
Interactive Election Campaigns on Social Media? Flow of Political Information Among Journalists and Politicians as an Element of the Communication Strategy of Political Actors
Kinga Adamczewska
Journal of Information, Technology & Politics, volume 21 issue 1 (2024), pp. 23–37

Chapter 5
The audience logic in election news reporting on Facebook: what drives audience engagement in transitional democracies of Albania and Kosovo?
Lindita Camaj, Erlis Çela, and Gjylie Rexha
Journal of Information, Technology & Politics, volume 21 issue 1 (2024), pp. 38–53

Chapter 6
One way or another? Discussion disagreement and attitudinal homogeneity on social networking sites as pathways to polarization in Czechia
Alena Macková, Martina Novotná, Lucie Čejková, and Lenka Hrbková
Journal of Information, Technology & Politics, volume 21 issue 1 (2024), pp. 54–68

Chapter 7
Soros's soldiers, slackers, and pioneers with no expertise? Discursive exclusion of environmental youth activists from the digital public sphere in Hungary and Czechia
Lenka Vochocová, Jana Rosenfeldová, Anna Vancsó, and Annamária Neag
Journal of Information, Technology & Politics, volume 21 issue 1 (2024), pp. 69–83

Chapter 8
Like, Share, Comment, and Repeat: Far-right Messages, Emotions, and Amplification in Social Media
Larissa Doroshenko and Fangjing Tu
Journal of Information, Technology & Politics, volume 20 issue 3 (2023), pp. 286–302

Chapter 9
Donetsk don't tell – 'hybrid war' in Ukraine and the limits of social media influence operations
Lennart Maschmeyer, Alexei Abrahams, Peter Pomerantsev and Volodymyr Yermolenko *Journal of Information, Technology & Politics*
DOI: https://doi.org/10.1080/19331681.2023.2211969

For any permission-related enquiries please visit:
www.tandfonline.com/page/help/permissions

Notes on Contributors

Alexei Abrahams is the Digital Lead for the Canadian Media Ecosystem Observatory, and an academic associate of the Center for Media, Technology, and Democracy, at McGill University's Max Bell School of Public Policy, Montreal, Canada.

Kinga Adamczewska is a researcher and lecturer at the Faculty of Political Science and Journalism, Adam Mickiewicz University, Poznan, Poland. Her research interests cover the fields of political communication, journalism studies and social network analysis.

Christian Baden is Associate Professor at the Department of Communication and Journalism at the Hebrew University of Jerusalem. His research focuses on the collaborative construction of meaning in dynamic, political public debates, with specific emphasis on the modeling and measurement of textual discourse.

Paweł Baranowski is Assistant Professor at the Department of Media Studies of the Institute of Journalism and Social Communication at the University of Wroclaw, Poland. His scientific interests oscillate around political communication, journalism studies and new media technologies.

Márton Bene (Ph.D.) is a senior research fellow at the Centre for Social Sciences, Hungarian Academy of Sciences Centre of Excellence, Hungary, and an assistant professor at the Faculty of Law, Eötvös Loránd University (ELTE), Hungary. His research interests are in political communication, social media and politics, and political behavior.

Lindita Camaj (Ph.D.) is Associate Professor at the Jack J. Valenti School of Communication, University of Houston, United States. Her research addresses the role of news media in political processes, with a focus on digital communication, media effects, access to information and journalism in South East Europe.

Lucie Čejková is a Ph.D. candidate at the Department of Media Studies and Journalism, Faculty of Social Studies, Masaryk University, Czech Republic. She deals with research on media trust and attitudes.

Erlis Çela (Ph.D.) is Assistant Professor at the Department of Communication Sciences, Beder University College in Tirana, Albania. His research interest includes the role of social media in journalism, disinformation and media literacy.

Andrea Ceron is Associate Professor at the University of Milan, Italy. His research interests include intra-party politics, text analysis and social media.

Larissa Doroshenko is Postdoctoral Teaching Associate at Northeastern University, United States. Her research interests are centered on the effects of new media on political campaigning, with a particular focus on "the dark side" of the Internet: populism, nationalism and disinformation campaigns.

Monika Eigmüller is Professor of sociology at the Europa-Universität Flensburg, Germany, and Director of the Interdisciplinary Centre for European Studies (ICES). In her research she deals with various fields of sociology of European integration. Main topics of interest are value conflicts and social inequality in the EU member states as well as EU social policy. Her latest book on *Sozialraum Europa* (Springer) has been published in 2021.

Miloš Gregor is an assistant professor at the Department of Political Science, Faculty of Social Studies, Masaryk University, Czech Republic. He is dealing with topics such as political communication and marketing, propaganda, disinformation and fake news.

Damian Guzek is an associate professor in digital media and communication at the University of Silesia in Katowice, Poland. His research is driven by questions related to media consumption and digital media, religions and politics.

Jörg Haßler is head of the junior research group "Digital Democratic Mobilization in Hybrid Media Systems" at the Department of Media and Communication at LMU Munich, Germany. His research interests include political communication, digital communication and empirical methods.

Lenka Hrbková is Assistant Professor at the Department of Political Science, Faculty of Social Studies, Masaryk University, Czech Republic. She has a doctoral degree in political science and in her research she focuses on the political attitudes, especially on the issue of affective polarization. She is principal investigator in the project "The Current Form and Sources of Political Conflict and Politically Motivated Division of Czech Society".

Daniel Jackson is Associate Professor of Media and Communication at Bournemouth University, United Kingdom. His research broadly explores the intersections of media, power and social change, including news coverage of politics, political communication, the mediation of sport and the dynamics of civic culture in online environments.

Kavyanjali Kaushik is a Ph.D. candidate at the Department of Social Sciences, Universidad Carlos III de Madrid, Spain. Her research focuses on the transformative impact of social media on political identities and actions, particularly analyzing the link between digital interactions and expressions with national identity development and mobilization for radical-right politics. She is also a pre-doctoral researcher for the project "Value Conflicts in a Differentiated Europe: The Impact of Digital Media on Value Polarisation in Europe" (ValCon), which examines the role of digital transformations in media in increasing conflicts over democratic values in Europe.

Karolina Koc-Michalska is Professor at Audencia Business School and Affiliated Researcher at CEVIPOF Sciences Po Paris, France, and University of Silesia, Poland. She studies the strategies of political actors in the online environment and citizens' political engagement. She employs a comparative approach focusing on the United States and European countries.

Simon Kruschinski is Research Associate and Ph.D. student in the Political Communication Division at the Department of Communication at the Johannes Gutenberg-University Mainz, Germany. His research focuses on election campaigns and how data, analytics and technologies are used to persuade or mobilize voters on- and offline.

Darren Lilleker is Professor of Political Communication at Bournemouth University, United Kingdom; co-editor of the *Journal of Visual Political Communication*; and Director of the Centre for Comparative Politics and Media Research.

Alena Macková is Assistant Professor at the Department of Media Studies and Journalism, Faculty of Social Studies, Masaryk University, Czech Republic. She has a doctoral degree in political science and is principal investigator in the project "Political Polarization in the Czech Republic: The Case of Multiparty System". She focuses in her research on changes in new information environment and their consequences for political communication.

Melanie Magin is Professor in Media Sociology at the Norwegian University of Science and Technology (NTNU), Norway. She works at the intersection of political communication, online communication (particularly social media and search engines) and comparative research. Her research focuses on the societal role and impact of traditional and new media as well as the chances and risks associated with them.

NOTES ON CONTRIBUTORS

Lennart Maschmeyer is Senior Researcher at the Center for Security Studies (CSS) at ETH Zürich. His research examines how technological change has altered the quality of subversion by comparing traditional subversion to contemporary "cyber subversion".

Annamária Neag is Research Fellow at Charles University, where she is leading an international research group that studies the civic engagement of children and youth (under 18-year-olds) and the skills needed for digital activism.

Martina Novotná is a Ph.D. candidate at the Department of Media Studies and Journalism, Faculty of Social Studies, Masaryk University, Czech Republic. Her research focuses on informal cross-cutting political talk online, emphasizing incivility and intolerance.

Matthew Placek is an Associate Professor of Political Science at the University of South Carolina Upstate, United States. His research focuses on the influence of social media and the internet on political attitudes in new democracies and non-democratic regimes. His work has been published in *Democratization*, *East European Politics*, the *International Journal of Communication* and *The Washington Post's Monkey Cage* blog.

Peter Pomerantsev is a senior fellow at Johns Hopkins University, United, States, and Co-director of the Arena Initiative. He is the author of several books about Russian and other authoritarian propaganda; the third of these, *How to Win an Information War: The Propagandist Who Outwitted Hitler*, was published in 2024.

Gjylie Rexha (Ph.D.) is Assistant Professor at the Faculty of Media and Communication, UBT Higher Education Institution, Kosovo. Her research addresses the role of journalists and media in political communication, especially focused on radio and television in Kosovo.

Jana Rosenfeldová is Researcher and Lecturer at the Institute of Communication Studies and Journalism, Faculty of Social Sciences, Charles University, Czech Republic. In her research she focuses on political communication and online political participation.

Uta Russmann is Professor of Media and Communication Studies with a focus on democracy research at the Department of Media, Society and Communication at the University of Innsbruck, Austria. Her research focuses on political communication, media and election campaigns, digital communication, (visual) social media, public relations and strategic communication.

Marko M. Scoric is Associate Professor at the Department of Media and Communication, City University of Hong Kong, where he leads the Political Communication and Culture Research Cluster and acts as the Ph.D. Program Coordinator. His research interests are focused on new media and social change, with a particular emphasis on the civic and political implications of digital technologies. He holds a Ph.D. in communication from the University of Michigan and a B.Sc. in psychology from the University College London.

Fangjing Tu is a Ph.D. candidate in the Department of Communication Arts at University of Wisconsin-Madison, United States. Her research is centered primarily on the question of how to cultivate informed and participatory citizens in the current media environment.

Anna Vancsó is Research Fellow at Charles University of Prague, Faculty of Social Sciences, Czech Republic, and an assistant research fellow at the Centre for Social Sciences, Hungarian Academy of Sciences Centre of Excellence, Hungary. Her main research interests are the transformation of the contemporary public sphere, with special focus on the role of online media in representing and shaping social realities.

Lenka Vochocová is Researcher and Lecturer at the Department of Media Studies, Faculty of Social Sciences, Charles University, Czech Republic. Her research interests cover the fields of gender media studies, online political participation, public sphere theories and political economy of communication.

Stefan Wallaschek is a postdoctoral researcher at the Interdisciplinary Centre for Europesan Studies (ICES), Europa-Universität Flensburg, Germany, and has worked in the project "Value Conflicts in a Differentiated Europe: The Impact of Digital Media on Value Polarisation in Europe" (ValCon). His research focuses on (digital) political communication, European politics as well as solidarity research.

Volodymyr Yermolenko is a Ukrainian philosopher, essayist, translator, doctor of political studies, candidate of philosophical sciences, and senior lecturer at the Kyiv-Mohyla Academy. He is a recipient of the Yurii Sheveliov Prize and of the Petro Mohyla Award.

Introduction: *Citizens, Participation and Media in Central and Eastern European Nations*

Karolina Koc-Michalska [iD], Darren Lilleker [iD], Christian Baden [iD], Damian Guzek [iD], Márton Bene [iD], Larissa Doroshenko [iD], Miloš Gregor [iD], and Marko M. Scoric [iD],

ABSTRACT

Central and Eastern Europe (CEE) countries faced significant political, economic, social, and technological transformations over the last four decades. Democratic processes, after relative stabilization, tremble again around polarizing values, populist leaders, or nationalistic ideologies. Online communication, especially social media platforms, play a vital role in shaping how citizens interact with the state, political actors, media, and other citizens. The book focuses on some of the challenges democratic institutions in the region face, in transforming and sustaining civil society and attempts to capture how the digital media environments mitigate or exacerbate those challenges. Included manuscripts focus on the role that online platforms play in the satisfaction with democracy in the CEE region, the interactions between journalists and political actors, the strategic media coverage of elections, affective polarization and political antagonism, and discursive attempts to discourage young people from civic engagement.

The countries in Central and Eastern Europe (CEE) have been going through tremendous changes and developments over the last forty years. The collapse of the Soviet Union saw these countries gain, or seize, their independence in largely bloodless transitions of power. Economic, social, and political developments profoundly changed how their societies have been functioning. The nations are largely flourishing market economies, but growing inequalities have fueled migration. Democratic institutions have been created, yet parties are not fully embedded and are often the political vehicles for charismatic personalities (see studies within Eibl & Gregor, 2019). The processes of transformation and development are well advanced in certain countries (especially those that joined the European Union (EU) in its enlargements of 2004 and 2013), but are still not fully achieved in others. Some nations did not democratize (Belarus), others struggled to resolve their independence or geopolitical situation (Ukraine, Kosovo, Northern Macedonia), many witness high political polarization and civic protest (Poland, Romania), and there are numerous examples where the CEE nations have witnessed a rise in support for populist politicians (Hungary and Poland).

The transitions to democratic market economies occurred at the same time as the nations of CEE witnessed sharp technological development. Just as democracy was becoming embedded, citizens gained access to a range of platforms that simplified interactions. New media, Internet-based platforms or social media, facilitated citizens' opportunities to express their opinions, engage in, or connect for collective action. However, there remain sharp digital divides in many CEE nations. Although access to the Internet is widespread, it is still lower than in the Western parts of Europe (especially broadband[1] access). There are also sharp divides between rural and urban areas, as well as skills divides (Esteban-Navarro et al., 2020). Certain groups of privileged citizens have unfettered access, while others have been left behind. The digital divide, often a consequence of infrastructural, educational, and financial inequalities, can complement incomprehension and polarization within the society. Restrictions in access to information, differential availability of internet affordances to spread civic knowledge, unequal abilities to participate in political discussion or to be active in political discourse lead to divided societies (Dragulanescu, 2002).

Table 1. Democracy Index rankings for nations included in the research (EIU, 2023).

Nation	Overall score	Global rank	Region rank	Electoral process & pluralism	Functioning of government	Political participation	Political culture	Civil liberties	Regime type
CEE	5.39	n/a	n/a	7.97	6.74	6.36	6.84	7.77	n/a
Czechia	7.97	25	1	9.58	6.43	7.22	7.50	9.12	Flawed
Poland	7.04	46	7	9.17	6.07	6.67	6.25	7.06	Flawed
Hungary	6.64	56	8	8.33	6.79	4.44	6.88	6.76	Flawed
Romania	6.45	60	11	9.17	6.43	5.56	3.73	7.35	Flawed
Albania	6.41	64	13	7.00	6.43	5.00	6.25	7.35	Flawed
Ukraine	5.06	91	19	5.58	3.07	7.22	5.00	4.41	Hybrid

It is perhaps all too easy to view the nations of CEE as being in a pre-development phase, held back by weak governance, insufficient resources, and the migration of many of the younger and brighter citizens. However, this important region is pivotal in terms of understanding how civil society can be built and maintained, and how democratic norms of thinking and acting can become embedded within society. It is equally important for understanding the challenges that democracy faces.

The problems confronted by citizens in CEE countries are not unique to this region, they are to differing extents shared by many nations across the continent of Europe and indeed globally (Berman & Snegovaya, 2019). The CEE region has faced severe challenges during the pandemic, but even more so since February 2022 with Russia's invasion of Ukraine. The war immediately caused instability, firstly due to an influx of refugees displaced from Ukraine that has impacted Poland and Romania in particular. Secondly, whereas Ukraine was known as the breadbasket of Europe, the protracted and stagnated conflict has caused economic challenges across the EU leading to increased costs of grain. Thirdly, since there has been reliance on Russian gas across the region, switching away from Gasprom supplies has increased fuel costs and so energy bills. The conflict has also opened further the social divisions within the societies, with Russian propaganda and disinformation fueling anti-EU and illiberal sentiments (Mandić & Klarić, 2023).

Facing these challenges successfully requires good governance and a strong, vibrant, and inclusive civil society. All the CEE nations are classified by the Democracy Index (EIU, 2023) as flawed democracies; they hold free and fair elections and basic civil liberties are respected, but there remain significant weaknesses in systems of governance, an underdeveloped political culture, and low levels of political participation. Of the sixteen nations that constitute CEE, our studies include the highest-performing nation, Czechia, two mid-table nations, Poland and Hungary, and two lower-performing nations with Romania and Albania. Kosovo does not have a separate entry within the index. The data shows that most of these nations perform overall better than CEE average but there are key weaknesses, not only in Albania but also deficiencies in civil liberties in Poland and Hungary, with political participation in Hungary and political culture in Romania being particularly low. Ukraine is a special case. Due to the government being on a war footing, Ukraine is classed as hybrid because its governance is a blend of democratic and authoritarian features, and hence pluralism, government functioning, political culture, and civil liberties have all suffered. The Democracy Index scores out of ten show a mixed picture for the region, although it is worth noting that in terms of their global rank, Czechia is just behind France, equal with Greece and ahead of Portugal and the USA. Poland and Hungary are ranked closely with nations of South America (Brazil and Argentina), Indonesia, and Thailand. Albania has a ranking similar to that of countries such as Ghana and Suriname. This offers a perception of the range of challenges faced in these nations.

It is equally interesting to note that over the history of the Democracy Index (2006–2022; Table 2), we notice a minor improvement for Albania but also minor decreases in performance for the other three nations. Ukraine has witnessed a gradual decline over the 2006–2022 period but the sharpest decline has been due to the invasion by Russia. Outside of Ukraine the changes are minor, but these changes do demonstrate the fragility of democracy

Table 2. Changes in the overall Democracy Scores 2006–2022 (EIU, 2023).

Nation	Overall score 2022	Overall Score 2006	Change
Czechia	7.97	8.17	−0.20
Poland	7.04	7.30	−0.26
Hungary	6.64	7.53	−0.89
Romania	6.45	7.06	+0.61
Albania	6.41	5.91	+0.50
Ukraine	5.06	6.94	−1.88

in the region. With attacks on media freedom, civil liberties, rights to free speech, and protest being infringed, there is a need for a strong civil society to defend core principles of democracy.

Though, since a democratic regime is considered embedded within societies, it is time to examine the relationship between technological developments and the sustainability of civil society within this region. The aim of this special edition is to raise questions regarding the ways in which digital technologies, and specific affordances of platforms, offer the potential for enhancing democratic culture and in what ways they undermine principles of pluralism and can support or hinder building a well-informed citizenry who are confident and able to debate political issues and reach a consensus.

The collection of the book chapters

The proposed book is divided into two parts: Part I looks at CEE countries from a comparative perspective, and Part II examines specific case studies within different CEE countries. The book consists of nine chapters covering CEE as a region (Chapter 1), in comparison with Western democracies (Chapters 2 and 3) and specific case studies from Albania and Kosovo (Chapter 5), Czechia and Hungary (Chapters 6 and 7), Poland (Chapter 4), and Ukraine (Chapters 8 and 9).

Chapter 1 by Matthew Placek offers a broad perspective drawing on six waves of the Eurobarometer data from 2014 to 2019 analyzing the relationship between social media use and its employment for information acquisition with the variation in satisfaction with democracy. The author indicates that those who are searching for information on social media are more critical toward democratic standards. They tend to be satisfied with the functioning of the democracy when the liberal democracy index and the electoral democracy index (v-dem.net) per country are above .7 and .8, respectively (with the score .6 for those not searching). These relations alter depending on the strength or backsliding of the democratic regime.

The next chapter by Paweł Baranowski, Simon Kruschinski, Uta Russmann, Jörg Haßler, Melanie Magin, Márton Bene, Andrea Ceron, Daniel Jackson and Darren Lilleker looks into the parties' use of negative campaigning on Facebook and examines its correlation with their ideological stance and national government or opposition status during the 2019 European Parliament campaign. Parties in Hungary, Poland, and Romania are compared to parties in the seven Western democracies. The results suggest that parties were producing fewer negative posts compared to positive and neutral ones. Notably, despite their lower frequency, negative posts received significantly more shares, which amplified their visibility on the platform. Thus, Facebook, where the dynamics of user engagement, algorithmic influence, and party strategy converge, becomes the primary catalyst behind the proliferation of negative campaigning, fundamentally changing the landscape of political discourse.

Chapter 3 by Stefan Wallaschek, Kavyanjali Kaushik and Monika Eigmüller explores the print media coverage and social media debates around the issue of the Independence of Judiciary (IoJ) from the Europeanization framework perspective. The manuscript compares Poland with Germany and Spain. The findings indicate that in cases where the independence of the judiciary is most under attack (Poland and Spain), the presence of EU actors and pro-EU perspectives in public debates is limited in both traditional and social media. This finding is crucial for understanding and enhancing the quality of democracy in the EU. The study advocates for a re-evaluation of the EU's approach to democratic value conflicts, for a greater emphasis on EU involvement in national debates and leveraging social media to diffuse pro-EU perspectives to bolster the integration.

Kinga Adamczewska in Chapter 4 examines relations on social media platforms between journalists and political actors in the context of the Polish parliamentary elections of 2015 and 2019. Surprisingly, the density of the links between media representatives and politicians dropped in time. The relations were measured based on reactions to posts by the journalists rather than on interactive exchanges of ideas. Between the two electoral periods, the most visible politicians, mainly from the opposition parties, amplified their online presence and visibility. The data highlights the growing absence of political actors from the ruling party and of journalists linked to public media.

The following chapter by Lindita Camaj, Erlis Çela and Gjylie Rexha studies the public's engagement with news posted by media in Albania and Kosovo. The authors build on the media logic and audience logic theoretical approaches to examine the reasons (interviews with editors) and effects (text analysis) of strategy- or issue-based personalization and negativity positing tactics within Facebook profiles of twelve news organizations. The audience tends to engage less with negative attacking posts and with posts focusing on issues, except for those covering social welfare, health, and immigration. The findings suggest that the audience-oriented modus operandi employed by the editors involves closely monitoring the community's reactions toward publications. The audience-oriented logic sets the tone for news choices by media but also the strategic behavior of political actors.

Alena Macková, Martina Novotná, Lucie Čejková and Lenka Hrbková in Chapter 6 examine the relations between social networking sites, affective polarization, and political antagonism in Czechia. The authors find substantial contrasts among the predictors: only the level of attitudinal homogeneity has the same effect on both polarization and antagonism, while other explanatory variables (experienced negativity, political unfriending, or political interest) are more context depending. The study suggests that a homogenous pattern of social media contribution to polarization may not exist and that the relationship is more nuanced.

Chapter 7 examines the discursive representation of the youth climate change-oriented movement in Czechia and Hungary. Lenka Vochocová, Jana Rosenfeldová, Anna Vancsó and Annamária Neag provide a study on normative assumptions around the exclusion of the youth from participating in the public sphere expressed via comments on various newspapers' profiles on Facebook. Findings show the general willingness to dismiss young people from politics. Two argumentation lines are prominent: firstly, denying expertise, experience, and rationality for political participation, and secondly, accusing youth of errant values and thus normatively incapable of participating in the democratic processes. Young people seem to be rather discouraged from political activities than being bolstered for further civic engagement.

Chapter 8 by Larissa Doroshenko and Fangjing Tu examines the role of emotions in online political participation, specifically in amplifying far-right posts on social media. Employing 2×3 mixed design survey experiment among Ukrainian students, they depict reactions toward far-right and centrist parties' messages following Euromaidan events. Results reveal that nationalist appeals evoked stronger emotional reactions and more engagement with these messages through likes, comments, and shares. Posts about national language policy were particularly successful: by stimulating hope and enthusiasm they generated more likes and shares. The chapter concludes with advice on how other political parties can use emotional appeals to encourage political participation when facing competition from far-rights.

In the concluding chapter, Lennart Maschmeyer, Alexei Abrahams, Peter Pomerantsev and Volodymyr Yermolenko compare theoretically and empirically the social media and television as vectors for influence operations targeting Ukraine (before 2022 war). It shows how and why decentralized and centralized media offer distinct opportunities and challenges for conducting influence operations, indicating that television has an advantage in both dissemination and persuasiveness. Watching television shows a strong correlation between exposure to an agreement with narrative elements and foreign policy preferences. Yet, the overall effects of such influence operations seemed limited.

This book is an attempt to bring together a collection of manuscripts dedicated to CEE to bring into the light the underrepresented in the international literature countries. However, still, the main limitation of the book remains the insufficient set of countries covered. We wish to encourage future research and publishing by scholars from the CEE countries. Similarly, to other non-Western regions, there is a need from the established research environments to support colleagues and contributors not only in critically reviewing but also to encourage and actively support the colleagues from less established academic institutions.

Note

1. World Bank Group. Fixed broadband subscriptions (per 100 people). https://data.worldbank.org/indicator/IT.NET.BBND.P2

ORCID

Karolina Koc-Michalska http://orcid.org/0000-0002-5354-5616
Darren Lilleker http://orcid.org/0000-0003-0403-8121
Christian Baden http://orcid.org/0000-0002-3771-3413
Damian Guzek http://orcid.org/0000-0002-8138-8128
Márton Bene http://orcid.org/0000-0003-0177-9717
Larissa Doroshenko http://orcid.org/0000-0001-6763-628X
Miloš Gregor http://orcid.org/0000-0002-0796-7121
Marko Scoric http://orcid.org/0000-0001-6578-9872

Bibliography

Berman, S., & Snegovaya, M. (2019). Populism and the decline of social democracy. *Journal of Democracy, 30*(3), 5–19.

Dragulanescu, N. G. (2002). Social impact of the "Digital Divide" in a Central–Eastern European country. *The International Information & Library Review, 34*(2), 139–151.

Eibl, O., & Gregor, M. (Eds.). (2019). *Thirty years of political campaigning in Central and Eastern Europe*. Cham: Palgrave Macmillan.

EIU. (2023). *Democracy Index 2022: Frontline democracy and the battle for Ukraine*. London: Economist Intelligence.

Esteban-Navarro, M. Á., García-Madurga, M. Á., Morte-Nadal, T., & Nogales-Bocio, A. I. (2020, December). The rural digital divide in the face of the COVID-19 pandemic in Europe—recommendations from a scoping review. *Informatics, 7*(4), 54.

Mandić, J., & Klarić, D. (2023). Case study of the Russian disinformation campaign during the war in Ukraine–propaganda narratives, goals, and impacts. *National Security and the Future, 24*(2), 97–140.

Part I
Central and Eastern Europe in a comparative perspective

Social media, quality of democracy, and citizen satisfaction with democracy in Central and Eastern Europe

Matthew Placek

ABSTRACT
The last decade has been tumultuous for democracy in Central and Eastern Europe (CEE). While the beginning of the 21st century saw many post-communist countries in the region democratize and become full members of the European Union, the last 10 years have been wrought with stagnation and democratic backsliding. By the 2020s, some of the strongest democratizers in the region had experienced significant issues. This study attempts to answer two questions related to whether social media users' satisfaction with democracy relies on a country's quality of democracy. The first question explores this relationship in the overall context of democracy, while the second examines the relationship with democratic backsliding. The findings show that social media use correlates with higher satisfaction with democracy when their country's democracy is more robust. Furthermore, as backsliding occurs, social media use is correlated with lower satisfaction with democracy.

Introduction

The last decade has been tumultuous for democracy in Central and Eastern Europe (CEE). While the late 20th and early 21st centuries saw many post-communist countries in the region democratize and become full members of the European Union, the last 10 years have been wrought with stagnation and democratic backsliding. By the 2020s, even some of the strongest democratizers in the region had experienced significant issues. For instance, in Hungary, Viktor Orban seemingly consolidated illiberal rule. Furthermore, the Law and Justice Party has significantly undermined the rights of minorities and the rule of law in Poland. In the Czech Republic, there were issues with judicial independence and corruption stemming from investigations into Andre Babis' personal finances.

Along with political turmoil, the region has also seen profound changes in access to digital technology and media production. Since 2008, global conglomerates that had quickly bought media outlets in CEE after initial economic liberalization have sold their investments to local oligarchs, who often have strong connections to political leaders (Stetka, 2012). Coupled with increased party control over state-run media outlets in many countries, political leaders have been able to weaponize mass media for partisan gain. Furthermore, most research on media's interaction with backsliding focuses on the legal aspects of the media concerning democratic backsliding (Guzek and Grzesiok-Horosz, 2022) or how political actors constrain critical media outlets (Bajomi-Lazar, 2012). However, little research has been devoted to understanding how social networking websites (SNS) affect politics in these changing democratic conditions. Previous studies have shown that SNS use leads to greater satisfaction with democracy before backsliding occurs (Placek, 2017), and online news consumption generally leads to government support (Placek, 2018). However, none have explored whether citizen satisfaction with democracy changes when governments restrict civil rights and liberties.

This study attempts to answer two questions related to whether SNS users' satisfaction with democracy relies on the quality of democracy in their country. Does SNS use lead to greater satisfaction with democracy in democratic countries with stronger protection of rights and liberties? In addition, as democratic backsliding occurs, does SNS use lead to lower satisfaction with democracy? Thus, this study explores the effect of SNS use on satisfaction with democracy in the overall context of democracy and democratic backsliding.

The study will proceed as follows. First, I examine previous literature on democratic backsliding and the quality of democracy in CEE. Further, I will review the literature on SNS and political attitudes before presenting expectations based on the extant literature. I will test these expectations using data from Eurobarometer, the Varieties of Democracy Project (VDEM), and the United Nations World Development Indicators (WDI). The findings show that SNS use increases a person's satisfaction when their country's democracy is rated higher according to the VDEM. Furthermore, as backsliding occurs, SNS use correlates with lower satisfaction with democracy than if democratic deepening occurs. The implications of these Results are discussed at the end of the paper.

Democratic backsliding, populism, and support for democracy in CEE

The countries in CEE provide interesting cases for studying whether SNS users' satisfaction with democracy is conditional on its functioning. These countries not only have a wide range of democratic outcomes, but also very distinct recent histories regarding democratic stability. Figure 1 shows the changes between the countries in this study. This variation is apparent in the graph. Some countries have remained stable, full democracies for both VDEM indices, while others have seen severe backsliding over the six-year period from which the survey data for this study came. Furthermore, Bulgaria and Romania had lower scores than the other countries in the region during the study period.

While the variation in democratic outcomes and histories in the region provides a compelling comparative context for exploring whether SNS users' satisfaction with democracy is conditional on the performance of democracy, there are substantive reasons why this study is essential. One of the primary conduits of democratic backsliding in the region is the appeal of illiberal populism (Vachudova, 2020). Historically, democratic

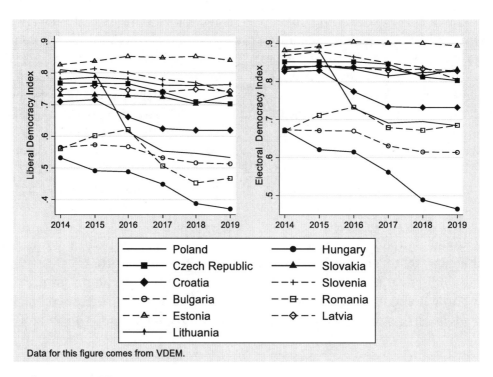

Figure 1. Change in democracy in CEE.

regression to authoritarianism has been characterized by rapid changes such as revolution and coup d'états (Levitsky & Way, 2010). However, liberal democracy has suffered from a much slower demise in the recent past, where elites whittle away at political institutions while enjoying support from portions of the mass public (Levitsky & Way, 2010).

As in other regions of the world, the rise of populism in CEE has seriously affected the quality of democracy in the region. By the late 2000s, several countries in the region, especially those that had joined the European Union, were considered consolidated democracies (Tomini, 2014). Such a designation would mean that these countries were on a path for continued democratic success that was impervious to backsliding (See Schedler, 1998).

However, the last decade has shown that democracy in the region may not have been as stable as previously thought (Stanley, 2019). Illiberal leaders have used various means to delegitimize civil society and create populist discourse to transform the political agenda (Enyedi, 2020). This dynamic makes this study even more critical because it examines whether the Internet can be a space that allows citizens to enact checks, balances, and other safeguards against democratic backsliding.

Social media in the context of CEE media systems

Alongside political changes since 1989, CEE has seen immense growth in information and communication technology (ICT). While the pattern mirrors that of other countries connected to the global marketplace, these technologies provide unique opportunities and pitfalls, given the unique political, social, and media dynamics present in the region. Therefore, this context is paramount for understanding how SNS use can alter citizens' political attitudes in the region.

Figures 2 and 3 detail the growth in Internet access and SNS use in each country from to 2014–2019. Figure 2 shows that access to broadband and internet use has grown over the period for each country in the following empirical analyses. Furthermore, Figure 3 shows that SNS use has grown immensely over time. In addition, while the use of SNS to follow news has grown, it still lags

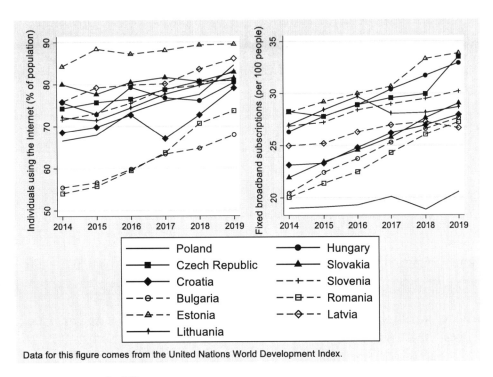

Data for this figure comes from the United Nations World Development Index.

Figure 2. Change in internet access in CEE.

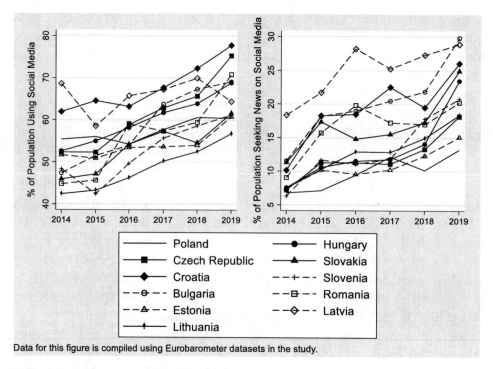

Figure 3. Change in SNS use in CEE.

precipitously for general use. Despite lower levels of information seeking, the overall growth of access to and use of ICTs increases the chances that SNS will impact politics in the region. This is because the interactive value of these networks increases exponentially as more users are added (Metcalfe, 2013).

While the growth of ICTs in CEE increases the likelihood that they will play a significant role in political life, the traditional media environment is also important, as the legal, business, and social frameworks of the media environment affect how people engage with digital media. Within the media system, several key trends coincided with the growth of SNS use in the region. First, in several countries, the capture of state media by ruling parties and the takeover of private media by government-aligned oligarchs have reduced overall press freedom (Bajomi-Lázár, 2014; Stetka, 2012). Therefore, in many countries, public media are under direct pressure from the ruling party, and private media can be subject to a complex process that leads to its use as a mouthpiece of the state (Bajomi-Lázár, 2014;). In addition to political pressure, the media in the region can also suffer from the need for corporatist media to turn profits. Indeed, other studies show that focusing on scandal- and tabloid-style presentations has become a crucial part of some private media outlets (Tworzecki & Semetko, 2012).

The coinciding trends in media capture and ICT growth underscore the opportunity for SNS use to alter support for democracy in the region. While traditional online media outlets often mirror tabloidization trends and focus on domestic news (Hladík & Štětka, 2017), SNS offer pathways for citizens to encounter information critical of political actors that would not be available elsewhere. For instance, Stetka, Surowiec, and Mazák (2019) showed that Facebook users in Czechia and Poland who encountered policy-related posts were likelier to leave critical comments than users who encountered campaigns or mobilization-related posts. Despite the need for more research on how SNS users in the region can use online resources to counter the potential state capture of media, this provides some evidence that ICTs and SNS can be used to create a public sphere outside state control.

Online media and political attitudes

Over the past 20 years, social scientists have sought to understand how the Internet and, more recently,

SNS influence individual and social behavioral patterns. As with other forms of media, researchers have found various associations between Internet and SNS use and political opinions and behavior. Despite the extensive research devoted to this subject, previous research shows a lack of consensus on how and whether digital media can support democratic politics.

Previous studies have found diverse associations between online media use and political opinions and behaviors. Research has found that Online media use has been associated with higher levels of political knowledge (Bode, 2016; Ceron, Curini, Iacus, & Porro, 2014) and engagement (Boulianne, 2009, 2015; Dimitrova, Shehata, Strömbäck, & Nord, 2014; Gil de Zuniga, Jung, & Valenzuela, 2012). Furthermore, it has influenced public attitudes toward elites and institutions (Ceron, 2015; Placek, 2017).

Despite these findings, others remain less convinced that online media elicit any effect on political attitudes (Newton, 2021). Beyond this, others have posited that it may adversely affect democracy. Much of these hypotheses hinge on the impact of media fragmentation leading to audience segmentation (Mancini, 2012) and minimal effects of media on political attitudes (See also Bennett & Iyengar, 2008). Beyond minimal effects, there is even a cause for concern regarding the detrimental effects of fragmentation, as this can lead to political apathy and exacerbate polarization (Prior, 2007; Stroud, 2008). Studies have shown that people tend to self-select news that reinforces their beliefs (Barberá, Jost, Nagler, Tucker, & Bonneau, 2015; Colleoni, Rozza, & Arvidsson, 2014; Feller, Kuhnert, Sprenger, & Welpe, 2011; Garrett, 2009). This realization becomes even more critical when we consider that non-democratic extremist groups can organize online (Simpson & Druxes, 2015), create imitated public spheres (Matay & Kaposi, 2008), and quickly spread misinformation online (Bode & Vraga, 2015; Del Vicario et al., 2016; Southwell & Thorson, 2015).Furthermore, other findings suggest that political polarization can influence the size and direction of SNS effects on political attitudes and satisfaction with democracy. Indeed, SNS use has been found to increase polarization through attitude reinforcement (Kubin & von Sikorski, 2021; Ohme, 2021). Further studies suggest that interactions with online opposition media can also exacerbate polarization (Bail et al., 2018), which is more likely to be realized through SNS use during heightened political conflict (Lee, 2016). Consequently, citizens may be more likely to believe their party's talking points, even if they are factually unsubstantiated (Druckman, Peterson, & Slothuus, 2013), and become less satisfied with democracy in their country (Wagner, 2021). Thus, SNS use could lead to lower democratic satisfaction and harm democracy by exacerbating polarization.

Despite concerns of fragmentation and the potential harm of the online sphere to democracy, there is reason to believe that it could produce positive effects for democracy. First, while some studies discuss the pervasiveness of filter bubbles and echo chambers, others contend that SNS and online discourse inadvertently expose people to news and political content that they otherwise would not search for (Anspach, 2017; Kahne et al., 2012; Wojcieszak & Mutz, 2009). Furthermore, other research points out that the finding that SNS use exacerbates polarization may not be generalizable, as most of the literature that finds increased polarization is hyper-focused on Twitter as a platform and the American public as a research audience (Kubin & von Sikorski, 2021). Even if this is not the case, there is still a substantial amount of disagreement in the literature, as other findings show that polarization is attenuated by cross-party contact (Wojcieszak & Warner, 2020) and even general SNS Use (Beam, Hutchens, & Hmielowski, 2018). Further evidence suggests that despite media fractionalization and a polarized social context, SNS users and online news seekers in CEE tended to be more supportive of democracy before democratic backsliding occurred in much of the region (Placek, 2017, 2018). Thus, while there are divergent views on whether Internet and SNS use can influence people's political attitudes and behavior, there is at least some evidence that online publics have different political views than their offline counterparts.

Expectations

The following empirical analysis examines whether SNS users' satisfaction with democracy in CEE is responsive to the quality of democracy in their country, and whether this support tends to change as democratic backsliding occurs. Although there is disagreement among previous studies regarding the Internet's ability to influence political attitudes, Bailard's (2014) theory of window opening and mirror holding conceptualizes how the process might occur.

Bailard's (2014) theory of the Internet's effects on political attitudes revolves around the fundamental principles of window opening – the ability to see how other forms of government function – and mirror holding – the ability of citizens to reflect on their government's performance. These two concepts provide a framework for considering how the Internet could affect political attitudes and how SNS use could do so. As with the Internet, SNS allow users to experience and understand events outside of their local areas. This certainly would include seeing how other governments function and how their government compares. The chance of this happening using SNS might be higher than that of general Internet use. While general Internet users must seek news to find information about government and politics, previous studies show that SNS users might be inadvertently exposed to political information (Lee & Kim, 2017; Wojcieszak & Mutz, 2009). Further, since inadvertent exposure is linked with information gain and recall (Lee & Kim, 2017), it seems likely that SNS users would have the opportunity to become more aware of political events that could link them to both "window opening" and "mirror holding" features of the digital sphere. Therefore, as SNS use increases, people's satisfaction with democracy increases when their country's democracy is performing well and decreases when democracy is performing poorly.

Additional reasons to believe that SNS use could produce positive effects on support for democracy come from the interaction between previous works detailing the attitudinal and cultural change process in new democracies and studies that describe the Internet and SNS's ability to engage the public. Previous studies have noted that technological and cultural changes can go hand in hand as a process of modernization (Hansen, Postmes, van der Vinne, & van Thiel, 2012; Inglehart, 2003). These functions fit Bailard's (2014) window-opening process, allowing SNS to expose people to new values, which would help sustain democracy (see Inglehart, 1988). Further, if we look at other studies of attitude change and support for democracy, we can see how mirror holding could allow SNS to affect satisfaction with democracy. For instance, Mishler and Rose (1997) show that attitudes toward a regime are not static and can be altered with updated information. Similar to Zaller's (1992) work on opinion change, Bailard's (2014) concept of mirror holding theorizes that the Internet, and by extension SNS use, should allow citizens to become better aware of the political discourse inside the country. Further, this effect could be more pronounced in countries that have seen democratic regression as partisan capture of traditional media, and restrictions on media freedom are the norm in such situations (Bajomi-Lázár, 2014; Stetka, 2012). Therefore, in these cases, the Internet and SNS may be the only media to provide information that criticizes political actors in power.

While there may be concerns that window opening and mirror holding could only occur through information seeking on SNS, evidence points to the contrary. There is ample evidence that general SNS use positively correlates with engagement in political and civic life (Boulianne, 2015, 2022; Theocharis et al., 2023). Further evidence expands on this finding and shows that even passive users are more likely to engage in offline political activity when inadvertently exposed to political media on SNS (Gainous, Abbott, & Wagner, 2021). Indeed, others have found that incidental exposure to political information positively correlates with many aspects of political life (Nanz & Matthes, 2022). Given the literature, it is certainly plausible that general SNS use can produce critical evaluations of democracy when backsliding occurs.

Aside from general SNS use, this study also explores whether a person's satisfaction with democracy is conditional on the democratic efficacy of SNS information seekers. Here, the pathways to "window opening" and "mirror holding" functions of SNS are slightly simpler. Previous research has shown that online information seeking raises political awareness (Bode, 2016; Ceron, Curini, Iacus, & Porro, 2014; Placek, 2020). Since information seekers are by choice seeking information and becoming more aware of political events, it seems plausible that they would encounter information that leads to "window opening" and "mirror holding." Thus, I expect SNS information seekers' satisfaction with democracy to depend on their country's democratic performance. Therefore, based on the previous literature, I offer the following hypotheses:

H1: *SNS use in countries with stronger democratic practices will correlate with higher satisfaction with democracy than does SNS use in countries with weaker democratic practices.*

H2: *Information seeking on SNS in countries with stronger democratic practices will correlate with higher satisfaction with democracy than does information seeking on SNS in countries with weaker democratic practices.*

H3: *As democratic backsliding occurs in a country, SNS use will correlate with lower satisfaction with democracy.*

H4: *As democratic backsliding occurs in a country, information seeking on SNS will correlate with lower satisfaction with democracy.*

Data and methods

The survey data used in this study come from six waves of Eurobarometer survey data collected every November from 2014 to 2019. Data from Bulgaria, Czech Republic, Croatia, Estonia, Hungary, Latvia, Lithuania, Poland, Romania, Slovakia, Slovenia are used in the analysis. Furthermore, data from the WDI and VDEM will provide insight into whether variations in the country-level context impact satisfaction with democracy. These datasets allow me to empirically test the association between SNS use and satisfaction with democracy, given the changing democratic context of CEE. Furthermore, the datasets enable me to control for individual- and country-level confounders.

While the data provide an opportunity to explore whether SNS users respond to changing democratic contexts, methodological challenges are prevalent in survey research. One of the key issues is that it is challenging to determine causality between political attitudes and media use because of consumers' self-selection of media content. While it is impossible for this or any survey-based study to fully untangle causality, methodological techniques can reduce complications arising from non-normally distributed data.

Before each of the following models, I will use entropy balancing to help doubly control for confounding variables that could impact a person's satisfaction with democracy and their likelihood of using SNS. I use SNS as the treatment variable and reweight the survey based on demographic and theoretical confounders so that the treatment and control groups have similar means, variance, and skewness for each variable (see Table A2 in the Appendix). This process reduces selection bias from the surveys, as the groups should have no observable differences. Therefore, it strengthens the claim of causality as outliers and model choice is less likely to drive the Results (see Hainmueller, 2012; Ho, Imai, King, & Stuart, 2007; Sekhon, 2009).

Beyond utilizing entropy balancing to reduce the bias associated with survey research, I will also use Hierarchical Linear Modeling. This approach is used to help control for country-level effects that could impact a person's satisfaction with democracy. In doing so, the study hopes to avoid committing Type I errors that when country-level effects are not controlled for in comparative analysis (see Robson & Pevalin, 2015; Steenbergen & Jones, 2002; Stegmueller 2013)

Dependent variable

Satisfaction with democracy

The dependent variable in this study is derived from[1] a question asking how satisfied a respondent is with how democracy works in their country. The variable is ordinal and ranges from 0–3, where zero denotes complete dissatisfaction with democracy and three means a person is very satisfied with democracy.[1]

While there is some debate on the usefulness of satisfaction with democracy as a measure of overall attitudes toward political regimes (see Canache, Mondak, & Seligson, 2001), this measure is helpful for this study because it is not meant to capture the concept of normative support for democracy. Further, it is not meant to capture a person's support for other pieces of regime legitimacy, such as economic efficacy or trust in the government (see Booth & Seligson, 2009). Although the variable cannot capture broad views of regime legitimacy, it appropriately measures individual evaluations of the actual performance of the democratic system (Linde & Ekman, 2003; Ridge, 2021).

Independent variables

Social media use

The first main independent variable, SNS use, comes from a question that asks how often a person uses SNS. The original variable is coded zero for never, one for less often, two for two or three times a month, three for once a week, four for two to three times a week, and five for daily. Because of issues with a large dispersion within the original coding, the variable was recoded to range from zero to three. Zero^2 means that a person never uses social media, one means that they use it less than daily, and two means that they use it daily.

The second variable, SNS news, is a dummy variable where zero indicates that a person does not use SNS to seek information and one means that they seek information on social media. It comes from a question that asks respondents where they get their news on national political matters. The original coding from Eurobarometer was one if a person mentioned using a medium for news and zero if they did not mention using the medium.

Country democracy rating

This study's main country-level independent variables are the two indices from the VDEM dataset. The first is a country's Electoral Democracy Index. This index captures how electoral democracy is achieved within a country. This index measures the notion that rulers are responsive to citizens through open electoral competition and that inclusive politics are guaranteed through extensive suffrage. The second index is the Liberal Democracy Index. This index denotes how liberal democracy is achieved within a country. In addition to accounting for electoral democracy, the Liberal Democracy Index emphasizes the importance of protecting individual and minority rights against the tyranny of the state and the majority.

While several reliable sources measure regime type exist (e.g., Freedom House, Polity IV, etc.) I chose the VDEM over the others for theoretical and empirical reasons. The VDEM was chosen because it measures multiple components of how democracy is conceptualized. Most notably, in this study, the distinctions between the Electoral and Liberal democracy indices allow for flexibility in noting whether changes to polyarchical or liberal democratic elements in a country's democracy can interact with social media to influence a person's support for democracy. This allows the study to provide a more nuanced analysis than other measures of democracy. Second, while other measures provide nuanced year-to-year measures of democracy, VDEM tends to capture more variation between countries (Vaccaro, 2021) and includes greater measurement coverage from year to year (Boese, 2019). Both these dynamics are important when measuring democracy but become even more integral when constructing measures of democratic change over time, as discussed below.

Democratic backsliding

Aside from country-year variables of the overall democratic context of a country, this study also uses variables that denote the year-over-year change in democracy score for both the Liberal Democracy Index and the Electoral Democracy Index from the VDEM. Further, it addresses longer-term changes by examining whether SNS use correlates with satisfaction with democracy, given a five-year shift in democracy ratings. The variables for yearly change in democracy score were created by subtracting the previous year's democracy score from the survey year's democracy score. For the variables of longer-term change, I subtracted the democracy score from five years earlier from the country's democracy score from the year the survey was conducted.[3]

Social media and democracy interactions

The main independent variables of interest in this study are a series of interaction variables that denote the interaction between SNS use and country-level democratic context. Therefore, interactions were created between the individual-level variables of SNS use and information seeking on SNS and the country-level variables of the VDEM liberal democracy index, electoral democracy index, and yearly and five-year changes in democracy scores in both indices. In the Results section, the yearly and five-year interactions contain two graphs. One graph for each interaction shows the predicted change in a person's satisfaction with democracy, based on the measured change in democracy ratings given for all countries in the region. A second graph for each extends this prediction to cover equal levels of democratic backsliding and democratic deepening. Since democratic backsliding has been more prevalent in both the one- and five-year change measures, I expand these measures to obtain an equal picture of how social media use might be associated with satisfaction with democracy in the case of democratic growth.

Control variables

At the individual level, the study controls for several socioeconomic and demographic factors that could influence satisfaction with democracy. First, it controls for the use of other media sources. There are control variables for how often a person uses the Internet, watches television, reads newspapers, or listens to the radio. Beyond this, it controls for sociopolitical factors such as political knowledge and political ideology. Finally, it controls for demographic factors such as life satisfaction, satisfaction with their household's financial situation, age, gender, educational attainment, size of the place where they live, self-identified social class, employment, and marital status.

The study also controls for country-level effects that could influence satisfaction with democracy using variables from the WDI. It controls for economics by using the natural log of each country's GDP and unemployment level. Furthermore, it controls for the percentage of the urban population and how many broadband internet subscriptions there are per 100 people.

Results

Figure 4 shows the marginal effects of SNS use and information seeking on SNS on satisfaction with democracy as the democratic[4] context changes. These findings support Hypotheses 1 and 2, respectively. As a country's democracy rating increases[5] in all models, SNS use and information seeking on SNS tend to increase satisfaction with democracy. This finding holds for both measures of democratic context.[6]

Perhaps the most interesting finding is that for general SNS use, those who use SNS daily tend to be more supportive of democracy when it is working well and more critical of it when it is not working well. However, people who use SNS less than daily tend to have static opinions of democracy, regardless of the democratic context.[7] One theoretical explanation is that people who use the medium more often could find relevant political information through active or passive means. In this scenario, daily users would therefore be more likely to consume news regarding democratic backsliding. Second, people who use SNS daily should be better skilled at using the medium, and technical skills could increase their ability to find and process relevant information.

Another interesting finding is that people who seek information on SNS tend to be more critical in their evaluations of democracy than general SNS users. The graphs in Figure 4 show that general SNS users are more satisfied with democracy when their country scores are near .6 on both indices. However, news users tend to become more supportive of democracy when their country's score is better than .7 on the liberal democracy index and .8 on the electoral democracy index. Theoretically, this could be due to the diversity of news sources that people could view on SNS. For instance, information-seeking on SNS could lead to more engagement in echo chambers than general SNS use.

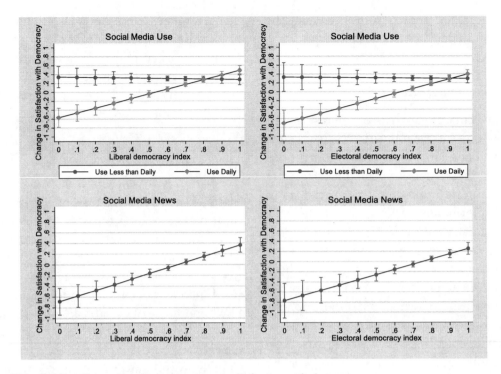

Figure 4. The effect of SNS and overall democracy rating on satisfaction with democracy.

While this is an interesting premise, unfortunately, the current data do not allow us to tease out the causal mechanism within this finding, as the Eurobarometer data do not provide any information on which news links SNS information seekers sought out. Thus, while this paper can provide insight into the effect of seeking news on SNS, it is severely limited in how much information can be gleaned about the impact of seeking specific types of news on SNS.

Figures 5 and 6 show the association between SNS use and satisfaction with democracy based on

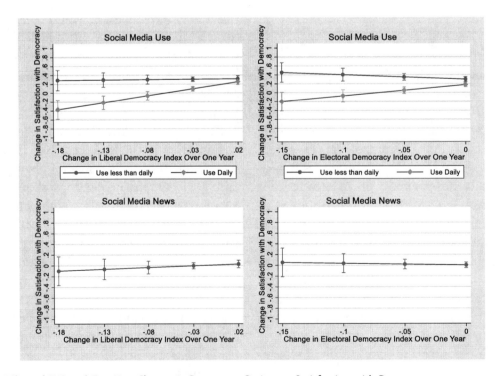

Figure 5. The Effect of SNS and One-Year Change in Democracy Rating on Satisfaction with Democracy.

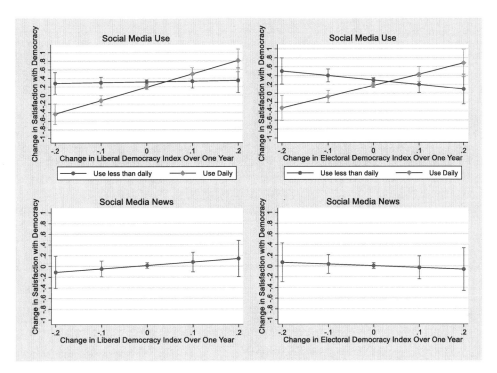

Figure 6. The effect of SNS and one-year change in democracy rating on satisfaction with democracy with predictions for extended democratic change.

a one-year change in a country's democracy rating. For each graph, the Y-axis denotes the predicted change in satisfaction with democracy and the X-axis describes the absolute value change in a country's democracy score over one year. Figure 5 shows the associations based on the minimum and maximum of the actual one-year changes in the democracy ratings. Figure 6 shows the predicted associations after extending the democracy rating to equal lengths of democratic growth or decay. The tables show that the impact of everyday SNS use on a person's satisfaction with democracy depends on how well a country's democracy has performed in the last year. In countries that have resisted backsliding, everyday SNS use leads to a slightly higher satisfaction with democracy. However, in countries with severe one-year declines, SNS use leads a person's satisfaction with democracy to decline somewhere between a quarter and three-quarters of a point. This is significant considering that the original scale for satisfaction with democracy has only four points.

In contrast, information seeking on social media in the context of a single year change in democracy has an insignificant impact on a person's satisfaction with democracy. While this is surprising given the other findings of the study, there are theoretical reasons for this finding. Research shows that active news seekers tend to acquire more knowledge (Prior, 2005) and are more resistant to opinion change (Zaller, 1992). Thus, active news seekers may only see opinion change if immense backsliding occurs in a single year or if it is sustained for a longer time.

Figures 7 and 8 show the association between SNS use and satisfaction with democracy relative to the five-year change in a country's democracy rating. For each graph, the Y-axis denotes the predicted change in satisfaction with democracy and the X-axis describes the absolute value change in a country's democracy score over a five-year period. As with the preceding figures based on a one-year shift in democracy ratings, Figure 7 shows the associations based on the minimum and maximum of actual five-year changes in democracy ratings. Figure 8 shows the predicted associations after extending the democracy rating to equal lengths of democratic growth or decay. Again, as with the one-year change in democracy rating, SNS use's impact on satisfaction with democracy is conditional on the change in the democracy rating. However, it is notable that the slope of the

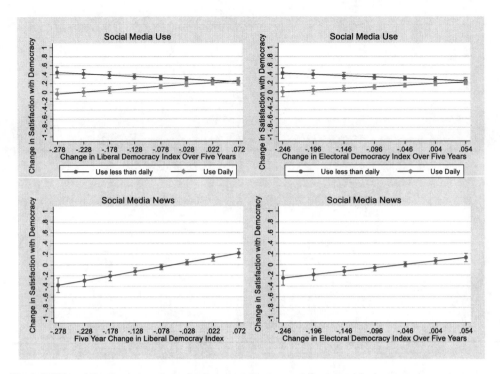

Figure 7. The effect of SNS and five-year change in democracy rating on satisfaction with democracy.

association is more robust for one-year change than for five-year change. This finding is interesting, as it signals that more significant one-year changes in democracy rating condition SNS use's impact on satisfaction with democracy more than longer-term slow backsliding. One reason is that short-term dynamics are more easily remembered, whereas long-term backsliding may not be a top-of-head in consideration of democracy for SNS users.

While general SNS use has more pronounced effects on a person's support for democracy after one year of democratic backsliding rather than longer-term backsliding, the effects of information-seeking on SNS seem to be more pronounced over the longer term. For example, Figures 5 and 6 show that news seekers are more satisfied with democracy when positive change occurs, but more dissatisfied when backsliding, especially significant ones, has happened over the five-year period.

Thus, the findings from the empirical models in Figures 5–8 provide tangential support for hypotheses 3 and 4. As democratic backsliding occurs, general SNS users are more likely to be dissatisfied in the short term. However, over longer periods of time, general SNS users' satisfaction with democracy hinges more on democratic deepening.

Further, as democratic backsliding occurs people who seek news on social media are unlikely to be less satisfied with democracy in the short term, but as long-term backsliding occurs, they are more likely to be dissatisfied with democracy in their country.

Discussion and conclusion

Previous scholarship has explored many political dynamics of backsliding in CEE and the effects that media, including SNS, have on support for the government, political issues, and political actors. This study analyzed whether SNS users in CEE are perceptive of the quality of democracy and changes to democracy in their country. The empirical Results suggest that SNS users can discern their country's overall quality and change to democracy. Further, both information seekers and general users tend to be perceptive of the overall quality and changes in the quality of democracy. The findings lend credence to previous studies of Internet use, which show that the medium may help users be more perceptive of their government's success or shortcomings (see Bailard, 2014).

Furthermore, this study fills an important gap in the literature by conducting a comparative analysis

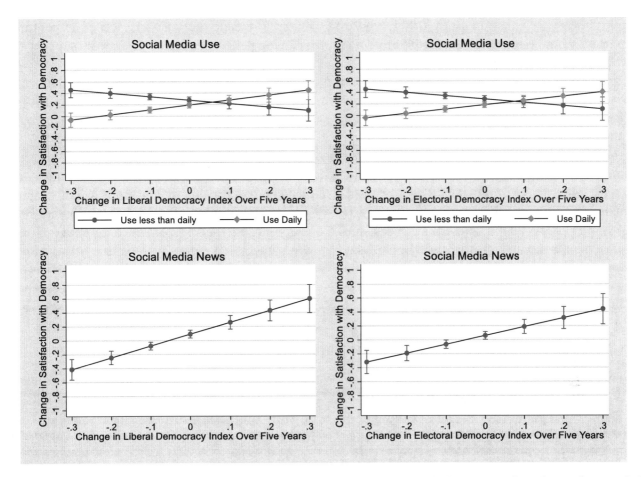

Figure 8. The effect of sns and five-year change in democracy rating on satisfaction with democracy with predictions for extended democratic change.

of the effects of SNS use on satisfaction with democracy in an understudied region. First, it uses a comparative approach that expands on existing studies in the region that usually focus on, at most, a handful of cases. This approach allows us to examine the dynamics of the region as a whole and to evaluate how country-level factors can interact with individual-level behavior because of the variety of democratic outcomes in the region. Furthermore, this study is novel in its methodology. By utilizing entropy balancing, robustness can be added to the findings. Previous studies have noted that internet use is skewed by multiple demographic factors. By using entropy balancing to create control and treatment groups within the survey data, we attempt to eliminate spurious correlations where the effect of SNS use on satisfaction with democracy is driven by a demographic variable rather than SNS use itself.

Finally, this study offers both theoretical and substantive importance in understanding SNS use and politics in CEE. The paper shows that both the general use of SNS and information seeking lead to greater satisfaction with democracy when democracy is working well and less satisfaction with democracy when backsliding occurs. Theoretically, the mechanism for this change attitude change is due to the internet's ability to provide opportunities of "window opening" and "mirror holding" as described by Bailard (2014). However, it is also important to consider that SNS use is more interactive than general internet use. Thus, general SNS use can provide additional opportunities for users to become inadvertently informed about politics. This can, therefore, enable greater numbers of citizens to be aware of potential backsliding because SNS have the potential to reach even inattentive audiences. From these findings, it seems that both the scope of information available and the interactive nature of SNS are the key reasons why it is different from other media.

Substantively, the findings in this study are important when we consider the future of democracy in CEE. As discussed earlier in this paper, the partisan capture of the state and oligarchization of corporate media are often developments that accompany democratic backsliding in the region. In such situations, the online public sphere is one of the few open conduits of communication outside the control of the governing party. The findings presented here show that SNS use might actually be able to strengthen the democratic norms of its users and thus provide a check against leaders that attempt to fix the rules of the game and dismantle liberal democracy. Of course, further research is needed to determine whether civil society and pro-democratic groups can effectively use this to their advantage, but the findings suggest that online communities may be more prone to support pro-democratic movements in the face of democratic backsliding.

While this study adds to the existing knowledge on SNS use and politics in CEE, it has limitations in both design and generalizability. First, it suffers from the common problems of plaque survey research design. In other words, selection bias in surveys makes it difficult to attribute causation. For instance, if something other than SNS use leads survey respondents' satisfaction with democracy to be conditional on the quality of democracy in their country, it will bias the Results of empirical models. To help mitigate some of this bias, the methodological technique of entropy balancing was used. This allowed me to control for theoretical demographic confounders before estimating the relationship among SNS use, democratic conditions, and satisfaction with democracy. While this does not allow attribution of causality, it emulates random trials and reduces overall bias in the Results.

A second limitation of this study is the overall generalizability of the Results. As noted in the early parts of the paper, CEE has a unique range of democratic outcomes and a unique history of democracy and democratization. Thus, while SNS users in CEE tend to perceive democratic backsliding and the quality of democracy, it is impossible to say that this phenomenon would occur globally or even in new democracies that are still in the transition or consolidation process. Indeed, further research outside the region is needed to continue evaluating the effects of SNS use on support for democracy.

Despite these limitations, the study shows that SNS users in CEE are perceptive of the quality of democracy and change to democracy in their country. It builds on studies such as Bailard (2014), which discusses how internet users may be perceptive to democratic conditions due to the medium's qualities of "mirror holding" and "window opening." It also builds on Placek's (2017) finding that SNS users in the region tended to support their governments before democratic backsliding occurred in many countries. However, the current study provides further evidence that SNS users perceive changes in democracy. Normatively speaking, these findings are beneficial in that SNS seem to allow users an open space to hold autocrats accountable for their actions. Certainly, the current study cannot discern whether this opportunity is realized, but the findings offer hope that this may be the case. As such, this paper provides evidence that, in some instances, SNS use might prove beneficial for democracy in the face of democratic backsliding.

Notes

1. See Table A1 in the Appendix for descriptive statistics of all dependent and independent variables.
2. The standard deviation of the original six-category variable was 2.28, whereas the variance for the three-category variable is .875.
3. For example, in 2014, Hungary's VDEM Liberal Democracy rating is .532. In 2009, their VDEM Liberal Democracy rating was .782. By subtracting 2009's rating from 2014 we get the Five-year change in democracy rating of -.25. Mathematically the annotation would be [2014 VDEM Liberal Democracy rating] - [2009 VDEM Liberal Democracy rating]= [Five -year change in democracy rating]. Thus, in our example .532 - .782 = -.25.
4. Full empirical results for each figure are found in Tables A3-A8 in the Appendix.
5. In all analyses, the reference category for social media use and social media news is "never use." Thus, all other findings are in reference to people who never use SNS or never use it to seek news.
6. All empirical models in the paper are hierarchical ordinal logistic regressions because of the ordinal coding of the dependent variable.
7. As noted in the Data and Methods section, entropy balancing is performed before all the empirical models. Full weighting statistics for entropy balancing are found

in Table A2 of the Appendix. The results show that entropy balancing was successful in reweighting the means of the control and treatment groups thus adding robustness to the findings in this section.

Disclosure statement

No potential conflict of interest was reported by the author(s).

Funding

The work was supported by the Office of the Vice President for Research, University of South Carolina .

References

Anspach, N. M. (2017). The new personal influence: How our Facebook friends influence the news we read. *Political Communication*, *34*(4), 590–606.

Bailard, C. S. (2014). *Democracy's double-edged sword*. Johns Hopkins University Press. doi:10.1353/book.72112

Bail, C. A., Argyle, L. P., Brown, T. W., Bumpus, J. P., Chen, H. ... Volfovsky, A. (2018). Exposure to opposing views on social media can increase political polarization. *Proceedings of the National Academy of Sciences*, *115*(37), 9216–9221. doi:10.1073/pnas.1804840115

Bajomi-Lázár, P. (2012). The party colonisation of the media: The case of hungary. *East European Politics and Societies*, *27*(1), 69–89. doi:10.1177/0888325412465085

Bajomi-Lázár, P. (2014). *Party colonisation of the media in central and Eastern Europe*. Central European University Press. doi:10.1515/9789633860427

Barberá, P., Jost, J. T., Nagler, J., Tucker, J. A., & Bonneau, R. (2015). Tweeting from left to right: Is online political communication more than an echo chamber? *Psychological Science*, *26*(10), 1531–1542. doi:10.1177/0956797615594620

Beam, M. A., Hutchens, M. J., & Hmielowski, J. D. (2018). Facebook news and (De)polarization: Reinforcing spirals in the 2016 US election. *Information communication & society*, *21*(7), 940–958. doi:10.1080/1369118X.2018.1444783

Bennett, W. L., & Iyengar, S. (2008). A new era of minimal effects? The changing foundations of political communication. *Journal of Communication*, *58*(4), 707–731. doi:10.1111/j.1460-2466.2008.00410.x

Bode, L. (2016). Political news in the news feed: Learning politics from social media. *Mass Communication & Society*, *19*(1), 24–48. doi:10.1080/15205436.2015.1045149

Bode, L., & Vraga, E. K. (2015). In related news, that was wrong: The correction of misinformation through related stories functionality in social media. *Journal of Communication*, *65*(4), 619–638. doi:10.1111/jcom.12166

Boese, V. A. (2019). How (not) to measure democracy. *International Area Studies Review*, *22*(2), 95–127. doi:10.1177/2233865918815571

Booth, J. A., & Seligson, M. A. (2009). *The legitimacy puzzle in latin America: Political support and democracy in eight nations*. Cambridge University Press. doi:10.1017/CBO9780511818431

Boulianne, S. (2009). Does internet use affect engagement? A meta-analysis of research. *Political Communication*, *26*(2), 193–211. doi:10.1080/10584600902854363

Boulianne, S. (2015). Social media use and participation: A meta-analysis of current research. *INformation Communication & Society*, *18*(5), 524–538. doi:10.1080/1369118X.2015.1008542

Boulianne, S. (2022). Standby ties that mobilize: social media platforms and civic engagement. *Social Science Computer Review*, 1–16. doi:10.1177/08944393211067687

Canache, D., Mondak, J. J., & Seligson, M. A. (2001). Meaning and measurement in cross-national research on satisfaction with democracy. *Public Opinion Quarterly*, *65*(4), 506–528. doi:10.1086/323576

Ceron, A. (2015). Internet, news, and political trust: The difference between social media and online media outlets. *Journal of Computer-Mediated Communication*, *20*(5), 487–503. doi:10.1111/jcc4.12129

Ceron, A., Curini, L., Iacus, S. M., & Porro, G. (2014). Every tweet counts? how sentiment analysis of social media can improve our knowledge of citizens' political preferences with an application to Italy and France. *New Media & Society*, *16*(2), 340–358. doi:10.1177/1461444813480466

Colleoni, E., Rozza, A., & Arvidsson, A. (2014). Echo chamber or public sphere? predicting political orientation and measuring political homophily in twitter using big data. *Journal of Communication*, *64*(2), 317–332. doi:10.1111/jcom.12084

Del Vicario, M., Bessi, A., Zollo, F., Petroni, F., Scala, A. ... Quattrociocchi, W. (2016). The spreading of misinformation online. *Proceedings of the National Academy of Sciences of the United States of America*, *113*(3), 554–559. doi:10.1073/pnas.1517441113

Dimitrova, D. V., Shehata, A., Strömbäck, J., & Nord, L. W. (2014). The effects of digital media on political knowledge and participation in election campaigns. *Communication Research*, *41*(1), 95–118. doi:10.1177/0093650211426004

Druckman, J. N., Peterson, E., & Slothuus, R. (2013). How elite partisan polarization affects public opinion formation. *The American Political Science Review*, *107*(1), 57–79. doi:10.1017/S0003055412000500

Enyedi, Z. (2020). Right-wing authoritarian innovations in central and eastern Europe. *East European Politics*, *36*(3), 363–377. doi:10.1080/21599165.2020.1787162

Feller, A., Kuhnert, M., Sprenger, T., & Welpe, I. (2011). Divided they tweet: The network structure of political microbloggers and discussion topics. *Proceedings of the Fifth International AAAI Conference on Weblogs and Social Media*, July 17-21, 2011, Barcelona Spain, 474–477.

Gainous, J., Abbott, J. P., & Wagner, K. M. (2021). Active vs. passive social media engagement with critical information: protest behavior in two asian countries. *The International Journal of Press/politics*, *26*(2), 464–483. doi:10.1177/1940161220963606

Garrett, R. K. (2009). Echo chambers online?: politically motivated selective exposure among internet news users. *Journal of Computer-Mediated Communication*, *14*(2), 265–285. doi:10.1111/j.1083-6101.2009.01440.x

Gil de Zuniga, H., Jung, N., & Valenzuela, S. (2012). Social media use for news and individuals' social capital, civic engagement and political participation. *Journal of Computer-Mediated Communication*, *17*(3), 319–336. doi:10.1111/j.1083-6101.2012.01574.x

Guzek, D., & Grzesiok-Horosz, A. (2022). Political will and media law: A Poland case analysis. *East European Politics and Societies*, *36*(4), 1245–1262. doi:10.1177/08883254211049514

Hainmueller, J. (2012). Entropy balancing for causal effects: A multivariate reweighting method to produce balanced samples in observational studies. *Political Analysis*, *20*(1), 25–46. doi:10.1093/pan/mpr025

Hansen, N., Postmes, T., van der Vinne, N., & van Thiel, W. (2012). Information and communication technology and cultural change: How ICT changes self-construal and values. *Social Psychology*, *43*(4), 222–231. doi:10.1027/1864-9335/a000123

Hladík, R., & Štětka, V. (2017). The powers that tweet. *Journalism Studies*, *18*(2), 154–174. doi:10.1080/1461670X.2015.1046995

Ho, D. E., Imai, K., King, G., & Stuart, E. A. (2007). Matching as nonparametric preprocessing for reducing model dependence in parametric causal inference. *Political Analysis*, *15*(3), 199–236. doi:10.1093/pan/mpl013

Inglehart, R. (1988). The renaissance of political culture. *The American Political Science Review*, *82*(4), 1203. doi:10.2307/1961756

Inglehart, R. (2003). Technological Change, Culture Change, and Society. In R. Breton & J. G. Rietz (Eds.), *Globalization and Society: Processes of Differentiation Examined*. Praeger.

Kahne, J., Middaugh, E., Lee, N.-J., & Feezell, J. T. (2012). Youth online activity and exposure to diverse perspectives. *New Media & Society*, *14*(3), 492–512. doi:10.1177/1461444811420271

Kubin, E., & von Sikorski, C. (2021). The role of (social) media in political polarization: A systematic review. *Annals of the International Communication Association*, *45*(3), 188–206. doi:10.1080/23808985.2021.1976070

Lee, F. L. F. (2016). Impact of social media on opinion polarization in varying times. *Communication and the Public*, *1*(1), 56–71. doi:10.1177/2057047315617763

Lee, J. K., & Kim, E. (2017). Incidental exposure to news: Predictors in the social media setting and effects on information gain online. *Computers in Human Behavior*, *75*, 1008–1015. doi:10.1016/j.chb.2017.02.018

Levitsky, S., & Way, L. A. (2010). *Competitive authoritarianism: hybrid regimes after the cold war*. Cambridge University Press. doi:10.1017/CBO9780511781353

Linde, J., & Ekman, J. (2003). Satisfaction with Democracy: A Note on Frequently Used Indicator in Comparative Politics. *European Journal of Political Research*, *42*(3), 391–408. doi:10.1111/1475-6765.00089

Mancini, P. (2012). Media fragmentation, party system, and democracy. *The International Journal of Press/politics*, *18*(1), 43–60. doi:10.1177/1940161212458200

Matay, M., & Kaposi, I. (2008). Radicals online: The hungarian street protests of 2006 and the internet. In K. Jakubowicz & M. Sükösd (Eds.), *Finding the right place on the map: Central and Eastern European media change in a global perspective* (pp. 277–296). Bristol, U.K: Intellect Books.

Metcalfe, B. (2013). Metcalfe's Law after 40 Years of Ethernet. *Computer*, *46*(12), 26–31. doi:10.1109/MC.2013.374

Mishler, W., & Rose, R. (1997). Trust, distrust and skepticism: Popular evaluations of civil and political institutions in post-communist societies. *The Journal of Politics*, *59*(2), 418–451. doi:10.1017/S0022381600053512

Nanz, A., & Matthes, J. (2022). Seeing political information online incidentally. effects of first- and second-level incidental exposure on democratic outcomes. *Computers in Human Behavior*, *133*, 107285. doi:10.1016/j.chb.2022.107285

Newton, K. (2021). Widespread reach, not much influence: online news and mass political attitudes and behaviour in the UK. *The Political Quarterly*, *92*(4), 716–726. doi:10.1111/1467-923X.13052

Ohme, J. (2021). Algorithmic social media use and its relationship to attitude reinforcement and issue-specific political participation – the case of the 2015 European immigration movements. *Journal of Information Technology & Politics*, *18*(1), 36–54. doi:10.1080/19331681.2020.1805085

Placek, M. (2018). Can the Internet aid democratic consolidation? online news and legitimacy in central and Eastern Europe. *International Journal of Communication*, *12*, 2810–2831.

Placek, M. (2020). Learning democracy digitally? the internet and knowledge of democracy in nondemocracies. *Democratization*, *27*(8), 1413–1435. doi:10.1080/13510347.2020.1795640

Placek, M. A. (2017). #democracy: Social media use and democratic legitimacy in central and Eastern Europe. *Democratization*, *24*(4), 632–650. doi:10.1080/13510347.2016.1202929

Prior, M. (2005). News vs. entertainment: How increasing media choice widens gaps in political knowledge and turnout. *American Journal of Political Science, 49*(3), 577–592. doi:10.1111/j.1540-5907.2005.00143.x

Prior, M. (2007). *Post-Broadcast democracy: How media choice increases inequality in political involvement and polarizes elections.* Cambridge University Press. doi:10.1017/CBO9781139878425

Ridge, H. M. (2021). Just like the others: Party differences, perception, and satisfaction with democracy. *Party Politics, 28*(3), 419–430. doi:10.1177/1354068820985193

Robson, K., & Pevalin, D. (2015). *Multilevel Modeling in Plain Language.* Sage Publications. doi:10.4135/9781473920712

Schedler, A. (1998). What is democratic consolidation? *Journal of Democracy, 9*(2), 91–107.

Sekhon, J. S. (2009). Opiates for the matches: Matching methods for causal inference. *Annual Review of Political Science, 12*(1), 487–508. doi:10.1146/annurev.polisci.11.060606.135444

Simpson, P. A., & Druxes, H. (2015). *Digital media strategies of the far right in Europe and the United States.* Lanham, MD: Lexington Books.

Southwell, B. G., & Thorson, E. A. (2015). The prevalence, consequence, and remedy of misinformation in mass media systems. *Journal of Communication, 65*(4), 589–595. doi:10.1111/jcom.12168

Stanley, B. (2019). Backsliding away? the quality of democracy in central and Eastern Europe. *Journal of Contemporary European Research, 15*(4), 343–353. doi:10.30950/jcer.v15i4.1122

Steenbergen, M. R., & Jones, B. S. (2002). Modeling multilevel data structures. *American Journal of Political Science, 46*(1), 218. doi:10.2307/3088424

Stegmueller, D. (2013). How many countries for multilevel modeling? a comparison of frequentist and bayesian approaches. *American Journal of Political Science, 57*(3), 748–761. doi:10.1111/ajps.12001

Stetka, V. (2012). From multinationals to business tycoons media ownership and journalistic autonomy in central and Eastern Europe. *The International Journal of Press/politics, 17*(4), 433–456. doi:10.1177/1940161212452449

Stetka, V., Surowiec, P., & Mazák, J. (2019). Facebook as an Instrument of election campaigning and voters' engagement: Comparing Czechia and poland. *European Journal of Communication, 34*(2), 121–141. doi:10.1177/0267323118810884

Stroud, N. (2008). Media use and political predispositions: Revisiting the concept of selective exposure. *Political Behavior, 30*(3), 341–366. doi:10.1007/s11109-007-9050-9

Theocharis, Y., Boulianne, S., Koc-Michalska, K., & Bimber, B. (2023). Platform affordances and political participation: How social media reshape political engagement. *West European Politics, 46*(4), 788–811. doi:10.1080/01402382.2022.2087410

Tomini, L. (2014). Reassessing democratic consolidation in central and Eastern Europe and the role of the EU. *Europe-Asia Studies, 66*(6), 859–891. doi:10.1080/09668136.2014.905387

Tworzecki, H., & Semetko, H. A. (2012). Media use and political engagement in three new democracies malaise versus mobilization in the Czech Republic, Hungary, and Poland. *The International Journal of Press/politics, 17*(4), 407–432. doi:10.1177/1940161212452450

Vaccaro, A. (2021). Comparing measures of democracy: statistical properties, convergence, and interchangeability. *European Political Science, 20*(4), 666–684. doi:10.1057/s41304-021-00328-8

Vachudova, M. A. (2020). Ethnopopulism and democratic backsliding in central Europe. *East European Politics, 36*(3), 318–340. doi:10.1080/21599165.2020.1787163

Wagner, M. (2021). Affective polarization in multiparty systems. *Electoral Studies, 69*, 1–13. doi:10.1016/j.electstud.2020.102199

Wojcieszak, M. E., & Mutz, D. C. (2009). Online groups and political Discourse: Do online discussion spaces facilitate exposure to political disagreement? *Journal of Communication, 59*(1), 40–56. doi:10.1111/j.1460-2466.2008.01403.x

Wojcieszak, M., & Warner, B. R. (2020). Can interparty contact reduce affective polarization? a systematic test of different forms of intergroup contact. *Political Communication, 37*(6), 789–811. doi:10.1080/10584609.2020.1760406

Zaller, J. (1992). *The nature and origins of mass opinion.* Cambridge University Press. doi:10.1017/CBO9780511818691

Patterns of negative campaigning during the 2019 European election: Political parties' Facebook posts and users' sharing behaviour across twelve countries

Paweł Baranowski, Simon Kruschinski, Uta Russmann, Jörg Haßler, Melanie Magin, Márton Bene, Andrea Ceron, Daniel Jackson, and Darren Lilleker

ABSTRACT
Focusing on the 2019 European Parliament campaign, we investigate parties' engagement in negative campaigning on Facebook and the relationship to a parties' ideology and their status as governing versus opposition party at the national level. Manual coding of 8,153 Facebook posts of parties from twelve European countries shows parties create less negative posts than positive and neutral ones. However, these negative posts attract more shares than positive, neutral, and balanced statements, which increases their prominence on the platform. Hence, users and algorithms create a negative campaign environment on Facebook to a greater extent than parties.

Negative campaigning is not only one of the most used, but also one of the most debated communication strategies in electoral campaigning (Haselmayer, 2019; Richardson, 2001). One reason for this is that studies analyzing the impact of negative campaigning report positive as well as negative effects on voters; thereby not providing a clear directive for campaigning parties. For instance, a positive effect is that voters can get information for political choices they would otherwise not get (Kahn & Kenney, 2000; Mattes & Redlawsk, 2014) and this can contribute to more informed voters. At the same time, at the societal level, negative messages can reduce trust in politics, potentially leading to disengagement of citizens in democratic processes (Ansolabehere & Iyengar, 1995; Papp & Patkós, 2019).

The aim of this study is twofold: first, we are interested in how parties use negative campaigning on Facebook and whether this varies according to their role in national government or opposition and their ideological standpoint. Second, we analyze how users respond to negative messages and whether their engagement is dependent on the parties that are posting the content. Hence, we do not assess the broader implications of the sharing of negative messages, whether they are positive in the sense of increasing voter's search for more information or negative in terms of, for example, reducing voter's trust in politics. But knowledge about users' sharing behavior is of great importance for campaigning parties as user engagement is an important indicator for the evaluation of a party's message. Indeed, the results presented by Ennser-Jedenastik and colleagues (2022) suggest that parties dynamically respond to the social media behavior of their potential voters by adapting Facebook communication depending on the received user feedback, leveraging the 'expected reception' (Kristensen, 2021) that negativity triggers.

We believe that our endeavor is relevant because research about negative campaigning on social media platforms, such as Facebook, is still limited (Haselmayer, 2019; for exceptions see Auter & Fine, 2016; Ceron & Curini, 2018; Gerbaudo, Marogna, & Alzetta, 2019; Heiss, Schmuck, & Matthes, 2019). Previous academic undertakings have shown notable differences in the degree, types and effects of negative messages between a broad range of communication channels – election manifestos, political advertisements, campaign posters, press releases, televised election debates, news coverage, websites (e.g., Ansolabehere & Iyengar, 1995; Geer, 2006; Holtz-Bacha, 2001; Johnston & Kaid, 2002; Kaid & Johnston, 1991; Lau & Pomper, 2004; Russmann, 2017; Schweitzer, 2010). As the media landscape evolves, Facebook has become the most important social media platform for political news across Europe (Newman, Fletcher, Schulz, Andı, & Nielsen, 2020), and political actors meanwhile use it as one of their central communication channels in electoral campaigns (Magin, Podschuweit, Haßler, & Russmann, 2017).

Moreover, with a few exceptions, comparative studies on the role of negative campaigning in multiple countries (Maier & Nai, 2020; Nai, 2020; Papp & Patkós, 2019; Valli & Nai, 2020; Walter, van der Brug, & van Praag, 2014) or in European Parliamentary elections (Ceron & Curini, 2018; Raycheva & Simunas, 2017; Schweitzer, 2010) are scarce. Therefore, we still know surprisingly little about the use of negative campaigning by parties in different countries – especially in Europe. Despite the stigma of the secondary character of EP elections (Reif & Schmitt, 1980), their importance (at least in terms of turnout) continues to grow (Ehin & Talving, 2021). From a scholarly perspective, however, they represent an arena of significant research interest. They have overlapping campaign durations, slight differences in voting systems and identical legal conditions in all EU countries. Hence, they are a unique opportunity for comparative research, the results of which can make an important contribution to the state of knowledge about election campaigns from a broad perspective.

Our study contributes to closing these gaps by presenting an exploratory investigating how parties from 12 countries have used Facebook for negative campaigning in the 2019 European election campaign. We provide novel, empirical descriptive insights on the use of negative campaigning in electoral communication on Facebook and users' reactions across multiple countries. More specifically, we investigate to what extent parties use negative campaigning and how often users share posts with negative compared to non-negative statements. We further explore how these patterns are affected by two party characteristics: (1) parties's role in government or opposition at the national level and (2) their ideological standpoint. Our analysis of 8,153 Facebook posts is the first to investigate negative campaigning on Facebook in such a broad range of countries and in a common political election contest. Thus, the analysis of a heterogeneous set of European countries in a single election contest increases the social significance and generalizability of the results compared to previous studies (Riffe et al., 1998).

Negative campaigning on Facebook as an amplification strategy

"Negative campaigning takes a variety of forms" (Haselmayer, 2019, p. 356). Following previous research (Ansolabehere & Iyengar, 1995; Geer, 2006) we define it as a campaign strategy used by political actors to attack political opponents by criticizing their behavior, ideologies, policy positions, set of values, or personal qualities. The aim of this strategy is to change recipients' attitudes in a negative way toward the political opponent. Hence, exaggerations and negative emotions such as fear, envy, blame and anger can be an aspect of negative campaigning (Raycheva & Suminas, 2017). Negative campaigning aims at gaining voters' support by downgrading their attitudes toward the political opponents (Haynes & Rhine, 1998), decreasing the utility that they expect by supporting the opponents, and/or reinforcing and strengthening extant negative associations voters have with the opponents (Iyengar & Krupenkin, 2018; Meffert, Chung, Joiner, Waks, & Garst, 2006). However, it cannot be taken for granted that these hopes of the political actors will necessarily be fulfilled.

Previous research suggests that, on balance, negative campaigning seems more likely to appeal to and mobilize a party's most loyal supporters such as Facebook followers rather than its opponents (Ansolabehere & Iyengar, 1995; Meffert et al., 2006) and to persuade neutral voters if the negative message resonates (e.g. Weeks, 2015). Overall, research has shown that parties resort to negative campaigning to get voters' support (Nai, 2020; Russmann, 2017) while demobilizing and depressing their opponent's voter base (Fridkin & Kenney, 2004). Negative messages are considered important for election campaigning since they are more memorable for voters and stimulate their knowledge about a campaign (Lau, Sigelman, & Rovner, 2007) and can gain high media attention (Haselmayer, Meyer, & Wagner, 2019; Maier & Nai, 2020).

Negative messages (also statements in Facebook posts) can be distinguished from positive, balanced, and neutral ones. Positive messages refer to highlighting, supporting and applauding a party's or politician's success, qualifications, accomplishments, and campaign tactics (Kaid & Johnston, 1991; Lau & Pomper, 2004). In digital communication, this "positive campaigning" has been used to "stress the effectiveness of hope-driven and positive content" (Gerbaudo et al., 2019) to elicit user reactions, "with the ultimate aim of maximizing motivation and engagement" (Gerbaudo et al., 2019). In balanced messages, negative as well as positive statements are used in about equal shares. That is, the sender both criticizes or attacks a political opponent but also supports and applauds the own party and its politicians or other political opponents in the same message (Richardson, 2001). Last, neutral messages include neither positive nor negative statements and usually have an informative character.

Facebook provides political actors with strategic affordances for negative campaigning which makes it a worthwhile strategy to use on the platform due to three reasons: first, political actors' negative messages can bypass the filter of the news media and directly reach users through Facebook posts. Certainly, negative messages can attract media attention (Haselmayer et al., 2019; Maier & Nai, 2020), but journalists often frame negative messages in a particular way, focusing on their strategic role rather than their substance (Pedersen, 2014), and giving them context by supplementing them with opponents' reactions or by interpreting and criticizing them. Hence, Facebook posts reflect how political actors position themselves and how they want to be seen by the public. Second, Facebook users are not only highly receptive to negative messages (Bene, 2017a; Heiss et al., 2019), but also often express negative and critical positions on the platform themselves (Bene, 2017b; Ziegele, Breiner, & Quiring, 2014). Consequently, negative campaigning fits well the overall atmosphere of this communication environment. The third reason is related to the attention-grabbing character of negative messages on Facebook: the main challenge for political actors is to compete for users' attention on the platform alongside the multitude of personal and entertaining content appearing on their News Feed. Negativity is a viable strategy in this context of information overload as users are more likely to pay attention to negative content (Meffert et al., 2006; Soroka, 2014).

The direct, organic communication of parties is only one part of campaigning on Facebook as user engagement largely affects the way voters perceive the campaign. In fact, the dissemination logic of Facebook is virality (Klinger & Svensson, 2015), where followers can make content visible for their friends by engaging with them (i.e., through liking or sharing). Additionally, the number of interactions with individual posts is one of the most important factors for Facebook's News Feed algorithm and may cause a popularity bias: Posts earning high engagement and already highly visible posts become even more visible compared to less engaged ones ("Matthew effect"; Bucher, 2012) – and a high number of shares is particularly efficient in this respect. According to Bossetta and colleagues (2018) shares are discursive acts and constitute a certain degree of political engagement on Facebook, which positively affects the algorithmic driven ranking and "organic" spreading of content across the platform. Shares are an extremely important form of interaction on Facebook because by forwarding a post to a user's network, the message is endorsed by the sharer among his/her friends, consequently offering additional verification of the shared material and ultimately being a more engaging activity than likingand commenting(Kim & Yang, 2017). Recent studies (Gerbaudo et al., 2019; Heiss et al., 2019) call for a more balanced understanding of the relationship between post characteristics and user engagement. In private settings, studies found a "positivity bias" in users' self-disclosure and in feedback processes (Ziegele & Reinecke, 2017), and news articles on Facebook were more likely to go viral if positive (Berger & Milkman, 2012). However, research on content published by political actors shows users are more likely to engage with negative posts than with neutral or positive content (Bene, 2017a; Ceron & D'Adda, 2016; Heiss et al., 2019). This phenomenon can be explained by psychological and sociological factors. The psychological approach argues that negative content triggers stronger psychophysiological reactions (Shoemaker, 1996) alongside greater attention (Meffert et al., 2006; Soroka,

2014) resulting in higher levels of cognitive involvement (Lau, Sigelman & Rover, 2007) that may lead to action (Heiss et al., 2019). The sociological explanation highlights that engaging with negative content may enable users to express political opinions in a way that does not require positive identification with existing political actors, which is generally avoided in front of a wide and heterogeneous network of Facebook friends (Bene, 2017b). Given these apparent incentives of going negative and assuming that political actors intentionally spread negativity with the expectation of triggering engagement due to their potential, our first hypothesis (H1) is that: *Facebook posts containing negative statements were more often shared than posts with (H1a) balanced, (H1b) positive, and (H1c) neutral statements in the 2019 European election campaign.*

Party characteristics as determining factors of negative campaigning and sharing behavior

Campaign strategies among parties usually differ (at least to a certain extent) and the decision for negative campaigning is dependent on structural conditions. A well-documented pattern is that negative campaigning is a less popular tactic in multiparty systems such as Germany, Denmark, and the Netherlands than in two-party systems like the U.S. (Elmelund-Præstekær, 2010; Holtz-Bacha, 2001; Russmann, 2017). The reason for this is the need to form coalitions in multiparty systems, which becomes more difficult if the former target of an attack has to become a partner in government later. However, being less likely does not mean non-existent. Despite the multiparty structure of the European parliament, negative campaigning has been used in European elections, both in traditional campaigning channels and on social media. Indeed, its use differs between countries and parties (Ceron & Curini, 2018; Raycheva & Šuminas, 2017). Previous research has consistently shown that differences in campaigns are often larger between parties than between countries, and party characteristics are particularly important in explaining negative campaigning (Kaid & Johnston, 1991; Magin et al., 2017; Walter et al., 2014). Moreover – as second-order elections – European elections typically focus on national concerns rather than EU issues (Reif & Schmitt, 1980).

Therefore, our study analyses negative campaigning from a party perspective. More specifically, we focus on two party characteristics – (1) parties' role in national parliaments and (2) their positions on the ideological spectrum – and investigate how these determine (a) different parties' degree of negativity on Facebook and (b) the number of shares of their negative posts. Based on the following theoretical and empirical findings, we expect these two party characteristics to be the main drivers of parties' strategic decision to use negative campaigning:

(1) Role in national parliaments. Previous studies show that challenger parties are more likely to go negative than incumbents (e.g., Auter & Fine, 2016; Elmelund-Præstekær, 2010; Nai, 2020; Russmann, 2017, StromerGalley et al., 2018). Geer (2006, p. 110) notes that a challenger is "serving its role as a critic of those in power" by going negative to make the voters aware of the incumbent's weaknesses. Challengers need to convince the voters of the advantages of themselves being in office, and the past actions of incumbents offer much scope for attack. In addition, when going negative leads to a backlash effect, challengers have less to lose than incumbents (Walter et al., 2014). Yet, given negativity on Facebook has the potential to increase user engagement (Bene, 2017a; Ceron & D'Adda, 2016; Heiss et al., 2019), smaller parties can use negativity as an equivalent of having lower prominence in traditional media. However, our current understanding of these dynamics comes from studies of negative campaigning in national contexts. European election campaigns differ significantly from national ones for two reasons: first, in contrast to national parliaments, there is no formal government and opposition in the European Parliament. Instead, governing coalitions tend to form on an issue-by-issue basis. Second, research has consistently shown that European elections are second-order elections in which campaigning parties focus more on national issues and constellations than on European ones (Reif & Schmitt, 1980). This is particularly salient for opposition parties, which are more likely to omit EU issues from their campaigns (Eugster et al., 2020) and try to translate EP elections into a national contest. Therefore, we assume that the government/opposition divide at the national level has more influence on each party's

level of negativity in the European election campaign and hypothesize: *H2: Parties in opposition in the national parliament used negative campaigning in their Facebook posts to a greater extent than parties in government at the national level in the 2019 European election campaign.*

User engagement can also depend on the role of the originator of negative posts in the national parliament. Parties in national government often have higher follower bases than opposition parties and can gain attention even from users that do not support them by addressing topics that they are responsible for in their government positions. Additionally, negativity can strongly influence committed party supporters and thus mobilize them to intensify their support (Ansolabehere & Iyengar, 1995), resulting as a part of mobilization strategy. Thus, previous research shows that posts by government members typically gain high levels of user-engagement (Steinfeld & Lev-On, 2020). Nevertheless, parties in national opposition are often more active on social media and have more extensive first-degree networks, which might act as a multiplier for engagement with their posts (Larsson & Kalsnes, 2014). Moreover, previous research has shown that opposition parties in national elections are far more inclined to use negative strategies in their election campaigns (Walter et al., 2014). Given these discrepancies in the current literature, we formulate the following research question: *RQ1: How did a party's status as a governing or opposition party in the national parliament determine how often its negative posts were shared in the 2019 European election campaign?*

(2) Ideology. Studies in national contexts show parties with more extreme ideological views take more extreme positions in their campaigns. Nai (2018) found that the ideological distance between parties fosters negative messages, because when parties disagree on key issues they are more likely to criticize each other. In that regard, studies found differences along parties' ideological lines (Lau & Pomper, 2004), with candidates and parties far from the ideological center (particularly far-right ones: Nai, 2020; Valli & Nai, 2020), more likely to use negative campaigning (Maier & Nai, 2020; Walter, 2014; Walter et al., 2014). A recent study on the 2019 EP election campaign found that ideology was a key aspect in parties' issue strategy (Haßler, Magin, Russmann, & Fenoll, 2021), therefore ideology is expected to also drive negativity in second-order elections. Consequently, we hypothesize: *H3: The further a party is ideologically away from the political center, the more negative were its Facebook posts in the 2019 European election campaign.*

Furthermore, the frequency with which users share negative posts might vary according to the parties' ideological standpoint. Some studies show that users tend to engage more with posts that align to their ideological worldview (e.g., Garrett, 2009). Moreover, the results of Hiaeshutter-Rice and Weeks' (2021) study of activity on various news portals' fanpages suggest higher activity among users on the left and right of the ideological spectrum in terms of shares. Putting these results into the context of political communication, this could indicate that party supporters may be exceptionally prone to promote negative posts. However, it is still unclear to what extent the sharing of posts is determined by the posts' overall ideological position. This leads to our final research question: *RQ2: How did the party's ideology of left, center and right determine how often its negative posts were shared in the 2019 European election campaign?*

Method

Sample and data collection

To test our hypotheses and answer our research questions, we conducted a quantitative content analysis of parties' Facebook posts during the 2019 European election campaign. Altogether, 8,153 Facebook posts of parties, which reached at least 5% of the votes during the 2019 European election campaign in 12 countries (Austria, Denmark, France, Germany, Hungary, Ireland, Italy, Poland, Romania, Spain, Sweden, and UK) were coded. We chose these 12 countries because they cover 82% of the European population and their parties represent a majority of the EP´s seats (540 of 751) before the 2019 EP election. Further justification is given by their systematically balanced selection regarding important structural dimensions (e.g., political and media systems, influence on the European level, geographic regions, citizens' attitudes toward the EU). Taken together, our country selection was driven by our effort to give robust insight into the European election campaign as a whole.

All posts of the selected parties were centrally saved at a daily interval in the month leading up to the election days (28 April to 26 May 2019, UK: 25 April to 23 May, Ireland: 26 April to 24 May) using the API-based software "Facepager" (Jünger & Keyling, 2019). The posts were coded separately in each country. Conducting a cross-national content analysis faces several methodological challenges, which we approached with the following steps (see for a comprehensive discussion Rössler, 2012; Lauf & Peter, 2001): First, to reduce a coder bias due to language skills, 29 coders (1 to 5 in each country) were trained on a joint coding scheme in English. Second, to address different coding capacities in the countries, random samples were drawn ensuring a proportional distribution of days and parties in Denmark, France, Poland, Sweden, and the UK (Table 1). Third, to test for reliability, a random sample of 50 English posts from European parties and groups was drawn to allow a comparison of coding where no country-specific background knowledge was necessary. The Holsti's CR values of all categories used in the current analysis show a common understanding (all Holsti ≥ 0.7; all Brennan & Prediger's κ ≥ 0.65; all Gwet's AC ≥ 0.94; for the detailed results see Table A1). Although the Holsti coefficient is considered too liberal in single country studies (Rössler, 2012), the complexity of our cross-national content analyses, the use of binary variables, and the careful selection, preparation and training of coders justify our decision to perform reliability testing for intercoder agreement based on the Holsti coefficient.[1]

Data and analysis

In order to analyze our data gathered from the content analysis, we use a descriptive approach using different non-parametric statistical tests of the following main variables:

Negative campaigning

The overall impression of all post elements (texts, pictures and videos) was manually coded in terms of *(1) positive* and *(2) negative statements* addressed to a specific target – an individual or collective political actor representing a particular political affiliation in the case of negative statements (the potential targets of the attack have been identified as separate variables in the codebook – see Table A1 for details). An example for a positive statement in a post is:

An example for a negative statement in a post is:

Table 1. Overview of the coded posts per country*.

Country	Number of published posts (n)	Number of posts coded manually (n)	Random sample (%)
Austria	824	818	100
Denmark	581	306	53
France	1074	697	65
Germany	532	531	100
Hungary	948	947	100
Ireland	304	303	100
Italy	4597	2003	44***
Poland	849	142	17
Romania	1060	995	100
Spain	789	779	100
Sweden	751	372	50
UK	570	260	43
Total	12879	8153	-

* Only original or shared posts created by the parties under investigation in the respective national language or in English were coded. Only national parties were coded in Spain. Percent values of the random sample deviating from round values derive from the fact that some posts could not be coded because they contained foreign language content or did not contain text and were deleted.
** Of national parties.
*** In the Italian sample, Lega alone posted 3234 posts. To reduce bias, a sample of 20% of the posts from Lega was drawn (while holding the share of posts per day constant). For all other Italian parties, the full sample was coded.

Posts were coded for the tone and the target of positive or negative statements (e.g. the host party, specific other parties, parties within the broader European grouping, the EU, etc.). All these variables were coded binary indicating whether a content criteria was present (=1) or absent (=0) (see Table A1 for a full description of the variables). Neutral posts are all posts that neither include positive nor negative statements. For example:

Posts that include both negative as well as positve statements are counted as balanced. For example:

Number of shares

Facebook users can share the content which was published by the analyzed parties on their Facebook pages. The number of how often party posts were shared was collected four weeks after the election to account for possible differences in the share numbers at the publishing time of a post and the time of data collection

Party ideology. We compared parties from 12 European countries. The use of the 'ideology' variable was a deliberate simplification to help verify the impact of the three main ideological orientations on user behavior (sharing). To analyze negative campaigning by parties depending on ideological positions, we used the 2019 Chapel Hill Expert Survey–CHES (Bakker et al., 2020), positioning European parties by various factors.

We used the 'lrgen' variable, which positions each party in terms of its overall ideological stance from 0 to 10, where 0 means 'extreme left' and 10 'extreme right'. For categorization of left, centre and right parties, lowest parties in the lowest quartile of CHES 'lrgen' variable were categorized as left, parties in the highest quartile were categorized as right and parties in the two quartiles in between were categorized as centre.

Findings

To get a first overview about the use of negative campaigning on Facebook, we analyzed the proportions between posts containing negative and positive statements as well as those identified as neutral and balanced. The results indicate that across the 12 countries, 17% of all posts were coded as negative, while 26% were positive, 49% neutral, and 8% balanced. Figure 1 provides a more detailed picture by European party groups. It shows significant but very weak associations between party groups and the tone of campaign messages ($\chi(27) = 752.117$, $p < .001$, $V = 0.18$). Negative statements were dominant only in the posts of Non-Inscrits (NI) party members, hence new parties (not present in the European Parliament before the 2019 election) used the negative strategy to a greater extent. All other parties posted with neutral (ALDE, ECR, ENF, EPP, Greens/EFA, GUE/NGL, NEW, S&D) and positive (EFDD) tone more frequently than with negative tone.[2]

The analysis of all posts and its shares provides significant evidence that, in line with *H1b* and *H1c*, users shared posts with negative statements more often than positive or neutral (Figure 2). However, differences between negative and balanced posts were not significant (Kruskal-Wallis test, H (3) = 475.95, $p < .001$; Wilcoxon rank sum tests, in all other comparisons: $p < .001$), which is why *H1a* is rejected. To control for different engagement levels on different party Facebook pages, z-standardization within individual parties was used. A more detailed analysis of the posts' shares by European party groups reveals significant differences in the sharing behavior of party posts across the groups in relation to the posts´ tone (Figure 3). Kruskal-Wallis tests show that the posts' tone significantly affects how often a post is shared (in each

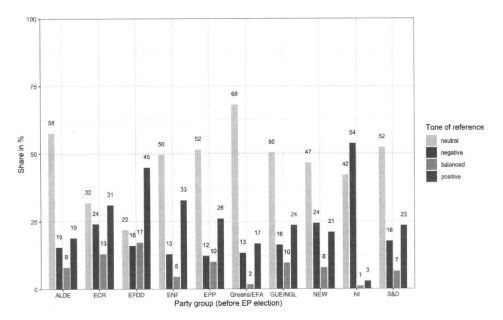

Figure 1. Overall distribution of posts with neutral, negative, balanced, and positive tone of references by European party groups. Note: 8153 coded posts. Chi-square = 752.117, df = 27, p < .001, V = 0.18

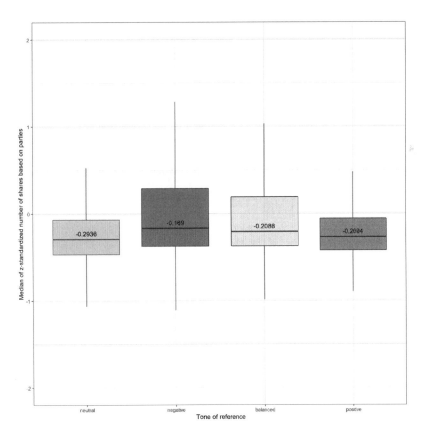

Figure 2. Median post shares differentiated between tone of references to other political actors. Note: N(neutral) = 3822, N(negative) = 1481, N(balanced) = 764, N(positive) = 2086; Kruskal-Wallis test: chi-squared = 475.95, df = 3, p-value < .001. Pairwise comparison using Wilcoxon rank sum test: balanced-negative: p > .05, all other comparisons: p < .001. Due to the highly skewed distribution there are less cases above the mean number of shares (=positive z) than below that (=negative z), this is the reason that the median is negative for each category.

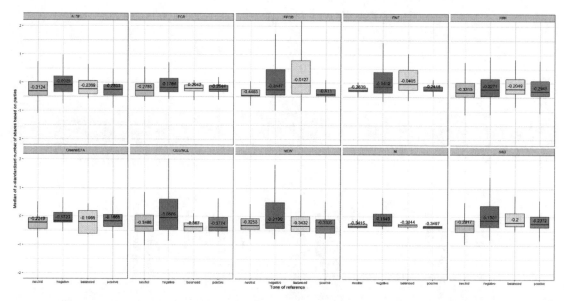

Figure 3. Median post shares differentiated between tone of references to other political actors by European party groups. Note:Results of Kruskal-Wallis tests and pairwise comparisons using Wilcoxon rank sum tests: **ALDE**: chi-squared = 23.595, df = 3, p-value < .001. Neutral-negative, negative-positive: p < .001; balanced-negative, balanced-positive: p < .05, all other comparisons: p > .05. **ECR**: chi-squared = 8.628, df = 3, p < .05. All comparisons: p > .05. **EFDD**: chi-squared = 79.217, df = 3, p < .001. Neutral-positive: p < .01, negative-balanced: p > .05, all other comparisons: p < .001. **ENF**: chi-squared = 51.605, df = 3, p < .001. Negative-balanced: p > .05, negative-positive: p < .05; all other comparisons: p < .001. **EPP**: chi-squared = 21.486, df = 3, p < .001. Negative-balanced, negative-positive: p > .05, balanced-positive, neutral-positive, negative-neutral: p < .05; balanced-neutral: p < .001. **Greens/EFA**: chi-squared = 11.514, df = 3, p < .01. Negative-neutral: p < .001, all other comparisons: p > .05. **GUE/NGL**: chi-squared = 10.557, df = 3, p < .05. Neutral-balanced, balanced-positive, neutral-positive: p > .05, all other comparisons: p < .05. **NEW**: chi-squared = 15.319, df = 3, p < .001. Negative-balanced: p < .05, neutral-balanced, balanced-positive, neutral-positive: p > .05, all other comparisons: p < .001. **NI**: chi-squared = 27.163, df = 3, p < .001. Neutral-negative: p < .001, all other comparisons: p > .05. **S&D**: chi-squared = 102.6, df = 3, p < .001. Negative-balanced, balanced-positive: p > .05, negative-positive: p < .01, all other comparisons: p < .001. Due to the highly skewed distribution there are less cases above the mean number of shares (=positive z) than below that (=negative z), this is the reason that the median is negative for each category.

case p < .05; see test statistics for each European party group in Figure 3). Negative posts published by all party groups were shared more often than those with neutral, positive and balanced statements. The only exception are negative posts by EFDD (*Mdn* = −0.2447), ENF (*Mdn* = −0.1412), and EPP (*Mdn* = −0.2271), where balanced posts were shared overall more frequently by Facebook users, although not significantly in all comparisons.

Party characteristic variables

Role in national parliaments. In the next step, we compare how party characteristics influence parties' use of negative campaigning, starting with a party's role in the national parliament. The number of posts with negative statements yields evidence supporting our assumption that opposition parties used negative campaigning (N = 1,090) in their Facebook posts to a greater extent than governing parties (N = 269) (*H2*). Table 2 shows the share of negative statements by status of parties on national level (government vs. opposition) in comparison to neutral, balanced and positive statements. The associations are significant but weak ($\chi(3)$ = 230.808, p < .001, V = 0.17). Parties in opposition at the national level use negative statements in

Table 2. Tone of references to political actors by status of party on national level (in %).

	Opposition parties (n = 5441) in %	Governmental parties (n = 2712) in %
neutral	50	47
negative	20	10
balanced	9	8
positive	22	35
Total	101	100

Note: 8,153 coded posts. Deviation from 100 due to rounding. Chi-square = 230.808, df = 3, p = 0.001, V = 0.17

nearly 20% of posts compared to only 10% in the case of governing parties. Relatedly, positive posts were more common in the case of governing (35%) compared to opposition parties (22%). The use of neutral and balanced posts does not differ according to the parties' role in the national parliaments. Altogether, H2 is supported by our data.

Regarding RQ1, the analysis indicates that posts with negative statements are shared significantly more often (Mdn = −0.1697) than balanced (Mdn = −0.2474), positive (Mdn = −0.2758) and neutral posts (Mdn = −0.3284) if they were posted by parties in national opposition (Kruskal-Wallis test, $H(3)$ = 169.36, $p < .001$; Wilcoxon rank sum tests, in each comparison $p < .05$) (see Figure 4). In contrast, this is not the case for posts from national governing parties. Here, users shared balanced posts significantly more frequently (Mdn = −0.059) than negative (Mdn = −0.1679), positive (Mdn = −0.2639) and neutral ones (Mdn = −0.2736) (Kruskal-Wallis test, $H(3)$ = 66.7, $p < .001$; Wilcoxon rank sum tests, in each comparison $p < .05$ except for the comparison of neutral and positive posts of ruling parties).

Ideology. To test *H3*, we analyzed how the parties' positions on the ideological spectrum influence the negativity of their Facebook posts. With the median as a measure of central tendency for both balance of post (mean value of the balance of negativity/positivity of the posts) and the

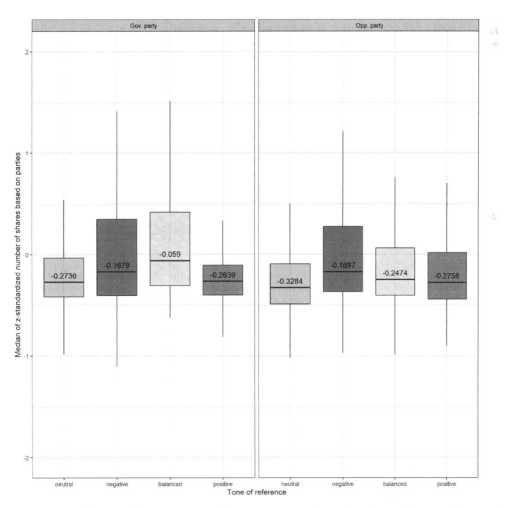

Figure 4. Median post shares differentiated between tone of campaigning to other political actors by national party role. Note: **Opp. party**: Kruskal-Wallis test: chi-squared = 169.36, df = 3, p-value < .001. Pairwise comparison using Wilcoxon rank sum test: balanced-positive: p < .05, all other comparisons: p < .001. **Gov. party**: Kruskal-Wallis test: chi-squared = 66.7 df = 3, p-value < .001. Pairwise comparison using Wilcoxon rank sum test: negative-balanced: p < .05, neutral-positive: p > .05, all other comparisons: p < .001. Due to the highly skewed distribution there are less cases above the mean number of shares (=positive z) than below that (=negative z), this is the reason that the median is negative for each category of sentiment.

position of the party in terms of its overall ideological stance (Figure 5), the analysis shows noticeable differences between political deviation from the theoretical center and negativity. Centrist parties, such as national parties affiliated with EPP or ALDE, used mostly positive campaigning in their electoral communication. The majority of political actors associated with the right-wing ECR group primarily used balanced communication in their campaigning. However, far-right parties belonging to EFDD (British Brexit Party and German Alternative für Deutschland) and ENF (French Rassemblement National and Austrian Freiheitliche Partei Österreichs) clearly show that the further a party is ideologically away from the political center, the more negative is its campaign, confirming H3. Looking at the left side of the political spectrum reveals comparable results. The main center-left party group, S&D, with the majority of parties arranged around a single ideological axis, demonstrates a rather balanced style of communication. Negativity of posts published by political actors associated with Green/EFA also did not show any relationship with ideological differences. However, far-left parties affiliated with GUE/NGL (especially German LINKE, Swedish Vänsterpartiet) and new parties on the left side of the ideological spectrum (Polish Wiosna and French La France Insoumise) are more likely to go negative.

To strengthen our argumentation, a Spearman rank correlation coefficient was performed to assess the relationship between a calculated extremity-score and the mean balance of a post, and indicates a significant positive correlation between the two variables (Spearman's $rho = .36$, $p < .01$). Thus, both far-right and far-left parties tend to use more negative campaigning in their Facebook posts.

Finally, to answer *RQ2*, we investigate if the parties' ideological position influences how often their posts are shared. Figure 6 reveals differences between the most shared posts by parties with different ideological stances. For negative campaigning, we do not find significant differences in terms of the overall share value for posts with negative statements published by parties of different ideology (Kruskal-Wallis test for negative campaigning: $H(2) = 0.511$, $p > .05$). This result indicates that regardless of the ideological stance of a party, negative campaigning can get more shares and therefore reach

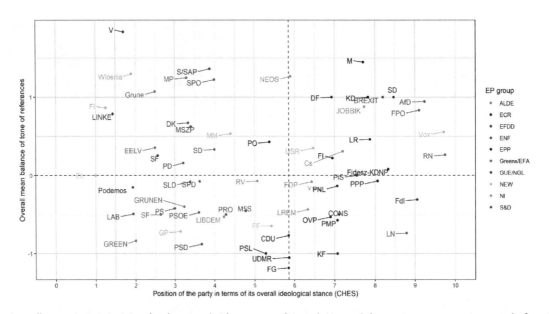

Figure 5. Overall tone in parties' Facebook posts (without neutral posts). Note: Colors represent party groups before European Parliamentary elections of 2019; dashed lines represent median values for both indicators. Overall balance = mean value of the balance of negative posts – positive posts per party. Pearson correlation between political deviation from the theoretical center (lrgen 5) and negativity: Spearman's rho = .36, p < .01.

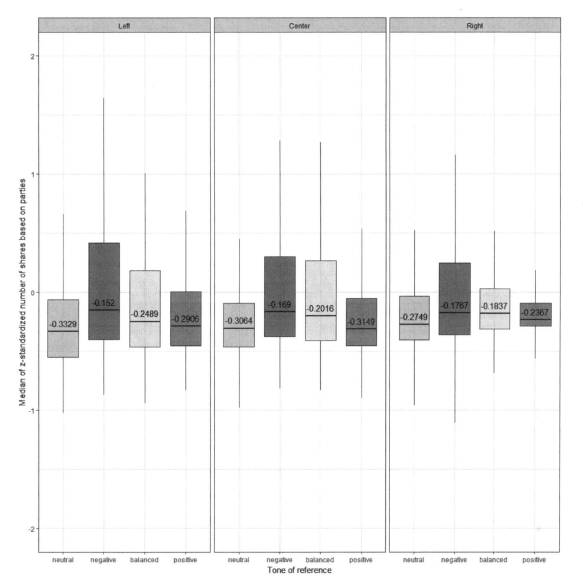

Figure 6. The median of shares on the ideological spectrum. Note: Kruskal-Wallis test for negative campaigning: chi-squared = 0.511, df = 2, p-value > .05. Due to the highly skewed distribution there are less cases above the mean number of shares (=positive z) than below that (=negative z), this is the reason that the median is negative for each category of sentiment.

a broader audience. However, a comparison of the unstandardized median share values reveals a significant difference for negativity in posts published by the parties of different ideologies (Kruskal-Wallis test for negative campaigning: $H(2) = 79.335$, $p < .001$) and significant divergence in terms of sharing and the parties' ideological stance (Wilcoxon rank sum tests, in each comparison $p < .05$). Facebook users shared posts containing negative statements of right-wing parties more often ($Mdn = 175$) than negative posts from left ($Mdn = 105$) and center parties ($Mdn = 75$).

Discussion and conclusion

Our exploratory descriptive analysis of data gathered from a cross-country content analysis breaks new ground in research on negative campaigning by (a) focusing on a broad range of countries in (b) a common political contest, and thereby, allowing for identifying and systematizing structural influences on parties' negative campaign communication on Facebook, which is the most important social media platform for political campaigning. Furthermore, it is the first study that (c) is taking user reactions to parties' negative posts into account. The findings show important common patterns for negative campaigning in European election campaigns and advances prior research in the field of political campaign communication.

Negative campaigning is clearly present, but not dominant on parties' Facebook pages in the 2019 European election; posts with positive and neutral statements were more frequent than negative ones. That said, the share of negative messages during the analyzed campaign is in line with previous research on negative campaigning on social media. Previous studies on Twitter campaigns in the United States, the Netherlands, and Italy report a share of negative posts around 15–18% (Ceron & Curini, 2018; Evans, Cordova, & Sipole, 2014; Hosch-Dayican, Amrit, Aarts, & Dassen, 2016). Moreover, the findings imply that the type of election plays a role in the use of negative, positive, and neutral posts. European elections are second-order elections with lower voter turnout than national elections, indicating a lower interest amongst voters for European elections than for national elections. By advancing the second-order elections literature, we argue that parties seem to try attracting their users' interest on Facebook by spreading positive messages to increase users' engagement and motivation (Gerbaudo et al., 2019). In comparison, parties in national elections typically use Facebook to go negative (e.g., Auter & Fine, 2016; Joathan, 2019; Steffan & Venema, 2020). The scope beyond national elections in this study and the differences in negative campaigning from national elections show that findings from one type of election are not necessarily transferable to other elections or non-election contexts. Given these dynamics, regional and local elections as well as non-election times should become the object of future studies.

The study shows that Facebook users' exposure to more or less negativity is dependent on the parties they and/or their friends follow. Consistent with the literature (Walter, 2014; Walter et al., 2014), parties located on the ideological extremes are more likely to use a negative strategy (*H3* confirmed). This applies to both far-right and far-left parties. Similarly (and perhaps because most ideologically extreme parties fall into this category), and in line with the existing scholarly research, parties in opposition at the national level are more inclined to adopt a negative campaigning strategy (*H2* confirmed). Particularly Non-Inscrits MEPs without a connection to a political group and new parties not present in the European Parliament before the 2019 election were going negative on Facebook. Hence, the main campaign strategy of these small, non-established parties was obviously to grab the media and voter attention by going negative. We do not find governmental parties eschew negativity; rather, their communication represents a mix of negative and positive content, while positive posts are rather infrequent for opposition parties. In sum, these findings confirm that party characteristics are important for explaining negative campaigning (Kaid & Johnston, 1991; Magin et al., 2017; Walter et al., 2014).

Our study provides evidence that "going negative" works in terms of engaging users. Posts with negative statements get significantly higher levels of shares than positive or neutral posts, while there are no differences for balanced posts (*H1* rejected). This result is in line with previous studies (Bene, 2017a; Heiss et al., 2019, Stromer-Galley et al., 2018) as well as with evidence that supporters find negative messages more compelling (Meffert et al., 2006; Weeks, 2015). This increases the probability that Facebook users with broad networks of politically active users will be exposed to negative content – both due to users' sharing behavior and the Facebook News Feed algorithm, which rewards post interaction with a greater visibility (popularity bias). Thus, our study advances previous literature in the field by showing that users and algorithms are driving negative campaign communication on Facebook to a greater extent than parties, and thereby, contributing to social media's reputation as an uncivil space. At the societal level, this finding indicates that even when parties are not overly negative in their communication strategies, the greater interactions with posts with negative statements mean that the campaign might *feel* more negative in its tone than it actually is. Unintended, but negative effects of this might be boosting citizens' disenchantment with politics and reducing their trust in politics, potentially leading to disengagement of citizens in democratic processes (Ansolabehere & Iyengar, 1995; Papp & Patkós, 2019).

Particularly, opposition parties benefit from adopting a negative campaigning strategy, because their posts containing negative statements were shared more often than those of national governing parties (*RQ1*). Similarly, right-wing parties benefit from their highly mobilized networks, which leads to their posts (particularly the negative and balanced ones) gaining higher engagement which increases their visibility through sharing thus making their arguments more prominent in the election campaign (*RQ2*).

A limitation of the findings on user engagement is that we only investigated how negative campaigning affects the number of shares. From a strategic perspective, the shares are more important than likes and comments since they increase parties' visibility on Facebook to a particular extent. However, restricting our analysis to shares means that we cannot determine the full spectrum of how users engage with negative messages on social media. This should be explored by future research. Furthermore, in the context of Facebook data, the possibility of social bots and Facebook advertising influencing the analyzed Facebook communication needs to be addressed (however, we cannot make any statement about possible bots or Facebook advertising in our material). Our focus is on the pure quantitative number of shares per post, because these are an indicator of visibility. In other words, we are interested in the visibility; independent of whether it was caused by shares of real users or of bots. Finally, it is important to note that even though our study covers 12 European countries, the generalizability of our findings to other contexts is limited. European elections are different from elections at other political levels, and Facebook is only one social media platform. Future research should use our codebook to investigate the use of Facebook compared to other platforms in the context of national, regional, and local elections. An increasing number of studies using the same measuring instruments would help increase the degree of generalizability of the findings.

Summing up, a party's decision to go negative is a tactical choice that is influenced by structural and situational conditions in different (electoral) contexts. This study has widened the scope of research on negative campaigning, but as outlined above, more research is necessary. Therefore, research needs to focus to a greater extent on the online context examining negative campaigning on other prominent social media platforms such as Twitter and Instagram, where parties fully control their communication and directly talk to citizens.

Notes

1. Because the central categories of the analysis were measured as binary variables some of which rarely occurred in the posts, kappa-based coefficients like Krippendorff's alpha appear to be too conservative and strict. To account for the zero inflation in the data that tends to cause bias when calculating these coefficients, we calculated Holsti values, also excluding codings where all decisions led to '0' with the result that all values still show a common understanding (robustness check: all Holsti CR ≥ 0.7)
2. See the Online Appendix for the acronyms of groups and the list of parties belonging to each category.

Acknowledgments

This publication is part of the work of the research network Campaigning for Strasbourg (CamforS), see https://digidemo.ifkw.lmu.de/camfors/.

Disclosure statement

No potential conflict of interest was reported by the author(s).

Funding

This publication is part of the work of the junior research group "DigiDeMo" which is funded by the Bavarian State Ministry of Science and the Arts and coordinated by the Bavarian Research Institute for Digital Transformation (bidt). It was also supported by the Incubator program of the Center for Social Sciences, Eötvös Loránd Research Network (project number: 03013645). Márton Bene is a recipient of the Bolyai János Research Fellowship awarded by the Hungarian Academy of Sciences (BO/334_20).

ORCID

Paweł Baranowski http://orcid.org/0000-0003-2916-4159
Simon Kruschinski http://orcid.org/0000-0002-3185-5656
Uta Russmann http://orcid.org/0000-0002-8684-6976
Jörg Haßler http://orcid.org/0000-0003-2907-5228
Melanie Magin http://orcid.org/0000-0003-2545-3594
Márton Bene http://orcid.org/0000-0003-0177-9717
Andrea Ceron http://orcid.org/0000-0002-6686-5969
Daniel Jackson http://orcid.org/0000-0002-8833-9476
Darren Lilleker http://orcid.org/0000-0003-0403-8121

References

Ansolabehere, S., & Iyengar, S. (1995). *Going negative: How political advertisements shrink and polarize the electorate.* New York, NY: Free Press.

Auter, Z. A., & Fine, J. A. (2016). Negative campaigning in the social media age: Attack advertising on Facebook. *Political Behavior, 38*(4), 999–1020. doi:10.1007/s11109-016-9346-8

Bakker, R., Hooghe, L., Jolly, S., Marks, G., Polk, J., Rovny, J., ... Vachudova, M. A. (2020). *2019 Chapel Hill Expert Survey. Version 2019.1* Retrieved from chesdata.eu. Chapel Hill: University of North Carolina.

Bene, M. (2017a). Go viral on the Facebook! Interactions between candidates and followers on Facebook during the Hungarian general election campaign of 2014. *Information, Communication & Society, 20*(4), 513–529. doi:10.1080/1369118X.2016.1198411

Bene, M. (2017b). Influenced by peers: Facebook as an information source for young people. *Social Media + Society, 3*(2). doi:10.1177/2056305117716273

Berger, J., & Milkman, K. L. (2012). What makes online content viral? *Journal of Marketing Research, 49*(2), 192–205. doi:10.1509/jmr.10.0353

Bossetta, M., Segesten, A. D., & Trenz, H. J. (2018). Political participation on Facebook during brexit: Does user engagement on media pages stimulate engagement with campaigns? *Journal of Language and Politics, 17*(2), 173–194. doi:10.1075/jlp.17009.dut

Bucher, T. (2012). Want to be on the top? Algorithmic power and the threat of invisibility on Facebook. *New Media & Society, 14*(7), 1164–1180. doi:10.1177/1461444812440159

Ceron, A., & Curini, L. (2018). e-Campaigning in the 2014 European elections: The emphasis on valence issues in a two-dimensional multiparty system. *Party Politics, 24*(2), 105–117. doi:10.1177/1354068816642807

Ceron, A., & D'Adda, G. (2016). E-campaigning on twitter: The effectiveness of distributive promises and negative campaign in the 2013 Italian election. *New Media & Society, 18*(9), 1935–1955. doi:10.1177/1461444815571915

Ehin, P., & Talving, L. (2021). Still second-order? European elections in the era of populism, extremism, and euroskepticism. *Politics, 41*(4), 467–485. doi:10.1177/0263395720986026

Elmelund-Præstekær, C. (2010). Beyond American negativity: Toward a general understanding of the determinants of negative campaigning. *European Political Science Review, 2*(1), 137–156. doi:10.1017/S1755773909990269

Ennser-Jedenastik, L., Gahn, C., Bodlos, A., & Haselmayer, M. (2022). Does social media enhance party responsiveness? How user engagement shapes parties' issue attention on Facebook. *Party Politics, 28*(3), 468–481. doi:10.1177/1354068820985334

Eugster, B., Jalali, C., Maier, M., Bathelt, S., Leidecker-Sandmann, M., Adam, S., ... Demertzis, N. (2020). When do European election campaigns become about Europe? *West European Politics.* Published online ahead of print. doi: 10.1080/01402382.2020.1778956.

Evans, H. K., Cordova, V., & Sipole, S. (2014). Twitter Style: An analysis of how house candidates used twitter in their 2012 campaigns. *PS, Political Science & Politics, 47*(2), 454–462. doi:10.1017/S1049096514000389

Fridkin, K. L., & Kenney, P. J. (2004). Do negative messages work? The impact of negativity on citizens' evaluations of candidates. *American Politics Research, 32*(5), 570–605. doi:10.1177/1532673X03260834

Garrett, R. K. (2009). Echo chambers online?: Politically motivated selective exposure among Internet news users. *Journal of Computer-Mediated Communication, 14*(2), 265–285. doi:10.1111/j.1083-6101.2009.01440.x

Geer, J. (2006). *In defense of negativity: Attack ads in presidential campaigns.* Chicago, IL: University of Chicago Press.

Gerbaudo, P., Marogna, F., & Alzetta, C. (2019). When "Positive Posting" Attracts Voters: User Engagement and Emotions in the 2017 UK Election Campaign on Facebook (pp. 5(4). Social Media + Society. 5(4), 1–11. https://doi.org/10.1177/2056305119881695

Gwet, K. L. (2019). *Package 'irrCAC.'* https://cran.r-project.org/web/packages/irrCAC/irrCAC.pdf. Accessed May 10, 2022.

Haselmayer, M. (2019). Negative campaigning and its consequences: A review and a look ahead. *French Politics, 17*(3), 355–372. doi:10.1057/s41253-019-00084-8

Haselmayer, M., Meyer, T. M., & Wagner, M. (2019). Fighting for attention: Media coverage of negative campaign messages. *Party Politics, 25*(3), 412–423. doi:10.1177/1354068817724174

Haßler, J., Magin, M., Russmann, U., & Fenoll, V. (Eds.). (2021). *Campaigning on Facebook in the 2019 European Parliament election: informing, interacting with, and mobilising voters.* Cham, Switzerland: Palgrave Macmillan.

Haynes, A. A., & Rhine, S. L. (1998). Attack politics in presidential nomination campaigns: An examination of the frequency and determinants of intermediated negative messages against opponents. *Political Research Quarterly, 51*(3), 691–721. doi:10.1177/106591299805100307

Heiss, R., Schmuck, D., & Matthes, J. (2019). What drives interaction in political actors' Facebook posts? Profile and content predictors of user engagement and political actors' reactions. *Information, Communication & Society, 22*(10), 1497–1513. doi:10.1080/1369118X.2018.1445273

Hiaeshutter-Rice, D., & Weeks, B. (2021). Understanding audience engagement with mainstream and alternative news posts on Facebook. *Digital Journalism, 9*(5), 519–548. doi:10.1080/21670811.2021.1924068

Holtz-Bacha, C. (2001). Negative campaigning: In Deutschland negativ aufgenommen [Negative campaigning: Negatively received in Germany]. *Zeitschrift für Parlamentsfragen, 32*(3), 669–677.

Hosch-Dayican, B., Amrit, C., Aarts, K., & Dassen, A. (2016). How do online citizens persuade fellow voters? Using twitter during the 2012 Dutch parliamentary election campaign. *Social Science Computer Review, 34*(2), 135–152. doi:10.1177/0894439314558200

Iyengar, S., & Krupenkin, M. (2018). The strengthening of partisan affect. *Political Psychology, 39*, 201–218. doi:10.1111/pops.12487

Joathan, Í. (2019). Negative campaign in the Brazilian presidential race: An analysis of the attacks posted on Facebook by the main candidates. *Contemporary Social Science, 14*(1), 71–88. doi:10.1080/21582041.2017.1369557

Johnston, A., & Kaid, L. L. (2002). Image ads and issue ads in US presidential advertising: Using videostyle to explore stylistic differences in televised political ads from 1952 to 2000. *Journal of Communication, 52*(2), 281–300. doi:10.1111/j.1460-2466.2002.tb02545.x

Jünger, J., & Keyling, T. (2019). *Facepager. An application for generic data retrieval through APIs.* Source code and releases available at https://github.com/strohne/Facepager/. Accessed April-May 2019.

Kahn, K. F., & Kenney, P. J. (2000). Negative advertising and an informed electorate: How negative campaigning enhances learning during Senate elections. In J. Thurber (Ed.), *Crowded airwaves: Campaign advertising in modern elections,* pp. 65-95, Washington, DC: Brookings.

Kaid, L. L., & Johnston, A. (1991). Negative versus positive television advertising in us presidential campaigns. *Journal of Communication, 41*(3), 53–64. doi:10.1111/j.1460-2466.1991.tb02323.x

Kim, C., & Yang, S. U. (2017). Like, comment, and share on Facebook: How each behavior differs from the other. *Public Relations Review, 43*(2), 441–449. doi:10.1016/j.pubrev.2017.02.006

Klinger, U., & Svensson, J. (2015). The emergence of network media logic in political communication: A theoretical approach. *New Media & Society, 17*(8), 1241–1257. doi:10.1177/1461444814522952

Kristensen, L. M. (2021). Audience Metrics: operationalizing news value for the digital newsroom. *Journalism Practice,* 1–18. doi:10.1080/17512786.2021.1954058

Larsson, A. O., & Kalsnes, B. (2014). 'Of course we are on Facebook': Use and non-use of social media among Swedish and Norwegian politicians. *European Journal of Communication, 29*(6), 653–667. doi:10.1177/0267323114531383

Lau, R. R., & Pomper, G. M. (2004). *Negative Campaigning: An Analysis of U.S. Senate Elections.* Lanham, MD: Rowman & Littlefield.

Lau, R. R., Sigelman, L., & Rovner, I. B. (2007). The effects of negative political campaigns: A meta-analytic reassessment. *Journal of Politics, 69*(4), 1176–1209. doi:10.1111/j.1468-2508.2007.00618.x

Lauf, E., & Peter, J. (2001). Die Codierung verschiedensprachiger Inhalte: Erhebungskonzepte und Gütemaße [Coding of content in different languages: Concepts of inquiry and quality indices. In E. Lauf & W. Wirth (Eds.), *Inhaltsanalyse: Perspektiven, Probleme, Potentiale [Content analysis: Perspectives, problems, potentialities]* (pp. 199–217). Cologne: Halem.

Magin, M., Podschuweit, N., Haßler, J., & Russmann, U. (2017). Campaigning in the fourth age of political communication. A multi-method study on the use of Facebook by German and Austrian parties in the 2013 national election campaigns. *Information, Communication & Society, 20*(11), 1698–1719. doi:10.1080/1369118X.2016.1254269

Maier, J., & Nai, A. (2020). Roaring candidates in the spotlight: Campaign negativity, emotions, and media coverage in 107 national elections. *The International Journal of Press/Politics, 1*(31). doi:10.1177/1940161220919093

Mattes, K., & Redlawsk, D. P. (2014). *The positive case for negative campaigning.* Chicago: University of Chicago Press.

Meffert, M. F., Chung, S., Joiner, A. J., Waks, L., & Garst, J. (2006). The effects of negativity and motivated information processing during a political campaign. *Journal of Communication, 56*(1), 27–51. doi:10.1111/j.1460-2466.2006.00003.x

Nai, A. (2018). Fear and loathing in populist campaigns? Comparing the communication style of populists and non-populists in elections worldwide. *Journal of Political Marketing,* 1–32. doi:10.1080/15377857.2018.1491439

Nai, A. (2020). going negative, worldwide: towards a general understanding of determinants and targets of negative campaigning. *Government & Opposition, 55*(3), 430–455. doi:10.1017/gov.2018.32

Newman, N., Fletcher, R., Schulz, A., Andı, S., & Nielsen, R. K. (2020). *Reuters Institute Digi-tal News Report 2020.* Reuters Institute for the Study of Journalism. http://www.digitalnewsreport.org/

Papp, Z., & Patkós, V. (2019). The macro-level driving factors of negative campaigning in Europe. *The International Journal of Press/Politics, 24*(1), 27–48. doi:10.1177/1940161218803426

Raycheva, L., & Šuminas, A. (2017). A negative touch in posters and spots. In C. Holtz-Bacha, E. Novelli, & K. Rafter (Eds.) *Political Advertising in the 2014 European Parliament Elections* (pp. 81–96). London: Palgrave Macmillan.

Reif, K., & Schmitt, H. (1980). Nine second-order national elections–a conceptual framework for the analysis of European Election results. *European Journal of Political Research, 8*(1), 3–44. doi:10.1111/j.1475-6765.1980.tb00737.x

Richardson, G. W.,sJr. (2001). Looking for meaning in all the wrong places: Why negative advertising is a suspect category. *Journal of Communication, 51*(4), 775–800. doi:10.1111/j.1460-2466.2001.tb02906.x

Riffe, D., Lacy, S., & Fico, F. G. (1998). *Analyzing media messages: Using quantitative content analysis in research*. Mahwah, NJ: Lawrence Erlbaum Associates.

Rössler, P. (2012). Comparative content analysis. In F. Esser & T. Hanitzsch (Eds.), *The handbook of comparative communication research* (pp. 459–468). Routledge.

Russmann, U. (2017). Negative campaigning in party-controlled communication channels: party communication strategies in campaign posters, newspaper advertisement, and press releases during the 2008 Austrian National Election Campaign. *Journal of Political Marketing, 16*(2), 95–117. doi:10.1080/15377857.2014.959693

Schweitzer, E. J. (2010). Global patterns of virtual mudslinging? The use of attacks on German party websites in state, national and European Parliamentary elections. *German Politics, 19*(2), 200–221. doi:10.1080/09644001003774149

Shoemaker, P. J. (1996). Hardwired for news: Using biological and cultural evolution to explain the surveillance function. *Journal of Communication, 46*(3), 32–47. doi:10.1111/j.1460-2466.1996.tb01487.x

Soroka, S. N. (2014). *Negativity in democratic politics: Causes and consequences*. Cambridge: Cambridge University Press.

Steffan, D., & Venema, N. (2020). New medium, old strategies? Comparing online and traditional campaign posters for German Bundestag elections, 2013–2017. *European Journal of Communication, 35*(4), 370–388. doi:10.1177/0267323120903681

Steinfeld, N., & Lev-On, A. (2020). MPs on Facebook: Differences between Members of Coalition and Opposition. *Digital Government: Research and Practice, 1*(2), 1–14. doi:10.1145/3363415

Stromer-Galley, J., Zhang, F., Hemsley, J., & Tanupabrungsun, S. (2018). Tweeting the attack: Predicting gubernatorial candidate attack messaging and its spread. *International Journal of Communication, 12*(22).

Unkel, J. (2021). *Tidycomm: Data Modification and Analysis for Communication Research*. https://joon-e.github.io/tidycomm/index.html. Accessed May 10, 2022.

Valli, C., & Nai, A. (2020). Attack politics from Albania to Zimbabwe: A large-scale comparative study on the drivers of negative campaigning. *International Political Science Review*, 1–17. doi:10.1177/0192512120946410

Walter, A. S. (2014). Choosing the enemy: Attack behaviour in a multiparty system. *Party Politics, 20*(3), 311–323. doi:10.1177/1354068811436050

Walter, A. S., van der Brug, W., & van Praag, P. (2014). When the stakes are high: Party competition and negative campaigning. *Comparative Political Studies, 47*(4), 550–573. doi:10.1177/0010414013488543

Weeks, B. E. (2015). Emotions, partisanship, and misperceptions: how anger and anxiety moderate the effect of partisan bias on susceptibility to political misinformation. *Journal of Communication, 65*(4), 699–719. doi:10.1111/jcom.12164

Ziegele, M., Breiner, T., & Quiring, O. (2014). What creates interactivity in online news discussions? An exploratory analysis of discussion factors in user comments on news items. *Journal of Communication, 64*(6), 1111–1138. doi:10.1111/jcom.12123

Ziegele, M., & Reinecke, L. (2017). No place for negative emotions? The effects of message valence, communication channel, and social distance on users' willingness to respond to SNS status updates. *Computers in Human Behavior, 75*, 704–713. doi:10.1016/j.chb.2017.06.016

Table A1. Coding scheme and intercoder reliability of variables used in the analysis.

Variable	Coding Scheme	Holsti[b]	Brennan & Prediger's κ[b]	Gwet's AC
Target actors[a] of negative statements and emotions	Coded when negative statements or emotions are addressed to a specific target actor. Target actors are either specific persons, such as politicians; or organized groups of people, such as parties. A target actor is coded if he/she/it is addressed explicitly by a negative statement or emotion.	Mean = 0.99 (Min = 0.94, Max = 0.99)	Mean = 0.95 (Min = 0.81, Max = 0.98)	Mean = 0.99 (Min = 0.95, Max = 1)
Target actors[a] of positive statements and emotions	Coded when positive statements or emotions are addressed to a specific target actor. Target actors are either specific persons, such as politicians; or organized groups of people, such as parties; A target actor is coded if he/she/it is addressed explicitly by a positive statement or emotion.	Mean = 0.97 (Min = 0.90, Max = 1.00)	Mean = 0.86 (Min = 0.65, Max = 0.98)	Mean = 0.98 (Min = 0.94, Max = 1)

[a]The precise identification of targets was achieved by listing them as binomial variables in the codebook. [b]To calculate Holsti and B&P's κ we used the R-package 'tidycomm': https://github.com/joon-e/tidycomm, Unkel (2021); [c]To calculate Gwet's AC we used the R-package 'irrCAC': https://cran.r-project.org/web/packages/irrCAC/irrCAC.pdf, Gwet (2019).

One conflict, two public spheres, three national debates: Comparing the value conflict over judicial independence in Europe across print and social media

Stefan Wallaschek, Kavyanjali Kaushik, and Monika Eigmüller

ABSTRACT
Conflicts over the independence of judiciary as one of the European Union's core democratic values is one indicator of democratic backsliding among its member states. Based on the Europeanization framework, we compare this conflict in German, Polish and Spanish print media and Twitter from 2019 to 2021. In the countries that are strongly affected by the value conflict, Poland and Spain, Europeanization is less evident. In contrast, the German discourse shows a high degree of Europeanization. We demonstrate that the print media is strongly elite-centric, while Twitter shows a higher actor visibility and inclusivity. However, we also identify important country differences.

Introduction

According to Article 2 of the Treaty of the European Union (TEU), rule of law is a fundamental value of the EU, along with other values such as democracy or equality. Yet, the EU is facing "by far the greatest risk – arguably the only truly existential risk – to the Union" (Kelemen, 2019, p. 247) due to a slow erosion of democratic institutions, processes and norms in some EU member states, also known as democratic backsliding (Bermeo, 2016; Jakab, 2022). A robust justice system, marked by impartiality and an unquestioned separation of powers, is central for the state of democracy in each EU member state. As the EU seeks closer integration, member states must treat each other as equals and recognize key institutions such as the Court of Justice of the European Union (CJEU). Scholars demonstrated that the rule of conflict impacted the intra-party working of the conservative European People's party and that the European Commission avoided enforcing sanctions against governments flouting this value (Emmons & Pavone, 2021; Kelemen, 2020).

Yet, despite its importance for national and EU politics – given its influence on the state of democracy in domestic politics, the functioning of the EU legal system and in maintaining supremacy of the EU law – scholars have largely overlooked how this value conflict is represented in the mass and digital media within EU member states. The manner in which conflicts are discussed, debated and understood within domestic public spheres matters for shaping public opinion over critical democratic values and has direct implications on policy decisions and democratic governance within the EU (Eriksen, 2005). Greater visibility of this conflict in the national media would signify a higher relevance of the EU agendas in domestic politics and more influence on the citizens' perception of EU matters. Consequently, we ask *to what extent the public debate about this value conflict is Europeanized in EU member states and who are the key actors shaping the media discourse over the conflict?*

Our study delves deep into the public debate on the value conflict of the independence of the judiciary (IoJ) in daily quality newspapers as well as on the social media platform Twitter (now rebranded as X) in Germany, Poland and Spain from 2019 to 2021. These countries have varying experiences of the value conflict over IoJ, with severe rule of law crises currently taking place in Spain and Poland but hardly any contestation over the value in Germany. Thus, the case selection provides a rich variation to test the resonance of the conflict across different national contexts and media environments.

We apply the Europeanization of public debates framework (Koopmans & Statham, 2010; Stier, Froio, & Schünemann, 2021), which investigates to what extent national public debates cover European policies and to what extent EU actors or other EU member states are present in national debates. A high Europeanization would indicate a high national relevance of EU norms and values and that EU actors significantly shape the national discourse over critical public debates. In contrast, low Europeanization points to a lack of EU influence in shaping national debates over such democratic debates and suggests a lack of EU legitimacy in these debates. Thus, the IoJ conflict, due to its transnational nature and direct implications for the EU integration project, serves as an ideal case to study within the Europeanization framework.

By doing a comparative analysis of the IoJ conflict, we advance the Europeanization approach in two ways: On the one hand, we compare the actor visibility across the online as well as offline media arena because social media platforms play an increasing role in public communication while traditional media remains an important actor shaping the political agenda-setting process (Chadwick, 2013; Grossman, 2022). Social media, especially Twitter, is an important channel to communicate, exchange information and mobilize around political issues (Stier, Froio, & Schünemann, 2021; Wallaschek et al., 2022). On the other hand, we compare three different countries and examine the key actors who are potentially driving the conflict and affecting the Europeanization of the debate.

Literature Review

Value conflicts and europeanization of media debates

The independence of the judiciary is a key democratic principle and one of the core values of the EU. The EU monitors and evaluates the IoJ in its member states and intervenes into their domestic politics when this core value is violated (Closa, 2019; Kelemen, 2020). Recent attempts to violate the value of IoJ have manifested through new legislations or constitutional amendments that overrule court decisions, changes to the retirement age of judges, and appointment of judges who reflect the preferences of political actors (for a general overview Kelemen, 2019). For instance, the Polish government annulled the appointment of judges for the country's Constitutional Tribunal in 2015 and shortened the term of office for the new judges, which was sharply criticized by the European Parliament and European Commission but without any consequences for Poland (Closa, 2019; Emmons & Pavone, 2021). This was the first step in a long, ongoing dispute between Poland and the EU that culminated (for the time being) in a ruling by the ECJ in 2021 in which it ruled these legislations violate the judicial independence and that the so-called "judicial reforms" in Poland undermine the legal integrity of EU law (Priebus, 2022).

In Spain, conflicts over the independence of Catalonia and Basque Country have led to crises of judicial independence since 2017 (Hernández & Closa, 2022). Another significant conflict surrounds the election of the General Council of the Judiciary (CGPJ), the highest self-governing body of the Spanish judiciary, which, among other functions, guarantees the independence of judges. The current conflict of judicial independence stems from the disagreement between the ruling left-wing Spanish Socialist Workers' Party (PSOE) and the opposition right-wing People's Party (PP) over the renewal of judges of CGPJ, which has been pending since 2018 and has prompted the EU to issue warnings to Spain (Urías, 2020).

Besides these two conflicts that also justify our case selection, there have been reports on the erosion of the rule of law in several EU member states such as Hungary, Italy and Romania in the last years, a tendency which brings the EU itself to the brink of a constitutional crisis (Kelemen, 2020) and is publicly debated as democratic backsliding (Bermeo, 2016).

The conflict over IoJ in several EU member states and the involvement of EU actors provides an ideal case to test the Europeanization framework. Scholars argued that the increase in competences and expanded policy areas for the EU has contributed to a higher salience of the EU in national politics which in turn has spurred political contestation and politicization of EU issues (Risse,

2010; Statham & Trenz, 2013). In particular, right-wing political parties use the EU as a blueprint to articulate their Euroscepticism and mobilize against further integration steps (Dutceac Segesten & Bossetta, 2019; Hutter, Grande, & Kriesi, 2016; Wallaschek, 2020).

Europeanization can be understood as the impact of EU decision-making and rules on domestic politics and policies of member states, as well as how the EU and European integration affects political cultures, ideas and attitudes at the national level (Auel & Tiemann, 2020, p. 7). In our study, we use the latter understanding and focus specifically on how different actors' visibility in the media shape public debates and to what extent the conflict over the IoJ is Europeanized.

Koopmans and Statham (2010) state in their ground-breaking study on the Europeanization of public debates that three dimensions are of importance: First, the *visibility* of actors and issues in the national debates of European countries. For European affairs and institutions to resonate among the policy agendas and citizens, Europe-related issues and actors have to be seen in public discourses in the media. Visibility of actors has a wider impact on the role and relevance of the EU within domestic politics. Second dimension is the *inclusivity* of actors, which implies a variety of actors appear and are involved in the public debate. This is a fundamental aspect of a liberal and plural democracy in which not only parties and politicians but also various interest groups, civil society organizations or other relevant actors are given space in the public sphere. This also includes European actors such as the European Commission, members of the European Parliament or EU lobby organizations. Finally, *contestation* is the third dimension and is viewed as the consequence of the aforementioned two dimensions. It is assumed that a higher visibility of (European) issues as well as a higher plurality of actor appearances leads to the public presentation of different ideas and interests, which may create more conflict among the featured actors. If actors disagree, they have to spell out their different visions on Europe which indicates to the public that Europe matters.

In our study, we use the first two dimensions (visibility and inclusivity) to measure the Europeanization of the public debate on the conflict of judicial independence. We understand contestation as the structural outcome of our results on visibility and inclusivity (see also section 3). Furthermore, we follow accounts that differentiate Europeanization into a vertical and horizontal dimension (Koopmans & Erbe, 2004). The *horizontal* dimension refers to linkages between member states, namely in cases in which actors of one EU member state refer to actors and/or issues in other EU member states. In contrast, *vertical* Europeanization occurs when discursive references are made from the national level to the EU, its institutions and actors, as well as European politics more generally. Koopmans and Erbe (2004) argue that identifying Europeanization is a relative matter and thereby, different degrees of horizontal or vertical Europeanization are possible. It is an empirical question to what extent and under which circumstances these processes occur or change.

Hence, we expect the EU's presence in the national media debates as an indicator of the Union's response to the rule of law challenges in member states, with the aim to prevent the erosion of democratic values and prevent the decline of democracy in these nations. Subsequently, in our study, we expect higher vertical Europeanization in Poland and Spain which are experiencing significant rule of law crises and challenges to the independence of their judiciaries. However, in Germany, which faces less severe challenges to IoJ and thus less direct intervention of EU actors in German domestic affairs, we expect low vertical Europeanization. Furthermore, this stability in the domestic matters might lead to more debates and comparative analysis on how other EU nations are handling challenges to IoJ, leading to our expectation that there will be higher horizontal Europeanization in Germany than in Poland and Spain.

Scholars have noted that such conflicts are predominantly based on mediatized structures. How people understand and perceive conflicts is a matter of mediatization in the online and offline media arenas (Hjarvard, Mortensen, & Eskjær, 2015). Conflicts are not neutrally channeled through media outlets; instead, media are influential intermediaries that shape how conflicts are framed and understood in the public. This holds true for legacy media as well as for social media platforms. These intermediaries create opportunities for different actors to present and share information, and provide opinion-based knowledge. This mediatization perspective is even more relevant for value conflicts. Values are unobservable, present ideals that are valid beyond concrete situations (Hitlin & Piliavin, 2004) and "refer to deep-rooted and enduring priorities and goals for individuals, organizations, and society" (Norris & Inglehart, 2019, p. 35). Thus, in order to study value conflicts, we have to pay attention to how these values are framed in the public debates, who is framing these in the public and to what extent these mediatized value conflicts change between different media arenas (Eigmüller & Trenz, 2020).

Based on recent work, we assume that the establishment of social media platforms has a positive effect on the promotion of the Europeanized public debate. It has been argued that social media create a cross-national public and reach citizens that are less concerned with EU-related issues (Bossetta, Dutceac Segesten, & Trenz, 2017; Ruiz-Soler, 2020). Moreover, with the costs to participate and get information low and the options to follow and receive news multifold, digital media help in the formation and democratization of the EU public sphere (Hänska & Bauchowitz, 2019). Hence, we expect higher horizontal Europeanization than vertical Europeanization on social media in all three countries.

Political agenda-setting in a hybrid media system

Building on the Europeanization of media debates and the IoJ conflict, it is important to understand how the Europeanization process takes place in a hybrid media environment as well as how different actors (including the EU, national governments, political parties, civil society organizations, and journalists) contribute to such publicly debated value conflicts, thereby influencing the agenda-setting.

According to Kingdon's (1995) classic account of policy-making, the policy process is significantly shaped by different ideas and interests as well as by the configuration of actors involved. While previous studies (such as Walgrave, Soroka, & Nuytemans, 2007) have investigated the agenda-setting relationship of the political and traditional media arenas, recent research highlights the influential role of digital and social media for agenda-setting processes (Grossman, 2022). In the contemporary political communication environment, termed "hybrid media system" by Andrew Chadwick (2013), agenda-setting is not only shaped by what politicians, interest groups or journalists say in public statements on TV or in parliament but also by what they tweet, post on Facebook or present on Instagram. This implies that these two media environments are interconnected and influence each other.

In the traditional media, powerful institutional actors such as government representatives and political parties and politicians are significantly more represented in Europeanized public debates than in debates on domestic topics. In turn, less-institutionalized actors such as NGOs, social movements or trade unions become marginalized from the discourse. Thus, Koopmans (2007) noted the former as the "winners of Europeanized public debates". Since the latter are better organized in the national context, have access to information and have a greater potential to mobilize around national issues, topics that refer to the European context add another layer of complexity for less-institutionalized actors with limited resources.

Journalists, however, have significant influence in Europeanization by providing public coverage of European issues in national media outlets (Pfetsch, 2008). Furthermore, civil society actors have a chance to intervene in Europeanized public debate during key events and increase their public visibility (Statham & Trenz, 2013). Moreover, specific non-institutionalized actor groups can shape the public debate and publicly mobilize if they highlight the directed impact of policies on people's lives (Chironi & Portos, 2021), strategically link domestic issues with European aspects to appeal to EU actors (Ayoub, 2013) or raise moral concerns that presents the protesters "'as guardians of the constitution'" as Matthes (2022, p. 14) highlights in her study of Polish judges criticizing the "judicial reform" in Poland. Yet, political parties and in particular right-wing political parties continue to strongly shape the debate on

EU issues (Hutter, Grande, & Kriesi, 2016). Interestingly, de Wilde (2023) recently showed that during the last crisis-ridden decade in the EU, EU actors also increased their visibility in national debates that cover European policies which might be explained by the growth in political authority in these policy areas. However, the increased visibility of EU institutions such as the European Parliament comes at the expense of national pro-European actors who are crowded out of the public debate. De Wilde argues that this may create more conflicts, because Eurosceptic and populist actors could better mobilize against the EU as a political force that intervenes in the domestic context. Against this backdrop, we expect that legacy media will be dominated by traditional actors such as political parties, politicians or EU institutions, rather than non-traditional actors such as civil organizations and associations, citizens or political groups.

In the networked, de-centralized and low-cost digital media environment, non-institutional actors and non-salient issues that were earlier marginalized from the traditional mass media gain the opportunity to shape the public discourse and the processes of Europeanization or transnationalization (Coleman & Blumler, 2009). Yet, the existing empirical evidence on the impact of social media networks such as Twitter and Facebook on facilitating Europeanization and transforming the traditional media environment into a hybrid one (Jungherr, 2014) is mixed. On the one hand, studies have shown that digital media dynamics remain embedded within the national public spheres and established powerful actors are as much central to the political debates online as they are in the offline world (Koopmans & Zimmermann, 2010; Wallaschek et al., 2022). On the other hand, online media have provided alternative stories, narratives and collective identities, eyewitness accounts, political watchdogs or citizen journalists to diffuse information in a large number of means and formats (such as videos, images or text) without time and location barriers (Nguyen, 2017; Rettberg, 2014). Thus, we expect to find both non-traditional and traditional media actors with similar public visibility in the social media debate over IoJ.

A cross-national and cross-media research design

Case selection

Comparing public debates by collecting data in different media systems with different language and cultural contexts and analyzing them across two levels of comparison – national and media contexts – is a challenging task (Von-Nordheim et al., 2021). The current study is designed to address these challenges in several ways. First, we compare the value conflict debate in three EU member states, Germany, Poland and Spain, which are experiencing varying degrees of the value conflict over IoJ between 2019 and 2021. In Poland and Spain, IoJ has been heavily contested internally and at the EU-level in the last half a decade as described in section 2.1. Comparing these two cases with Germany allows us to analyze and contrast the process of Europeanization over a core democratic value when it is not under attack, because Germany is the least affected from the conflict out of the three countries.

Second, we conduct a cross-media analysis between traditional print newspapers and the social media platform Twitter. Specifically, we select two quality daily newspapers belonging to the liberal and conservative ideological leanings and tweets from each of the three countries over the 3-year time period to a) systematically identify the actors who appear in the offline public to advance a claim on the value (visibility dimension) and b) study whether social media broaden the debate to non-mainstream actors (inclusivity dimension). By doing so, we aim to measure Europeanization of the value conflict across different national contexts and media arenas.

Data collection and operationalization in two media arenas

We collect data from both newspapers and Twitter using several keywords that combine the term "independence" with relevant domains of the judiciary, including terms such as "judicial," "justice," "judiciary," "courts," "judges" and name of the highest court in each country (for the complete keyword queries see Appendix).

We collected articles from a center-left and center-right leaning daily quality newspaper in each of the three countries using the FACTIVA database. In Germany, we used the center-left newspaper *Süddeutsche Zeitung* and center-right *Die Welt/Welt am Sonntag*; Polish newspapers were the center-left *Gazeta Wyborcza* and the center-right *Rzeczpospolita*; and *El Pais* (center-left) and *El Mundo* (center-right) were selected as the two Spanish newspapers. These media outlets have also been used in previous studies on the Europeanization of the public framework (i.e. Koopmans & Statham, 2010; Statham & Trenz, 2013). The highest number of articles in the three-year period were collected from Poland (5480 articles), while 714 and 901 articles were collected from Germany and Spain, respectively (total 7095 articles).

Based on the claim making analysis (de Wilde, 2023; Koopmans & Statham, 2010), we wrote a comprehensive codebook with detailed instructions (see Codebook in the Appendix). Before coding the sample of articles from each of the countries by the respective coders, a moderate Fleiss' Kappa (mean) score of 0.67 was reached among the four coders by coding English articles on IoJ from *The Financial Times*. However, the coding of the actor categories reached a substantial level of 0.76 (Fleiss' Kappa). While these results are not completely satisfactory, we have to take into account that we trained the coder with an extra-corpus and expect that based on country expertise and language skills of the native language speaking coders, the score would be higher for the respective coding of the country case. We then draw random samples of 20%, 5% and 15% articles per newspaper per year from Germany, Poland and Spain (see Appendix Table A1-A2 for sample overview). The varying sample sizes stem from the different total numbers of newspaper articles. To reach an appropriate level of comparability across countries and still account for higher or lower levels of publicity for this issue, we opted for these context-dependent sample sizes. Then, a four-member team manually coded the newspaper article according to the codebook (more details in the Codebook included in the Appendix).

We used the Twitter API for Academic Research to collect tweets from all three countries between 2019 and 2021, resulting in a corpus of 47,126 tweets from Germany 26,841 tweets from Poland and 4,875 tweets from Spain[1] (total 78,842 tweets) (see Appendix Figure A1-A3 for the timeline of tweets by country). The data includes original tweets as well as replies, mentions, retweets and quoted tweets. In this study, we focus on retweets to highlight which actors gained the most visibility and how many actors are included in the discourse, two of the three dimensions of the Europeanization framework. Retweets connect two users if one rebroadcasts another's content and thus are responsible for increasing the visibility of actors if they are retweeted by others (Boyd, Golder, & Lotan, 2010; Conover et al., 2021).

Next, we employ network analysis on both the coded traditional media data and the retweets data from Twitter to identify the structure of the public debate on independence of judiciary. Network analysis enables us to visualize the interactions between actors and how these patterns of interconnectedness shape the flow of information, ideas and opinions contributing to the process of Europeanization over IoJ. Our manual coding allows us to trace these communicative relationships between actors who express a position and take an action on the value of IoJ and those actors to whom this action is directed toward. Thus, we construct networks where an actor (node) is connected (edges) to another actor if they have directed the action or expression over the value toward that actor. The number of nodes in each network indicates the number of actors that get coverage in the traditional media debate or get retweeted on Twitter by others due to an action they take or an opinion they express over the value of independence of the judiciary. The number of edges between two nodes imply the number of times two actors engage with each other to exchange information, take action toward each other, communicate with each other (in the case of traditional media coverage) and retweet each other (in case of Twitter). These actors can include EU institutions, national government, politicians and political parties, judges and courts, legal experts, journalists, civil society associations and others. To take into account issue cycles and the changing saliency of issues, the traditional media networks and the retweet networks are constructed in each country for each of the 3 years (total 18 networks). We then focus only on the main component – the largest set of connected nodes (actors) – in each of the traditional media and retweet networks. We calculate the eigenvector centrality for each node to measure the visibility of an actor within this largest set of interconnected actors (we consider here the top 10 most visible actors in the main network). Actors with high eigenvector centrality scores are those who are connected to other also highly connected actors (Bonacich, 1987). Since an actor can only have a high eigenvector score if they are mentioned in the media or retweeted by other actors who are also highly mentioned and retweeted, it allows us to identify their overall high influence and visibility in the debate on IoJ.

To measure vertical and horizontal Europeanization, the proportion of highly visible EU and member state actors other than Germany, Poland and Spain in the respective country cases is calculated. To measure inclusivity, we calculate the proportion of traditional (government, opposition and media) and non-traditional actors (alternative media, public figure, academic scholar, NGO/civil society, trade union, citizens, and others) in the networks. It is important to note here that while we rely on the extensive codebook for the print media, we manually classified only the actor's name, nationality and function in tweets.

Results

The empirical analysis compares the actor constellation in the debates over judicial independence in the three countries. Section 4.1 presents the results from the print media network analysis in order to identify the Europeanization of the debate and Section 4.2 presents the results from the social media network analysis, with the results compared across the three cases. Finally, the findings from both media arenas are brought together to discuss their implications and challenges. Moreover, we split the time period into years taking into account that Europeanization may change in the course of a 3-year period. Thus, the following results for the legacy and social media not only contain a country comparison but a within-comparison regarding the time dimension as well. In order to facilitate the interpretation of several comparison layers, Figures 1 and 2 present an overview of the main findings (absolute numbers by country, media arena and year are documented in the Appendix Tables A3-A5 for legacy media and Tables A6-A8 for social media).[2]

Traditional media

We begin with the results of traditional media networks in each country. In Germany, very few nodes (36) and edges (25) imply not many actors advance a position and interact with each other in the

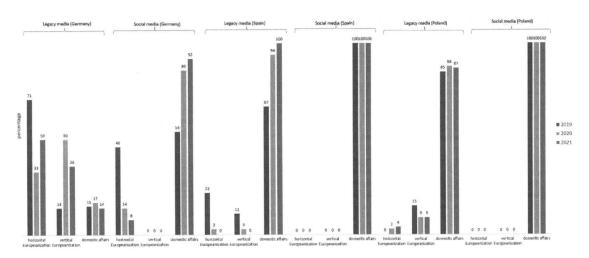

Figure 1. Levels of Europeanization in legacy and social media in Germany, Poland and Spain. Note: The percentages add up for the same colored bars per year and country's media arena. E.g., in the 2019 German traditional media debate network, 71% are actors from other member states (horizontal Europeanization), while 14% are EU actors (vertical Europeanization) and 15% are German actors (domestic affairs).

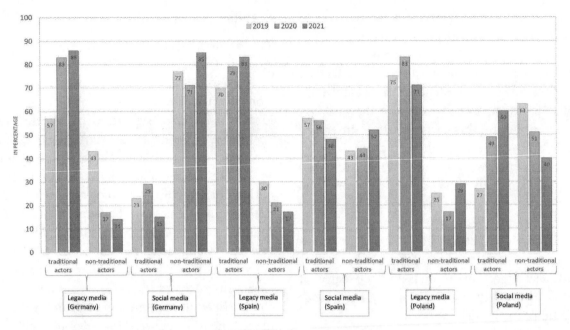

Figure 2. Actor constellations in legacy and social media in Germany, Spain and Poland. Note: The percentages add up for the same colored bars per year and country's media arena. E.g., in the 2021 Polish social media debate network, 60% are traditional actors, while 40% are non-traditional actors.

debate over independence of judiciary, indicative of the low level of conflict over the value in the country. Yet, despite the low number of nodes and edges in the main component, the level of horizontal and vertical Europeanization in the traditional media debates is high, with a significant presence of non-German actors, particularly from Poland and the European Court of Justice. Except for the vertical Europeanization score in 2019, the relative share is always above one-third or even above 50% (Figure 1). German actors are hardly featured in the main component, except for the journalists commenting on the situation in Poland. This result is underlined by the eigenvector centrality analysis (Appendix Table A16-A18), where non-German actors such as the Polish government or EU actors (ECJ, European Parliament, European Commission) in each year rank higher and are thus more visible and influential in the media debate on IoJ in Germany. In terms of inclusivity, the German discourse in all 3 years mainly includes traditional actors such as governments, journalists or members of EU institutions (at least 50% share) and marginalizes non-traditional actors such as civil society organizations (see Figure 2 and Appendix Table A16-A18).

In contrast to the German discourse, the Spanish debate displays more discursive intensity with more actors (52) involved in the debate and higher number of interactions between them (43). However, despite the higher number of actors taking part in the conflict over the value and unlike the German traditional media debate, the Spanish traditional media is hardly Europeanized (Figure 1). The relative horizontal and vertical Europeanization is decreasing in the main component over time. While non-Spanish actors, namely actors from other EU member states or EU actors themselves, are hardly present in the overall discourse in 2019, the debate on judicial reforms and a biased judiciary in other countries such as Hungary or Poland forms a second large community within the Spanish network in 2020 and especially in 2021 (Appendix Table A22-A24). Regarding the inclusivity of the discourse, traditional actors such as government, opposition or media actors are dominant in each year (a share of at least 70% each year) as shown in Figure 2.

The Polish legacy media network is the largest of the three and the most intense, with the highest number of actors (90) and the most number of interactions between them (93). However, like Spain and in contrast to Germany, the level of vertical and horizontal Europeanization remains very low in Polish traditional media debate on IoJ (Figure 1). The only EU actor which is prominently featured in every year is the European Court of Justice and hardly any actors from other EU member states appear in the Polish print media debate. Regarding the inclusivity, and as we show in Figure 2, the share of traditional actors is similar to the other two countries with a high presence of traditional actors such as government, judiciary and media actors (at least a share of 70%).

To conclude, based on our print media network findings, we reject the expectation that Poland and Spain will have a higher share of vertical Europeanization than Germany. Instead the German discourse displays higher levels of it, except in 2019 in which the main component of the Polish discourse includes slightly more EU actors (15%) than the German discourse (14%). However, the second expectation that German discourse will exhibit higher horizontal Europeanization is supported with the country's traditional media debate networks adding a higher share of non-domestic actors every year, more than the Spanish or Polish media. The expectation of higher visibility of traditional actors than non-traditional actors in the mass media is also supported, because in each country and year, these actors (government, opposition, media, EU actors) are dominant in the main component while non-traditional actors are featured much less. It should be nonetheless highlighted that two actor groups – legal actors as well as academic scholars – show a high visibility in all three countries which is remarkable, given that these actors are hardly present in other studies on Europeanization (see e.g. Koopmans & Statham, 2010; Statham & Trenz, 2013).

Social media

Social media debates on independence of judiciary are in sharp contrast to legacy media, with the German online public sphere containing much more intense debate on the value than Poland and Spain with higher number of actors and edges between them.

In Germany, the number of users, indicated by the nodes present in the networks, steadily increases from 2019 to 2021. Despite the large number of users and an intense online public debate, the lack of any of the EU actors in top 10 most visible actors as indicated by a high eigenvector centrality indicates that there is no vertical Europeanization in any of the years in the online media debates in Germany on IoJ (Appendix Table A9-A11 for full eigenvector measures). However, there is some horizontal Europeanization observed in 2019, with half of the most visible actors coming from countries other than Germany (including Spain, Italy, Austria and Poland). This trend completely disappears in 2020 with no horizontal Europeanization, and in 2021, only a few Austrian actors are present in the discourse that indicates very weak horizontal Europeanization (Figure 1 and Appendix Table A10-A11). In terms of inclusivity, the main components – largest community of interconnected actors within a network – of the 2019 and 2020 networks almost encompass the total nodes present in the network, indicating many different actors are connected to each other and take part in the debates in these years. The share of non-traditional actors is high, with 77.3% and 71.4% in 2019 and 2020, respectively (Figure 2). However, only 11 accounts in 2019 and 5 accounts in 2020 have the eigenvector centrality greater than zero. In contrast, the main component of 2021 is barely represented by 6% of the total nodes present. And again, even though non-traditional actors represent 85% of the main component, only nine of them have eigenvector centrality greater than zero.

The Polish Twitter discourse is less intense than the German discourse with low numbers of users and edges between them, despite being a highly affected country with an ongoing IoJ crisis (Appendix Table A7). Despite the value being intensely debated between the Polish government and EU institutions, and members of other EU states condemning actions that have resulted in weakening of the rule of law, the online discourse in Poland contains neither any vertical nor any horizontal Europeanization in terms of actor visibility of EU and non-Polish actors on the networks across all 3 years (Figure 1). The discourse remains highly nationalized as the top 10 actors with highest eigenvector centrality scores from 2019 to 2021 are all Polish actors. According to Figure 2, results of the inclusivity analysis show that in sharp contrast to Germany and similar to the traditional media Polish newspapers, the Polish online networks are dominated by traditional politicians, media and judicial actors (Appendix Table A11-

A13). The exception is the year 2019 since 51% of those in the main component comprise citizens and more than half of them have eigenvector centrality scores greater than zero. This implies that in 2019, the Polish Twitter discourse was more inclusive of non-traditional actors, even if no horizontal and vertical Europeanization is observed.

Finally, the Spanish online discourse on independence of judiciary is the least intensive one, with the lowest number of users and edges between them (Appendix Table A8). Like the German and Polish Twitter networks, the eigenvector centrality scores highlight the absence of vertical Europeanization on Spanish Twitter with complete lack of EU actors present in the top 10 most visible actors (Appendix Table A14-A16). Unlike Germany and similar to Poland, Spanish Twitter discourse is also devoid of any horizontal Europeanization and remains highly nationalized with no presence of any actors from other EU member states (Figure 1). Results of the inclusivity analysis reveal nearly 43% of actors in 2019 and 44% of the actors on the Spanish networks are non-traditional actors, with almost half of them with eigenvector centrality scores higher than 0. These results as visualized in Figure 2 indicate that non-traditional actors such as citizens, NGOs, scholars or alternative media received a fair share of say in the online discourse on independence of judiciary in 2019 and 2020. However, this trend is not observed in 2021 because despite 52% of the accounts that form the main component in the network are non-traditional actors, all of them have an eigenvector centrality of zero.

Overall, we can confirm that horizontal Europeanization will be more prevalent on social media discourses only in the case of German Twitter discourse, while in the case of Poland and Spain, this expectation is not met. Going against our final expectation, the findings demonstrate that non-traditional actors such as citizens, alternative media and NGOs do not have equal visibility as traditional actors. Though there is a high inclusivity and expansion of the debate to non-traditional actors on social media, these actors have eigenvector centrality scores of zero and thus do not influence the discourse. Therefore, it still remains dominated by traditional actors, who have high eigenvector centrality scores in the networks.

Discussion

Our study highlights several dimensions of the relationship between value conflicts, Europeanization and the hybrid media system. Research on Europeanization often assumes that a higher relevance of European issues and significant events, such as a value conflict, may spur a more Europeanized debate within national domains (Ruiz-Soler, 2020; Statham & Trenz, 2013). Instead, we identified that domestic actors engaging with other domestic actors gain prominence while EU actors play a peripheral role, despite the broader implications of value conflicts such as the IoJ conflict for democracy across the EU. These findings go against the conventional view that the EU suffers from democratic deficit itself, with its failure to include national publics in the EU-level decisions and its lack of a heterogenous and shared public sphere (Habermas, 2012). Recent literature highlights that EU's interventions in fact matter in order to defend democratic values in member states, and that comparative perspective can shed light on when the EU is able to intervene in national politics and how that affects democratic backsliding (Kelemen, 2017). Our study similarly found that when a core democratic value is under attack in a member state, there is less participation and diffusion of EU's politics at the national-level debates, pointing toward the EU's constrained role in resolving these conflicts and upholding democratic values.

We also identified strong differences across media arenas as well as countries. Countries affected by the conflict over judicial reforms or the independence of judges, i.e. Poland and Spain, did not see any horizontal Europeanization in the media debates – neither on Twitter nor in print newspapers. The debate on the IoJ value instead turns domestic and creates a national discourse steered by traditional actors such as government, opposition parties and politicians, and journalists. If at all, the print media included EU actors to some extent in the debates in Poland and Spain, indicating a weak vertical Europeanization.

Our contrasting case, Germany, offers interesting variation. Being relatively unaffected by the conflict over IoJ led to more Europeanized, both vertical and horizontal, rather than domestic debates in the country, with heavy presence of the EU and other member states' actors in both print and social media discourses. However, this could also be due to Germany's leading role in EU affairs and signal to the national audience that this debate does not concern the German public and is only a matter of other EU member states.

Hence, we can explain the different degrees of Europeanization by the countries' affectedness of and involvement in the conflict over a democratic value. This also implies that conflicts about democratic values such as the IoJ lose their European foundation as the debates become more contentious and turn into domestic conflicts dominated by traditional national actors, as observed in Poland and Spain.

It is noteworthy that Twitter – often perceived as providing a public space for transnational debates (Hänska & Bauchowitz, 2019; Ruiz-Soler, 2020) – is strongly national oriented. This is evident in the similar tendencies of actor visibility and inclusivity in the Spanish and Polish discourses. Except for Germany in 2019, which stands out due to the inclusion of Austrian and Spanish actors, Twitter debates remain predominantly national. Nonetheless, the core of the German Twitter discourse consists of non-traditional actors who are absent from the print media, such as right-leaning journalists and media outlets, politicians from the right-wing populist party AfD and citizens who are more on the periphery of the main component, but are still connected to the debate. One explanation for this differing actor constellation in Germany could be that these right-wing actors leverage alternative media channels such as Twitter to communicate their ideologies and beliefs away from the mainstream debates. So, while the actor constellation in Spain and Poland is in both media arenas relatively similar, the two German media arenas present two different discourses on the same value conflict – a Europeanized legacy media debate and a mainly domestic but alternative social media debate.

Conclusion

This study investigated the ongoing value conflict over independence of judiciary in EU member states, assessing the Europeanization of the public debate and the actors driving the conflict. We argued for the need to study democratic value conflicts in the EU as rule of law forms a crucial part of the larger integration project and thus the Union's involvement in the conflict matters to ensure the democratic values are protected and advanced. This focus on Europeanization sheds light on the comparative contexts where the EU can or cannot intervene in addressing democratic backsliding. To this end, we examined the legacy media and Twitter in Poland, Spain and Germany between 2019 and 2021.

Our study makes two crucial contributions to the literature. First, contrary to our expectation, when a country is affected by a European value conflict, it does not translate into Europeanization itself – neither in the legacy media nor on a digital media platform such as Twitter. The value conflict is predominantly discussed among domestic, traditional actors in Spain and Poland. Although the print media shows a stronger Europeanization in Germany, the country remains largely unaffected by the conflict itself. So, even in the most-likely case scenario, the Europeanization of the public is weakly present and disappears as soon as the conflict becomes domestically heated.

Second, we identified similarities between the print media and Twitter in Poland and Spain, characterized by weak to non-existing Europeanization and a strong visibility of traditional actors. The latter supports our expectation on the presence of traditional actors in the print media but goes against our expectation regarding Twitter. The presence of oppositional parties in Spain and judicial actors in Poland can be explained by the country context, with the conflict in Spain mainly perceived as a political dispute between the social democratic government and the conservative opposition, while the conflict in Poland centered around judges, lawyers and courts publicly opposing the policy changes by the right-wing nationalist government (see also Matthes, 2022). In contrast, the legacy media and Twitter in Germany differ significantly, with the former being highly Europeanized but consisting of traditional powerful actors while the latter being more national yet leaning toward more alternative right-wing voices.

Language barriers across countries, different issue cycles and public attention waves play a big role on a social media platform whose main function is not to create a public for deliberation and inform citizens, but to connect users, share opinions with the followers and create attention for issues through shared use of hashtags. While it is often assumed that the two media arenas coexist and influence each other in a hybrid media system, the findings point to the persistent power of traditional actors in shaping the discourse even in the online networks in Poland and Spain, while any effect of the digital public sphere on the mass media is not observed. In contrast, the study shows the growing power of alternative voices, especially far-right actors, in the German Twitter discourse. This variation could be a result of historical background and the media landscape of the countries. Marginalized right-wing voices feel sidelined in Germany and hence are more likely to leverage social media to express their opinions and operate within algorithmic echo chambers that reinforce their views. However, it could also be likely that because German actors are not directly involved in any domestic conflict, they do not feel the need to maintain a strong presence in the online debates while the right-wing actors might seize the EU-wide saliency of topic to express Eurosceptic narratives. In Poland and Spain, the highly contentious level of the debate over the value makes it crucial for national traditional actors to shape the narratives in both mass and social media. Such insights into the sociopolitical conditions under which these online networks complement, or work in isolation from, the mainstream mass media, is crucial to shape communication strategies in the hybrid media system as it affects the quality of democratic deliberation and the evolving role of media in democratic societies.

Our study bears nonetheless limitations. First, the research focused on the actor dimensions of visibility and inclusivity in the Europeanization framework, leaving out the analysis of the content of the debates. Future studies should examine how different actors frame democratic value conflicts and how this contestation within a hybrid media system affects the European integration process and the democratic quality of the EU member states. Furthermore, the comparative perspective should be extended to other national contexts, social media platforms and democratic values to investigate how specific political cultures, diversity of digital platforms beyond Twitter and other values such as gender equality or freedom of expression could influence the degrees of Europeanization.

Our study has crucial implications for the analysis of mediatized value conflicts and the Europeanization of the public. While values such as the independent judiciary are inscribed in the EU treaty, they do not have an a priori European dimension, but are rather transferred to the national context. Thus, EU actors might not be in a favorable position to intervene in on-going national debates and instead pro-European domestic actors have much more capabilities in supporting such European values (see also de Wilde, 2023). Moreover, the optimistic view on social media platforms such as Twitter as drivers of Europeanization should be seen more critically. Our study suggests that the communicative environments of these platforms are embedded in and shaped by national contexts. Taken together, these patterns of Europeanization across diverse national contexts and media environments underscore the strategic opportunity right-wing Eurosceptic as well as alternative pro-European domestic voices have to influence internal national debates, particularly those of EU-wide importance, in a hybrid media environment. A deeper understanding of these dynamics of domestic national and media contexts is essential for EU policy-making and agenda-setting that lie at the heart of the integration project.

Notes

1. Location filter by country ensures tweets from other countries containing the same keywords are not captured during data collection. However, the total number of tweets collected in Germany and Spain is strongly affected when using the location filter. While it was necessary in the Spanish context to avoid capturing tweets from other Spanish-speaking countries, in Germany the location filter yielded a very low number of tweets. This could be because Twitter users can choose not to divulge their location information. Thus, all German-language tweets were collected without the location filter and then tweets from other German-speaking nations such as Austria and Switzerland were removed during the data cleaning process. The Polish case was not as affected and

a similar number of tweets were captured with or without the use of a location filter, and thus the location filter was used to ensure minimum noise in the data.
2. For detailed network characteristics such as number of nodes/actors and links/edges between them, average degree centrality and modularity scores, and descriptive statistics on vertical and horizontal Europeanization on traditional and social media networks, see Appendix Tables A3-A8.

Acknowledgments

We would like to thank the anonymous reviewers as well as the editors of the special issue for their constructive feedback on our work. We also highly appreciate the helpful comments from colleagues at the ECPR General Conference 2022 where we presented a previous version of our manuscript. We are thankful to Julia Martyniewicz and Lara Fuge for outstanding research assistance.

Disclosure statement

No potential conflict of interest was reported by the author(s).

Funding

This work was supported by the Volkswagen Foundation in the project "Value Conflicts in a Differentiated Europe: The Impact of Digital Media on Value Polarisation in Europe (ValCon)" (2020-2024)

ORCID

Stefan Wallaschek http://orcid.org/0000-0002-3758-1799
Kavyanjali Kaushik http://orcid.org/0000-0001-8612-0051
Monika Eigmüller http://orcid.org/0000-0003-2065-0951

References

Auel, K., & Tiemann, G. (2020). *Europeanising European public spheres*. Brussels: Policy Department for Citizens' Rights and Constitutional Affairs (European Parliament).

Ayoub, P. M. (2013). Cooperative transnationalism in contemporary Europe: Europeanization and political opportunities for LGBT mobilization in the European Union. *European Political Science Review*, 5(2), 279–310. doi:10.1017/S1755773912000161

Bermeo, N. (2016). On Democratic Backsliding. *Journal of Democracy*, 27(1), 5–19. doi:10.1353/jod.2016.0012

Bonacich, P. (1987). Power and centrality: A family of measures. *American Journal of Sociology*, 9(5), 1170–1182. doi:10.1086/228631

Bossetta, M., Dutceac Segesten, A., & Trenz, H.-J. (2017). Engaging with European politics through Twitter and Facebook: Participation beyond the national? In M. Barisione & A. Michailidou (Eds.), *Social Media and European politics* (pp. 53–76). Palgrave. doi:10.1057/978-1-137-59890-5_3

Boyd, D., Golder, S., & Lotan, G. (2010). Tweet, tweet, Retweet: Conversational aspects of retweeting on Twitter. *2010 43rd Hawaii International Conference on System Sciences*, 1–10. 10.1109/HICSS.2010.412

Chadwick, A. (2013). *The hybrid media system: Politics and power*. Oxford: Oxford University Press.

Chironi, D., & Portos, M. (2021). 'Together we stand': Coalition-building in the Italian and Spanish feminist movements in times of crisis. *European Journal of Politics and Gender*, 4(2), 291–309. doi:10.1332/251510821X16135837027525

Closa, C. (2019). The politics of guarding the treaties: Commission scrutiny of rule of law compliance. *Journal of European Public Policy*, 26(5), 696–716. doi:10.1080/13501763.2018.1477822

Coleman, S., & Blumler, J. G. (2009). *The internet and democratic citizenship: Theory, practice and policy*. Cambridge University Press. doi:10.1017/CBO9780511818271

Conover, M., Ratkiewicz, J., Francisco, M., Goncalves, B., Menczer, F., & Flammini, A. (2021). Political polarization on Twitter. *Proceedings of the International AAAI Conference on Web & Social Media*, 5(1), 89–96. doi:10.1609/icwsm.v5i1.14126

de Wilde, P. (2023). More power, less influence: European union actors in media debates on fiscal policy after the eurocrisis. *Journal of European Integration*, 45(2), 239–255. doi:10.1080/07036337.2022.2115485

Dutceac Segesten, A., & Bossetta, M. (2019). Can euroscepticism contribute to a European public sphere? The Europeanization of media discourses on euroscepticism across six countries. *JCMS: Journal of Common Market Studies*, 57(5), 1051–1070. doi:10.1111/jcms.12871

Eigmüller, M., & Trenz, H.-J. (2020). Werte und Wertekonflikte in einer differenzierten EU. In A. Grimmel (Ed.), *Die neue Europäische Union: Zwischen Integration und Desintegration* (pp. 33–56). Baden-Baden: Nomos.

Emmons, C., & Pavone, T. (2021). The rhetoric of inaction: Failing to fail forward in the EU's rule of law crisis. *Journal of European Public Policy*, 28(10), 1611–1629. doi:10.1080/13501763.2021.1954065

Eriksen, E. O. (2005). An emerging European public sphere. *European Journal of Social Theory*, 8(3), 341–363. doi:10.1177/1368431005054798

Grossman, E. (2022). Media and policy making in the digital age. *Annual Review of Political Science*, 25(1), 443–461. doi:10.1146/annurev-polisci-051120-103422

Habermas, J. (2012). Hat die Demokratie noch eine epistemische Dimension? Empirische Forschung und normative Theorie. In *Ach, Europa: Kleine politische Schriften XI* (pp. 138–191). Frankfurt am Main: Suhrkamp.

Hänska, M., & Bauchowitz, S. (2019). Can social media facilitate a European public sphere? Transnational communication and the Europeanization of Twitter during the Eurozone crisis. *Social Media + Society*, 5(3), 205630511985468. doi:10.1177/2056305119854686

Hernández, G., & Closa, C. (2022). The challenge of Catalan secessionism to the European model of the rule of law. *Hague Journal on the Rule of Law*, 14(2–3), 257–285. doi:10.1007/s40803-022-00177-7

Hitlin, S., & Piliavin, J. A. (2004). Values: Reviving a dormant concept. *Annual Review of Sociology*, 30(1), 359–393. doi:10.1146/annurev.soc.30.012703.110640

Hjarvard, S., Mortensen, M., & Eskjær, M. F. (2015). Introduction: Three dynamics of mediatized conflicts. In M. F. Eskjær, S. Hjarvard, & M. Mortensen (Eds.), *The dynamics of mediatized conflicts* (pp. 1–27). New York: Peter Lang.

Hutter, S., Grande, E., & Kriesi, H. (Eds.). (2016). *Politicising Europe: Integration and mass politics*. Cambridge: Cambridge University Press.

Jakab, A. (2022). Three misconceptions about the EU rule of law crisis. *Verfassungsblog*. doi:10.17176/20221017-162426-0

Jungherr, A. (2014). *Twitter in politics: A comprehensive literature Review*. SSRN. https://ssrn.com/abstract=2402443

Kelemen, R. D. (2017). Europe's other democratic deficit: National Authoritarianism in Europe's democratic Union. *Government and Opposition*, 52(2), 211–238. doi:10.1017/gov.2016.41

Kelemen, R. D. (2019). Is differentiation possible in rule of law? *Comparative European Politics*, 17(2), 246–260. doi:10.1057/s41295-019-00162-9

Kelemen, R. D. (2020). The European Union's authoritarian equilibrium. *Journal of European Public Policy*, 27(3), 481–499. doi:10.1080/13501763.2020.1712455

Kingdon, J. W. (1995). *Agendas, alternatives, and public policies*. New York: Longman.

Koopmans, R. (2007). Who inhabits the European public sphere? Winners and losers, supporters and opponents in Europeanised political debates. *European Journal of Political Research*, 46(2), 183–210. doi:10.1111/j.1475-6765.2006.00691.x

Koopmans, R., & Erbe, J. (2004). Towards a European public sphere? Vertical and horizontal dimensions of Europeanized political communication. *Innovation: The European Journal of Social Science Research*, 17(2), 97–118. doi:10.1080/1351161042000238643

Koopmans, R., & Statham, P. (2010). *The making of a European public sphere. Media discourse and political contention*. Cambridge: Cambridge University Press.

Koopmans, R., & Zimmermann, A. (2010). Transnational political communication on the internet: Search engine results and hyperlink networks. In R. Koopmans & P. Statham (Eds.), *The making of a European public sphere. Media discourse and political contention* (pp. 171–194). Cambridge: Cambridge University Press.

Matthes, C.-Y. (2022). Judges as activists: How Polish judges mobilise to defend the rule of law. *East European Politics*, 38(3), 468–487. doi:10.1080/21599165.2022.2092843

Nguyen, D. (2017). *Europe, the crisis, and the Internet: A web sphere analysis*. Palgrave. doi:10.1007/978-3-319-60843-3

Norris, P., & Inglehart, R. F. (2019). *Cultural backlash: Trump, Brexit, and Authoritarian populism*. Cambridge: Cambridge University Press.

Pfetsch, B. (2008). Agents of transnational debate across Europe: The Press in Emerging European public sphere. *Javnost - the Public*, 15(4), 21–40. doi:10.1080/13183222.2008.11008980

Priebus, S. (2022). The Commission's approach to rule of law backsliding: Managing instead of enforcing democratic values? *JCMS: Journal of Common Market Studies*, 60(6), 1684–1700. doi:10.1111/jcms.13341

Rettberg, J. W. (2014). *Blogging*. Cambridge: Polity Press.

Risse, T. (2010). *A community of Europeans? Transnational identities and public spheres*. New York: Cornell University Press.

Ruiz-Soler, J. (2020). European Twitter networks: Toward a transnational European public sphere? *International Journal of Communication, 14*, 5616–5642.

Statham, P., & Trenz, H.-J. (2013). *The politicization of Europe: Contesting the constitution in the mass media.* London: Routledge.

Stier, S., Froio, C., & Schünemann, W. J. (2021). Going transnational? candidates' transnational linkages on twitter during the 2019 European Parliament elections. *West European Politics, 44*(7), 1455–1481. doi:10.1080/01402382.2020.1812267

Urías, J. (2020). *Spain has a problem with its judiciary.* Verfassungsblog. doi:10.17176/20200120-125805-0

Von-Nordheim, G., Bettels-Schwabbauer, T., Di-Salvo, P., Kennedy, P., Kiss, K.-R. ... Telo, D. (2021). The state of europeanisation: Between clash and convergence. A comparison of the media coverage of the 2019 European elections in seven countries. *Revista Mediterránea de Comunicación, 12*(1), 95–113. doi:10.14198/MEDCOM000021

Walgrave, S., Soroka, S., & Nuytemans, M. (2007). The mass media's political agenda-setting power: A Longitudinal analysis of media, Parliament, and government in Belgium (1993 to 2000). *Comparative Political Studies, 41*(6), 814–836. doi:10.1177/0010414006299098

Wallaschek, S. (2020). Analyzing the European parliamentary elections in 2019: Actor visibility and issue-framing in transnational media. In M. Kaeding, M. Müller, & J. Schmälter (Eds.), *Die Europawahl 2019* (pp. 219–230). Springer VS. doi:10.1007/978-3-658-29277-5_18

Wallaschek, S., Kaushik, K., Verbalyte, M., Sojka, A., Sorci, G., Trenz, H.-J., & Eigmüller, M. (2022). Same same but different? Gender politics and (trans-)national value contestation in Europe on Twitter. *Politics & Governance, 10*(1), 146–160. doi:10.17645/pag.v10i1.4751

Part II
Country case studies

Interactive election campaigns on social media? Flow of political information among journalists and politicians as an element of the communication strategy of political actors

Kinga Adamczewska

ABSTRACT
This study examined politicians' communication strategies with journalists in Poland within the context of the flow of information on social media (Facebook and Twitter). The main questions posed in the article concerned which entities used which patterns of information flow, and whether during election campaigns, politicians communicated with journalists on social media by reacting to the latter's published posts. The study focused on pre-electoral periods of two consecutive parliamentary elections in Poland conducted in 2015 and 2019. The results showed that politicians rarely reacted to journalists' Twitter posts. If they did, they most often used reactive communication. Additionally, political actors from opposition parties more intensely used information flow patterns with a higher level of interactivity in 2019 than in 2015.

Introduction

The emergence and popularization of social media changed the possibilities for exchanging information between political communication actors. Both journalists (Bruns & Nuernbergk, 2019) and politicians (Haman & Školník, 2021; Jungherr, 2016; Praet, Martens, & Van Aelst, 2021; Vargo, Guo, McCombs, & Shaw, 2014) now view platforms such as Facebook and Twitter as a tool for their work. The growing popularity of both platforms has prompted these entities to communicate on social media, especially during ongoing election campaigns.

Although traditional media is predominant (including in Poland[1]) as the main source of information about politics (Lilleker & Vedel, 2013; Owen, 2014), the widespread use of online forms of communication during election campaigns (Gibson, 2015; Lilleker & Jackson, 2010) has forced political communication actors to switch to the hypermedia mode (Howard, 2006). In this mode, online media is treated as a supplement to traditional media (Štětka, Mackova, & Fialova, 2014). These changes have given politicians and journalists a wide range of strategic choices: should they observe other actors on social media or should they actively react to others' activities? If they choose the latter, to which entities should they react and in what way should they do so – by liking, sharing, or commenting? What strategy is the best?

The research problem of this paper is identifying communication strategies Facebook and Twitter politicians use during election campaigns. From the point of view of running an election campaign, politicians can be partners with media actors, they can actively participate in the flow of information journalists generate, or they can limit their online activities and be a present, passive entity in political news. By being active users, politicians can attract journalists' and the news media's attention and deliver a message to people. This message is crafted for a specific purpose and with conscious intention (Blach-Ørsten, 2016; Blach-Ørsten, Eberholst, & Burkal, 2017). At the same time, social media is a double-edged sword for politicians. Their activities may pose a threat to their image, so a "passive" strategy in their relations with journalists may seem safer to them. The communication network that social media has shaped is an interesting case study topic because analyzing this network can reveal the "hidden relationship" (its presence, type, and intensity) and the pattern of information flow between politicians and journalists.

Flow of information

Information flow, the mechanism of transmitting messages among structurally connected entities, is strongly associated with the concept of interactivity, perceived as a process-related variable (Kelleher, 2009; Rafaeli, 1988). Rafaeli (1988, p. 111) defined interactivity as the extent to which messages in a sequence relate to each other and, in particular, the extent to which each third or later message is related to earlier messages (Rafaeli & Sudweeks, 1997). From this perspective, there are three possible types of messages in the communication process: one-way – produces declarative communication; two-way – creates responsive (reactive) communication; and a third type (the basis of interactive communication) – two-way, repeated flow of messages between the sender and the receiver (Ariel & Avidar, 2015).

In the first information flow model, which refers to interactivity, four main patterns are included: allocution, registration, consultation, and conversation (Bordewijk & van Kaam, 1986). The allocution pattern equates to a one-way flow of messages – from the central entity to the periphery. Registration is based on the collection of information peripheral entities sent at the center's request. Consultation is the response of the central entity to a request for information from peripheral entities. Conversation involves the exchange of messages between peripheral entities, bypassing the central entity.

This model predates the advent of websites and the widespread use of the internet and therefore does not fully take into account the way digital media works. First, the model does not support a situation in which two central entities communicate with each other. Second, central and peripheral entities are defined not empirically but theoretically (as producers or consumers of information). Third, the registration pattern (collecting information about peripheral entities) is an inherent feature of the internet. Therefore, the model requires modification to enable the study of information flow in the new media environment today.

This paper proposes combining two concepts (interactivity and patterns of information flow) and creating a new theoretical approach to study the flow of information on social media. The proposed model has two dimensions: (1) level of interactivity of the distributed messages – non-interactive, reactive, or interactive; and (2) centrality and peripherality of the entity, defined as the structure of the real connections of this entity with others. It results in the introduction of three different message flow patterns (allocution, reaction, and conversation) and their types (Table 1).

In line with Bordewijk and van Kaam (1986), it is assumed that an exchange of messages may take place between central and peripheral entities in the proposed model. However, the way in which these entities are defined and categorized has changed. Previously, the center and the periphery were separated because of control over the production and distribution of messages. In the new approach, these entities are identified empirically through the centrality measures used (Krnc, Sereni, Skrekovski, & Yilma, 2020). Thus, the identification of central and peripheral entities is based on the structure of their real connections, not on the potential possibilities and resources (e.g. in access to information).

Additionally, in one social network, it is possible to have not only many peripheral entities but also many central entities that can communicate with each other on social media. This significantly influences the number of identifiable information flow patterns – the new model has a total of eight patterns, twice as many as in Bordewijk and van Kaam's model (Bordewijk & van Kaam, 1986). Such a processual approach has not yet been proposed in research on the flow of information on social media.[2]

Table 1. Proposition for a new information flow model on social media.

		The Level of Message Interactivity		
		Interactive	Reactive	Non-interactive
Type of Entity	**Central**	Conversation	Reaction	Allocution
	Peripheral	Mixed Conversation	Mixed Reaction	x
		Conversation	Reaction	Allocution

In line with the new theoretical proposal for information flow on social media, allocution occurs when a given entity publishes a post without using any social media functionality (liking, sharing, commenting, mentioning). Reaction takes place when a given entity publishes a post using the abovementioned functionalities. Conversation, characterized by the highest level of interactivity, consists of at least three exchanges of messages between two entities using the commenting function. Exchanging messages at least three times is necessary to fulfil the condition that later information interacting entities provide refers to earlier messages and to encourage further exchange between the entities.

Analysing the use of specified patterns of information flow by journalists and politicians, which are a manifestation of the communication strategy these entities have chosen, will help provide insights into their mutual relations, created and manifested through social media. Verifying the model using empirical research involves recognizing the level of interactivity of the messages sent between two entities to define the flow pattern used and then determining the centrality measures of the analyzed network actors. Actors who are best connected with others occupy the central position. They are perceived as the most important and the most influential entities in the whole network. Such entities, communicating with each other, create elite sub-networks, further strengthening their own visibility on social media. In the context of election campaigns, this form of communication between politicians and journalists seems desirable. Thus, after the initial recognition of the patterns of information flow between politicians and journalists on the network level, a detailed empirical analysis (actor level) is conducted that covers central entities, and the pattern of central reaction and central conversation is analyzed.

Politicians and journalists on social media

In the last few years, the use of social media (especially Twitter) in the context of political discussions has attracted great interest from academics. Numerous studies have focused on the performance of specific political actors (politicians and parties) on social media during election campaigns (e.g. Bruns & Highfield, 2013; Daniel & Obholzer, 2020; Graham, Broersma, Hazelhoff, & Van't Haar, 2013; Paatelainen, Kannasto, & Isotalus, 2022; Silva & Proksch, 2021, Vergeer, Hermans, & Sams, 2013; Stier, Bleier, Lietz, & Strohmaier, 2018). Analyses of the role of journalists and news media in online political debates have also been carried out (e.g. Bruns & Burgess, 2011; Fincham, 2019; Heiberger, Majó-Vázquez, Castro Herrero, Nielsen, & Esser, 2021; Larsson & Moe, 2012; Molyneux & Mourão, 2019). Finally, researchers have been paying greater attention to relations between politicians and journalists in online media (Broersma & Graham, 2016; D'heer & Verdegem, 2014, Ekman & Widholm, 2015; Metag & Rauchfleisch, 2017; Nuernbergk & Conrad, 2016; Verweij, 2012).

Politicians can use Twitter in a variety of ways: to comment on something or express their views and opinions (Silva & Proksch, 2021; Stier, Bleier, Lietz, & Strohmaier, 2018; Verweij, 2012), to conduct an individual-oriented election campaign, and to bypass political party gatekeeping (Golbeck, Grimes, & Rogers, 2010; Kruikemeier, 2014; Kruikemeier, van Noort, Vliegenthart, & de Vreese, 2013). They can also monitor social media to gain insights into the important issues of the day (Hanusch & Nölleke, 2018). By being active users, politicians can also attract the attention of journalists and news media and relay a specific message to people. This message is sent for a specific purpose and with conscious intention, avoiding traditional media filters (Blach-Ørsten, 2016; Blach-Ørsten, Eberholst, & Burkal, 2017). How do politicians communicate with journalists, who are public figures, and social media users? Politicians and journalists are dependent on each other – each side has something to offer and needs the other to achieve its own goals (Davis, 2007; Van Dalen, 2021). Journalists need politicians as information sources, and politicians through journalists and their publications can reach potential voters with their message. It seems, therefore, that especially during the election campaign, their mutual relations will be frequent on social media. However, because of social media's limitations and threats (online reputation risk, negative media attention, and limited resources), these mutual relations offer benefits and pose threats. Both entities should carefully think about and control these relations during elections. From this point of view, establishing such relations can be treated as a strategic action, not a spontaneous one.

Politicians are journalists' natural partners in the political communication process, especially during election campaigns. Journalists report more often and more positively about politicians they have personal contacts with (Van der Goot, Van der Meer, & Vliegenthart, 2021). Further, establishing two-way communication with journalists gives politicians the opportunity to influence public and media policy (Metag & Rauchfleisch, 2017). Politicians, formerly outside the sphere of media institutions, are now incorporating social media in election campaigns to implement their own communication strategies (Ekman & Widholm, 2014). Alternatively, studies have demonstrated that politicians face the hostile media phenomenon, which makes them less likely to contact journalists and more likely to use conflict and drama to gain public attention (Matthes, Maurer, & Arendt, 2019).

The above studies concerned traditional media and offline contacts between politicians and journalists. Relations between journalists and politicians in online media are more complicated. On the one hand, research has shown that journalists often appear in politicians' tweets as interaction partners (D'heer & Verdegem, 2014; Nuernbergk & Conrad, 2016). They are mutually involved in the direct exchange of messages (Broersma & Graham, 2016). Nuernbergk (2016) found that political journalists mainly interact with other journalists and politicians through @mentions in their tweets. Hanusch and Nölleke (2018), who reported that Australian journalists interact in a journalism-centered bubble, especially in their @mentions, echoed Nuernbergk (2016). Additionally, Molyneux and Mourão (2019) found that journalists interact more with other journalists and the political elite, confirming the "echo effect".

Meanwhile, political journalists indicated that they rarely interact with other actors of political communication in public through social media (Revers, 2014). The reason for this is the lack of time for deeper discussions and a reluctance to reveal the issues they are working on to other journalists (Broersma & Graham, 2016). Rega (2021) pointed out that although Twitter, thanks to its functionalities, enables interactive exchange of messages and two-way flow of information, its use by media entities seems limited.

Journalists and politicians on social media in central and eastern Europe

Most research on politician-journalist relations comes from Western European countries and the United States, but greater attention is being paid to the use of social media during election campaigns in Central and Eastern European countries (Appelberg, Johansson, Nygren, & Baranowski, 2014; Baboš & Világi, 2018; Cutts & Haughton, 2021; Domalewska, 2018; Hladík & Štětka, 2017; Johansson & Nożewski, 2018; Macková & Štětka, 2016; Matuszewski & Szabó, 2019; Murray Svidronova, Kascakova, & Bambusekova, 2019; Vesnic-Alujevic, Jurišić, & Bonacci, 2021). This is especially interesting because, in terms of political communication, some similarities (common goals of political actors, mobilization of voters, duplication of election campaign patterns in Western countries by political actors in the relatively young democracies of Central and Eastern Europe, campaigning in a new hybrid media environment) as well as differences (stability of party systems, lack of roots and organizational structures of Central and Eastern European parties, no experience in conducting democratic election campaigns because of the communist regime, tradition of professional and independent journalism) can be expected between these regions (Cutts & Haughton, 2021; Hladík & Štětka, 2017).

Research shows that social media allows politicians to collect voter feedback, disseminate their own plans after elections, increase their visibility, promote new political actors (Murray Svidronova, Kascakova, & Bambusekova, 2019), inform other actors of political communication about their presence in traditional media, present the results of their work, and criticize their political opponents (Domalewska, 2018). Political parties implement different campaign strategies on social media to influence people. Implementing two-way communication strategies generates more participation from people than unidirectional communication strategies (Baboš & Világi, 2018). Over the past few years, political actors in Central and Eastern Europe have increased the use of social media in election campaigns, surpassing even politicians in Western Europe in this respect (Cutts & Haughton, 2021). However, they still do not seem to take full advantage of the opportunities this new communication channel offers (Baboš & Világi, 2018). Indeed, in Poland, politicians use Twitter as an instrument to reach both voters and the media, but Polish politicians tend to rely on sharing tweets rather than publishing original content and to be followed rather than follow other profiles (Domalewska, 2018). This shows that they use social media in a reactive way.

Research on the use of social media by journalists in most cases has focused on information sources. In 2012, Czech journalists, active mainly on Facebook, declared that they rarely used this platform as a source of information. Additionally, they were aware that their privacy on social media was limited, so they had to carefully publish their statements on the website. At the same time, they were aware of the impact of social media on their profession (Hladík & Štětka, 2017). The results of Croatian research, however, showed the opposite tendency: Facebook was treated as a regular source of political information. The dominant sources were political actors, indicating that social media did not change the practices journalists used in this area (Vesnic-Alujevic, Jurišić, & Bonacci, 2021). In Sweden and Poland, social media are incorporated into regular work in the newsroom (Anikina, Dobek-Ostrowska, & Nygren, 2013), but journalists still prefer direct contact with politicians rather than asking them questions on Twitter (Johansson, 2019).

Vesnic-Alujevic, Jurišić, and Bonacci (2021) also suggested that collecting and filtering information has ceased to be the domain of journalists; it has also become a task that politicians perform. Media actors can now only report on what politicians decide to make public, thus changing the power relations between them and politicians and changing the role of journalists as gatekeepers. This may be one of the main differences in the way journalists from different regions of Europe function on social media. Other studies have shown that Swedish journalists have more opportunities to act as gatekeepers on Twitter; in Poland, it is more the political side (Johansson & Nożewski, 2018).

In conclusion, the relations that politicians form with other social media users, including journalists, during an election campaign fit in with the hybrid communication strategy. This strategy has been "interpreted as a synergy of mass communication strategies and messages targeted at individual follower networks on social media" (Stier, Bleier, Lietz, & Strohmaier, 2018, p. 66). The interactions between politicians and journalists can bring the former some benefits (e.g. greater visibility on social media[3]) and be a useful element of campaign strategies, but when candidates manage to use diverse forms of interaction (Kreiss, 2016). The current article adopts similar assumptions. The purpose of the article is to examine the distinct patterns of information flow (allocution, reaction, and conversation) between political and media actors during the election campaigns in Poland in 2015 and 2019 on Facebook and Twitter. Determining the extent to which politicians engaged in journalists' posts about politics, published on social media, will make it possible to indicate what communication strategy politicians adopted in this regard just before the parliamentary elections.

Two research questions are posed:

RQ1: What patterns of political information flow existed in the political communication process between politicians and journalists on social media during the election campaigns in 2015 and 2019 in Poland?

RQ2: How intense was the information flow entities in a central position in the network generated during the parliamentary election campaigns in Poland in 2015 and 2019?

The answer to the first question will reveal the level of interactivity at which journalists and politicians communicated with each other, assuming such communication took place at all on social media. A non-interactive pattern (allocution) would indicate that their activity on social media was aimed only at publishing posts without establishing structural relations with other actors. A reactive pattern (reaction) would indicate an intent to establish such relations to a limited extent. An interactive pattern (conversation), meanwhile, would indicate that journalists and politicians were highly engaged in the exchange of information.

The second research question concerns the characteristics of the communication process between the most important entities in the entire social network. The question is posed from the point of view of their ability to control the flow of information. Mutual communication between the entities with the greatest resources and the ability to disseminate and block information seems to be particularly important during an election campaign. Central media entities, from the point of view of election campaign strategies, should be the most desirable partners in the communication process for politicians.

Methods

The research period covered the two weeks preceding the election silence before the parliamentary elections in Poland in 2015 and 2019.[4] The election campaign in 2015 resulted in a change in the ruling party in Poland. After an eight-year-rule by Civic Platform (PO), Law and Justice (PiS) gained power. For the first time since 1989, the victorious election committee won a parliamentary majority to form an independent government. In 2019, after the parliamentary election campaign, Law and Justice remained in power.

The research sample was prepared in several stages:

(1) Journalists who published political information in Polish traditional and online media during the research period were identified. Data on 2905 publications from seven media outlets were collected. The number of identified political journalists (the authors of collected publications) totaled 187 in 2015 and 134 in 2019. Identification of individual journalists as the authors of the publications was possible in 47% of cases. The other publications either did not contain information about the author of the publication or had only initials or a pseudonym.

(2) Data on active Facebook and Twitter[5] accounts of identified political journalists were collected. Only public profiles were included in the analysis. In 2015, only 99 out of 187 journalists were active on Facebook or Twitter, and in 2019, only 72 out of 134 journalists were active on Facebook or Twitter (Graph 1).

All Facebook and Twitter posts by political journalists concerning political issues prevalent in the research period were monitored and collected.[6] Data on public profiles of journalists on social media were collected using NodeXL Pro software in the week after the elections. Next, all datasets were manually integrated into one file for further analysis (Graph 2).

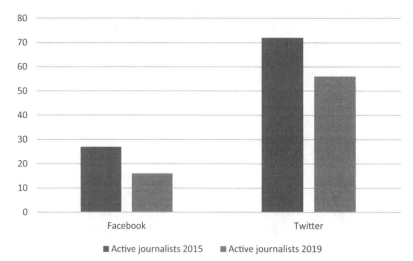

Graph 1. Differences in the number of active journalist accounts on Twitter and Facebook in 2015 and 2019.

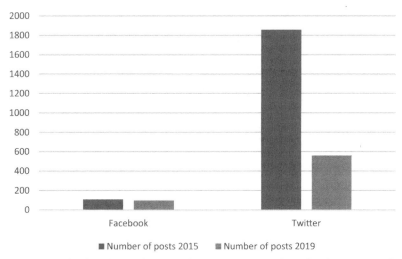

Graph 2. Differences in the number of political posts by journalists on Twitter and Facebook in 2015 and 2019.

(3) In the coding phase, each social media post was characterized in terms of the sender of the message, the social media functionality the sender used (like, share, comment, @mention), and the name of the entity with which the message sender (the post author) had established a relationship by using the listed functionalities. Which journalists and politicians reacted to a journalist's published post was also monitored. For each post, the information flow pattern the author used (sender perspective) was coded:

- The allocution pattern was identified when a given entity published a post on social media without using any social media functionalities (like, share, comment, @mention).
- The reaction pattern was identified when a given entity published a post using the above-mentioned functionalities, reacted to previous posts, and dynamized the flow of information.
- The conversation pattern was identified when a given entity exchanged messages with another using the commenting function, provided that the exchange took place at least three times (A to B, B to A, again A to B, ...).

In the empirical research, social network analysis (SNA) was used. The methodological approach was based on the Gephi software SNA method for obtaining statistical data and visualizing networks. This method demonstrates how actors are related to each other and how they communicate within a social network. Actors in SNA are marked as nodes (vertices), and the connections between them are marked as edges (ties) (Hevey, 2018). Three statistics were calculated for the created network. The first statistic was density, which is understood as the number of connections in the network as a proportion of the total number of possible connections that are present (Robins, 2015). It is a measure of the effectiveness of interconnection, using which one can answer the question of how many connections actors use for all possible links. A density coefficient close to 1 represents a well-connected network, and a density coefficient close to 0 represents a poorly connected network (Johansson & Nożewski, 2018).

The second statistic, one of the simplest characteristics of a node's position, was the degree of connection – the number of direct relationships of a given node with other nodes. In a directed network, it is possible to distinguish the degree of relations a given node initiates (out-degree) and the degree of relations a given node accepts (in-degree). The last measure is also an indicator of the popularity or prestige of a given node in the network (Batorski & Zdziarski, 2009).

The third statistic was betweenness centrality. It describes the position of the node in the network structure and determines its validity, significance, and influence on other nodes in the network (Hevey, 2018). Centrality is fundamental in research on the phenomenon of flows and processes taking place in the network (Borgatti, 2005). Thus, it is important from the point of view of the current paper as well. Betweenness centrality refers to the identification of actors in the social network that function as a bridge or a broker between nodes (Zhang & Ho, 2022). If the value of this indicator is large, the given node plays an important role as a medium (Kim & Kim, 2020). Additionally, the degree statistic correlates strongly with measures of centrality, making it a powerful summary index (Butts, 2008).

In the created social network, 628 media and political actors were identified in 2015 and 433 actors were identified in 2019. The journalists who authored the posts included in the research sample appeared on the social network as senders of information. However, if in their posts they referred to other actors (political or media), these new entities were included in the network through an established connection. A similar procedure was followed when other political or media actors reacted to a journalist's post by liking, sharing, commenting or mentioning it. Although the number of politicians involved in the information flow process was almost identical for both analyzed periods, significantly fewer journalists were active in 2019 (Graph 3). This may be related to the decrease in the number of active accounts of media actors on Twitter compared to 2015.

Results

Regarding RQ1, in 2015, the dominant pattern of information flow was allocution. Journalists used allocution for 49% of the analyzed posts. This means that they published a post without using any social media functionalities (like, share, comment, @mention). Meanwhile, in 2019, this percentage decreased significantly to 6%. The opposite trend can be observed in the case of two other patterns: in 2019, an increase in both reaction and conversation patterns was identified compared to 2015. Reaction as a pattern of information flow was still the most frequently observed pattern, but every third post generated a flow of information between politicians and journalists in the conversation pattern. Graph 4 shows the proportions of the use of the three patterns of information flow separately for the two research periods.

Using SNA, two directed networks were visualized. These networks included entities (journalists and politicians) communicating with each other. Based on the analysis, the allocution pattern, which assumed no connections between journalists and politicians, was excluded. The 2015 network consisted of 379 nodes (297 journalists and 82 politicians). Between these entities, a total of 1030 relations (edges) had occurred. A high degree of dispersion ($\Delta d = 0.014$) characterized the structure of the network – the density was at a very low level, which means there were many entities that were not connected to each other.

The second network, in 2019, consisted of a similar number of nodes ($N = 412$; 303 journalists and 109 politicians) and fewer relationships between them ($N = 669$), making the density even

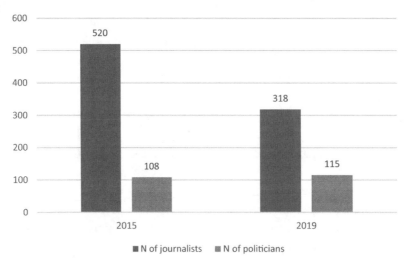

Graph 3. Differences in the proportion of media and political actors present in the analysed social networks in 2015 and 2019.

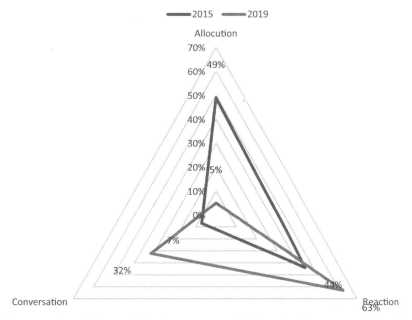

Graph 4. Differences in the proportion of the use of the three patterns of information flow among journalists and politicians in 2015 and 2019.

lower (Δd = 0.008). A comparison with a study that obtained data on two social networks of similar sizes using the same technique and methodology (Stevens, 2010) used in the current study showed that in 2019, the flow of information between journalists and politicians was less intense (Graph 5).

In the next step, it was checked how often politicians established relations with journalists using a more interactive pattern of information flow: reaction and conversation. In the analyzed directed networks, the number of politicians' outgoing connections with journalists was calculated. In 2015, 55 politicians generated such connections 80 times. The most active had a 5-to-3 out-degree. In 2019, fewer political actors, 47, established more relationships with journalists – 172 in total. The intensity of interactive communication with journalists was also higher – the five most active politicians generated between 9 and 20 connections (Table 2).

In the last step, both networks were analyzed to identify entities that held a central position in

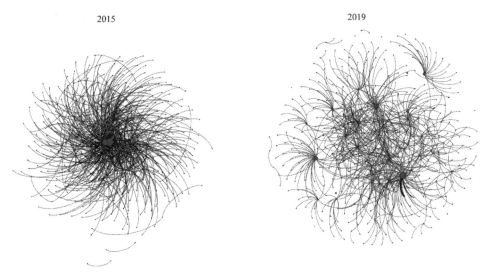

Graph 5. The network of journalists and politicians who participated in the social media communication process. The colours of the nodes correspond to the types of actors (media – blue, politicians – red). The sizes of the nodes were selected based on betweenness centrality. Layout: Fruchterman-Reingold.

the network and could act as bridges or information brokers. Betweenness centrality indicates how often a given node appears in the shortest paths between pairs of nodes. Potentially, these nodes have greater control over the flow of information in the network (Batorski & Zdziarski, 2009). This indicator work illustrates the importance of a given node in terms of information propagation in the network. Using the model presented in the theoretical part, it was checked which entities held the central, that is, the most influential (regarding the flow of information), position in the network.

In 2015, the 20 most important nodes in terms of information flow were identified. A total of 143 relationships existed between them (Bc between 0.01 and 0.07).[7] Interestingly, in this network, only journalists were present. In turn, in 2019, with the same or higher level of betweenness centrality ratio (Bc between 0.01 and 0.24), a larger network consisting of 47 nodes but connected by a similar number of relationships (141), was created. Additionally, four politicians, all from opposition parties, appeared on this network (Borys Budka, Adam Szłapka, Anna Maria Żukowska, Michał Boni). Among the central entities, no representative of the Polish public media or the ruling party was identified (Graph 6). By using the betweenness centrality score of any node in the social network, it was possible to identify the most efficient "spreaders" in a network. Such identification can be a very important step to optimize the use of available resources and to ensure the more efficient spread of information, especially in election campaign contexts.

Table 2. The most active politicians using a reaction or conversation pattern to communicate with journalists on social media.

	Name of Politician (Affiliation)	Out-Degree
2015	Marek Magierowski (Law and Justice)	5
	Marek Łapiński (Civil Platform)	5
	Barbara Nowacka (Your Movement)	3
	Jarosław Gowin (Poland Together)	3
	Przemysław Wipler (KORWIN Party)	3
2019	Michał Boni (Civil Platform)	20
	Borys Budka (Civil Platform)	13
	Anna Maria Żukowska (Democratic Left Alliance)	11
	Joanna Kluzik (Civil Platform)	10
	Tadeusz Truskolaski (Civil Platform)	9

Discussion

The research showed how politicians engaged in communication processes with journalists during the parliamentary election campaigns in Poland in 2015 and 2019 on social media. Among three distinguished patterns of information flow, allocution, reaction and conversation, the second one was dominant over time. Politicians and journalists were more likely to respond by liking, sharing, or commenting on messages than by engaging in lengthy conversations. This result is in line with those of previous studies – political and media actors do not fully use the interactive potential of social media (Baboš & Világi, 2018; Herrera & Requejo, 2012; Meyer & Tang, 2015; Rega, 2021). The result may be a starting point for in-depth research on the causes of this phenomenon. Perhaps the phenomenon is related to making a rational choice about costs (time, money, energy, potential negative impact on the image of the politician) and benefits (greater visibility on social media, interest of journalists in a particular candidate), which may result from more interactive

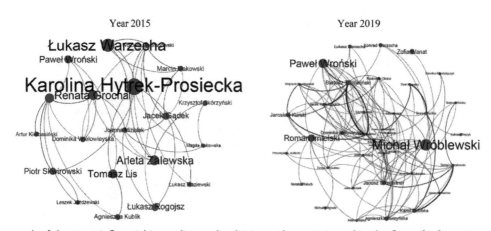

Graph 6. The network of the most influential journalists and politicians who participated in the flow of information on social media. The colours of the nodes correspond to the types of actors (media – blue, politicians – red). The sizes of the nodes were selected in terms of the betweenness centrality. Layout: Fruchterman-Reingold.

communication between these entities (Hong, Choi, & Kim, 2019).

From 2015 and 2019, a low level of density was noted for social networks. This is typical when they include a large number of nodes (Borgatti, Everett, & Johnson, 2018, p. 175). However, the lower network density in 2019 shows that in the second research period, fewer entities were connected to each other compared to 2015. This may reflect the disintegration of the journalistic and political community in Poland after 2015. Law and Justice (the ruling party) introduced practices limiting access to officials for journalists from private media outlets and began to financially support pro-government media (Mong, 2018; Newman et al., 2021). The situation of journalists who worked in public media outlets changed significantly – those who (in official statements) presented a different perspective from the ruling party were dismissed. Other journalists resigned from public media in favor of private media. New journalists who were often young and unknown in the journalist community took their place (Censki, 2016; Maslak, 2016). The lower network density in 2019 could therefore be a symptom of the weakening of relations among the group of journalists and between journalists and politicians not only offline but also on social media at the level of their structural connections.

Politicians can establish connections with political journalists on social media as a part of their broader communication strategy during an election campaign. We observed that they initiated such relations with greater intensity in 2019. However, politicians with the largest number of out-degrees came from opposition parties. Given the electoral context, it seems that their more interactive communication could have been a planned action aimed at drawing journalists' attention to specific politicians and increasing these politicians' visibility on social media. It was likely an attempt to intercept the flow of information to maximize politicians' media exposure during the election campaigns. This is consistent with the results of American researchers, which showed that opposing party politicians, underdogs, and extremists are more likely to become active political tweeters (Hong, Choi, & Kim, 2019).

The introduced information flow model was tested at the level of central entities. However, it also provides an opportunity for further exploration of the behavior of politicians on social media. For example, do the communication activities of politicians with a central position differ from the communication activities of politicians with a peripheral position in the network? Do politicians generate relations more often with journalists in a central position or in a peripheral position? How do politicians highlight their presence in the process of political communication on social media and with whom (which journalist) do they engage? These are strategic questions politicians must answer when calculating the cost-benefit of each of their decisions, especially before elections. The discussed model also holds promise for theory development. It brings together concepts found in earlier models of mass communication (information flow, interactivity) and integrates them with empirical measures of centrality and peripherality using SNA.

Important limitations can be indicated in the conducted study. First, the obtained results seem to contradict research showing that journalists often appear in the tweets of politicians as interaction partners (D'heer & Verdegem, 2014; Nuernbergk & Conrad, 2016). However, it should be borne in mind that such interaction was coded if it occurred at the structural level (e.g. by @mention): mentioning a politician in the content of a post without marking them did not generate a structural link in the analyzed network. In this respect, the analysis was carried out at the level of structural links between politicians and journalists, not semantic ones.

Second, SNA, as a quantitative method, enabled visualization of the structure of connections within the analyzed social network and calculation of the degree and betweenness centrality index for each actor in the network. Thus, only an estimate of who had more potential to exert a more influential role in the whole communication structure was possible. Combining SNA with other research methods, such as media content analysis, could help paint a more complete picture of the communication strategy of politicians and journalists by answering these questions: About what issues do politicians and journalists communicate with each other on social media in a reactive and interactive way?

What is the tone of this communication? On the whole, the current study's results may provide inspiration to undertake this type of analysis in the future.

Notes

1. Public opinion polls conducted in Poland in 2015 showed that television remains the most popular source of information about politics: most Poles learned about candidates running in parliamentary elections from TV news (79%), and 31% used the internet for this purpose (CEBOS, 2015). Similar results were obtained in 2019: the most popular source of information was again news broadcast on television (70%), and every third respondent (31%) learned about campaign content on the internet (CEBOS, 2019).
2. Earlier studies have identified other information flow patterns. McMillan (2002) distinguished four patterns of information flow: monologue, feedback, responsive dialogue, and mutual discourse. In 2019, Johnson proposed modes of communication on Facebook and Twitter. Jensen (2016) also introduced four prototype meta-communication patterns into the digital media environment. In each case, however, the flow of information was treated as a variable related to a given medium and not to the communication process itself.
3. Political journalists, as intermediaries between politicians and citizens, produce important and visible content on the one hand, but on the other hand, they are burdened with important social and democratic expectations (Bruns & Nuernbergk, 2019). Potentially, the high activity of some politicians on social media, shared as a source of information by leading political journalists, can increase the visibility of specific political contents and candidates. According to López-Rabadán and Mellado (2019, p. 4), "Since tweets are typically quoted in their entirety and with little journalistic mediation, they can generate a notorious direct impact on the electorate and public opinion."
4. In 2015, elections took place from 9 to 23 October (parliamentary elections took place on 25 October 2015), and in 2019, elections took place from 28 September to 11 October (parliamentary elections took place on 13 October 2019).
5. This was because Facebook and Twitter are becoming increasingly popular in Poland, and interest among politicians in these communication channels is growing (Adamik-Szysiak, 2019). The number of Facebook users forms around 80% of all Polish internet users. In 2019, the popularity of both platforms increased (Digital 2020 Report, 2020). Additionally, Twitter has mainly Polish journalists and politicians (Czarkowska & Gumkowska, 2017)
6. Only posts that contained political information (about political actors and their activities) were collected.
7. The value of the betweenness centrality index was presented on a standardized scale.

Disclosure statement

No potential conflict of interest was reported by the author.

Funding

Data collection and analysis were funded by the National Science Center (2018/29/N/HS5/00723).

ORCID

Kinga Adamczewska http://orcid.org/0000-0003-0755-0788

References

Adamik-Szysiak, M. (2019). Social media as a tool of political permanent campaign on the example of the activity of polish politicians. *SWS Journal of Social Sciences and Art*, *1*(2), 1–12. doi:10.35603/ssa2019/issue2.01

Anikina, M., Dobek-Ostrowska, B., & Nygren, G. (2013). *Journalists in three media systems: Polish, Russian and Swedish journalists about values and ideals, daily practice and the future.* Moscow: Lomanosov Moscow State University.

Appelberg, J., Johansson, E., Nygren, G., & Baranowski, P. (2014). Social media in the professional work of Polish, Russian and Swedish journalists. *Journal of Print and Media Technology Research*, *3*(2), 107–118.

Ariel, Y., & Avidar, R. (2015). Information, interactivity, and social media. *Atlantic Journal of Communication*, *23*(1), 19–30. doi:10.1080/15456870.2015.972404

Baboš, P., & Világi, A. (2018). Just a show? Effects of televised debates on political attitudes and preferences in Slovakia. *East European Politics and Societies*, *32*(4), 720–742. doi:10.1177/0888325418762050

Batorski, D., & Zdziarski, M. (2009). Analiza sieciowa i jej zastosowania w badaniach organizacji i zarządzania. [Network analysis and its applications in organization and management research]. *Problemy zarządzania*, 7(4), 157–184. 26

Blach-Ørsten, M. (2016). Politikkens medialisering: Et nyinstitutionelt perspektiv. [The mediatization of politics: A new institutional perspective. In I. S. Hjarvard (Ed.), *Medialisering: Mediernes rolle i social og kulturel forandring. [Mediatization: The role of the media in social and cultural change]* (pp. 185–216). Copenhagen, Denmark: Hans Reitzel.

Blach-Ørsten, M., Eberholst, M. K., & Burkal, R. (2017). From hybrid media system to hybrid-media politicians: Danish politicians and their cross-media presence in the 2015 national election campaign. *Journal of Information Technology & Politics*, 14(4), 334–347. doi:10.1080/19331681.2017.1369917

Bordewijk, J. L., & van Kaam, B. (1986). Towards a new classification of tele-information service. *InterMedia*, 14 (1), 16–21.

Borgatti, S. P. (2005). Centrality and network flow. *Social Networks*, 27(1), 55–57. doi:10.1016/j.socnet.2004.11.008

Borgatti, S. P., Everett, M. G., & Johnson, J. C. (2018). *Analyzing social networks*. London: Sage.

Broersma, M., & Graham, T. (2016). Tipping the balance of power: Social media and the transformation of political journalism. In A. Bruns, G. Enli, E. Skogerbø, A. O. Larsson, & C. Christensen (Eds.), *The Routledge companion to social media and politics* (pp. 89–103). New York: Routledge. doi:10.4324/9781315716299-7

Bruns, A., & Burgess, J. (2011). #ausvotes: How Twitter covered the 2010 Australian federal election. *Communication, Politics and Culture*, 44, 2–37.

Bruns, A., & Highfield, T. (2013). Political networks on Twitter: Tweeting the Queensland state election. *INFORMATION COMMUNICATION & SOCIETY*, 16(5), 667–691. doi:10.1080/1369118X.2013.782328

Bruns, A., & Nuernbergk, C. (2019). Political journalists and their social media audiences: New power relations. *Media and Communication*, 7(1), 198–212. doi:10.17645/mac.v7i1.1759

Butts, T. C. (2008). Social network analysis: A methodological introduction. *Asian Journal of Social Psychology*, 11(1), 13–41. doi:10.1111/j.1467-839X.2007.00241.x

Censki, J. (2016, July 11). Polish media veers back to pre-1989. *Politico*. Retrieved from https://www.politico.eu/article/polish-tv-viewers-turn-off-tune-out-drop-out-poland-kaczynski/

Cutts, D., & Haughton, T. (2021). Winning votes and influencing people: Campaigning in central and Eastern Europe. *East European Politics*, 37(2), 239–266. doi:10.1080/21599165.2020.1767076

Czarkowska, M., & Gumkowska, A. (2017). Facebook, Twitter, Instagram, Pinterest – nowe perspektywy badawcze [Facebook, Twitter, Instagram, Pinterest – new research perspectives]. *Adeptus*, 10(10). doi:10.11649/a.1519.

Daniel, W. T., & Obholzer, L. (2020). Reaching out to the voter? Campaigning on Twitter during the 2019 European elections. Retrieved from *Research & Politics*, 7(2), 205316802091725. doi:https://doi.org/10.1177/2053168020917256

Davis, A. (2007). *The mediation of power. A critical introduction*. London: Routledge.

D'heer, E., & Verdegem, P. (2014). Conversations about the elections on Twitter: Towards a structural understanding of twitter's relation with the political and the media field. *European Journal of Communication*, 29(6), 720–734. doi:10.1177/0267323114544866

Domalewska, D. (2018). The permanent campaign in social media: A case study of Poland. *Central and Eastern European eDem and eGov Days*, 331, 461–468. doi:10.24989/ocg.v331.38

Ekman, M., & Widholm, A. (2015). Politicians as media producers: Current trajectories in the relation between journalists and politicians in the age of social media. *Journalism Practice*, 9(1), 78–91. doi:10.1080/17512786.2014.928467

Fincham, K. (2019). Exploring political journalism homophily on Twitter: A comparative analysis of US and UK elections in 2016 and 2017. *Media and Communication*, 7(1), 213–224. doi:10.17645/mac.v7i1.1765

Gibson, R. K. (2015). Party change, social media and the rise of 'citizen-initiated' campaigning. *Party Politics*, 21(2), 183–197. doi:10.1177/1354068812472575

Golbeck, J., Grimes, J. M., & Rogers, A. (2010). Twitter use by the U.S. Congress. *Journal of the American Society for Information Science and Technology*, 61(8), 1612–1621. doi:10.1002/asi.21344

Graham, T., Broersma, M., Hazelhoff, K., & Van't Haar, G. (2013). Between broadcasting political messages and interacting with voters: The use of Twitter during the 2010 UK general election campaign. *INFORMATION COMMUNICATION & SOCIETY*, 16(5), 692–716. doi:10.1080/1369118X.2013.785581

Haman, M., & Školník, M. (2021). Politicians on social media. The online database of members of national parliaments on twitter. *Profesional de la información*, 30(2), e300217. doi:10.3145/epi.2021.mar.17

Hanusch, F., & Nölleke, D. (2018). Journalistic homophily on social media. *Digital Journalism*, 6(7), 1–23. doi:10.1080/21670811.2018.1436977

Heiberger, R., Majó-Vázquez, S., Castro Herrero, L., Nielsen, R. K., & Esser, F. (2021). Do not blame the media! The role of politicians and parties in fragmenting online political debate. *The International Journal of Press/Politics*. Retrieved from https://journals.sagepub.com/doi/full/10.1177/19401612211015122

Herrera, S., & Requejo, J. L. (2012). 10 good practices for news organizations using Twitter. *Journal of Applied Journalism & Media Studies*, 1(1), 79–95. doi:10.1386/ajms.1.1.79_1

Hevey, D. (2018). Network analysis: A brief overview and tutorial. *Health Psychology and Behavioral Medicine*, 6(1), 301–328. doi:10.1080/21642850.2018.1521283

Hladík, R., & Štětka, V. (2017). The powers that tweet: Social media as news sources in the Czech Republic. *Journalism*

Studies, 18(2), 154–174. doi:10.1080/1461670X.2015.1046995

Hong, S., Choi, H., & Kim, T. K. (2019). Why do politicians tweet? Extremists, underdogs, and opposing parties as political tweeters. *Policy & Internet*, 11(3), 305–323. doi:10.1002/poi3.201

Howard, P. N. (2006). *New media campaigns and the managed citizen*. Cambridge, New York, Melbourne, Madrid, Cape Town, Singapore, São Paulo: Cambridge University Press.

Jensen, K. B. (2016). Been there, done that: Communication, meta-communication and presence. *Nordicom Review*, 37(1), 7–22.

Johansson, E. (2019). Social media in political communication: A substitute for conventional media? In K. M. Johansson & G. Nygren (Eds.), *Close and distant political executive – Media relations in four countries* (pp. 149–173). Gothenburg: Nordicom.

Johansson, E., & Nożewski, J. (2018). Polish and Swedish journalist-politician Twitter networks: Who are the gatekeepers? *Central European Journal of Communication*, 11(2), 129–150. doi:10.19195/1899-5101.11.2(21).2

Jungherr, A. (2016). Twitter use in election campaigns: A systematic literature review. *Journal of Information Technology & Politics*, 13(1), 72–91. doi:10.1080/19331681.2015.1132401

Kelleher, T. (2009). Conversational voice, communicated commitment, and public relations outcomes in interactive online communication. *Journal of Communication*, 59(1), 172–188. doi:10.1111/j.1460-2466.2008.01410.x

Kim, S. Y., & Kim, B. Y. (2020). Big data analysis of AI news and robot journalism trends. *Technology*, 11(10), 1395–1402.

Kreiss, D. (2016). *Prototype politics: Technology-intensive campaigning and the data of democracy*. Oxford University Press. doi:10.1093/acprof:oso/9780199350247.001.0001

Krnc, M., Sereni, J. S., Skrekovski, R., & Yilma, Z. (2020). Eccentricity of networks with structural constraints. *Discussiones Mathematicae Graph Theory*, 40(4), 1141–1162. doi:10.7151/dmgt.2180

Kruikemeier, S. (2014). How political candidates use Twitter and the impact on votes. *Computers in Human Behavior*, 34, 131–139. doi:10.1016/j.chb.2014.01.025

Kruikemeier, S., van Noort, G., Vliegenthart, R., & de Vreese, C. H. (2013). Getting closer: The effects of personalized and interactive online political communication. *European Journal of Communication*, 28(1), 53–66. doi:10.1177/0267323112464837

Larsson, A. O., & Moe, H. (2012). Studying political microblogging: Twitter users in the 2010 Swedish election campaign. *New Media & Society*, 14(5), 729–747. doi:10.1177/1461444811422894

Lilleker, D. G., & Jackson, N. A. (2010). Towards a more participatory style of election campaigning: The impact of web 2.0 on the UK 2010 general election. *Policy & Internet*, 2(3), 67–96. doi:10.2202/1944-2866.1064

Lilleker, D., & Vedel, T. (2013). The internet in campaigns and elections. In W. Dutton (Ed.), *Oxford handbook of internet studies* (pp. 401–420). Oxford: Oxford University Press. doi:10.1093/oxfordhb/9780199589074.013.0019

López-Rabadán, P., & Mellado, C. (2019). Twitter as a space for interaction in political journalism. Dynamics, consequences and proposal of interactivity scale for social media. *Communication & Society*, 32(1), 1–18. doi:10.15581/003.32.37810

Macková, A., & Štětka, V. (2016). Walking the party line? The determinants of facebook's adoption and use by Czech parliamentarians. *Media Studies*, 7(14), 157–175. Retrieved from. https://repository.lboro.ac.uk/articles/journal_contribution/Walking_the_party_line_Determinants_of_facebook_s_adoption_and_use_by_Czech_parliamentarians/9473099

Maslak, P. (2016). Poland's conservative government puts curbs on state TV. *The New York Times*. Retrieved from https://www.nytimes.com/2016/07/04/world/europe/polands-conservative-government-puts-curbs-on-state-tv-news.html

Matthes, J., Maurer, P., & Arendt, F. (2019). Consequences of politicians' perceptions of the news media: A hostile media phenomenon approach. *Journalism Studies*, 20(3), 345–363. doi:10.1080/1461670X.2017.1377102

Matuszewski, P., & Szabó, G. (2019). Are echo chambers based on partisanship? Twitter and political polarity in Poland and Hungary. *Social Media + Society*, 5(2), 1–14. doi:10.1177/2056305119837671

McMillan, S. J. (2002). A four-part model of cyber-interactivity: Some cyber-places are more interactive than others. *New Media & Society*, 4(2), 271–291. doi:10.1177/14614440222226370

Metag, J., & Rauchfleisch, A. (2017). Journalists' use of political tweets: Functions for journalistic work and the role of perceived influences. *Digital Journalism*, 5(9), 1155–1172. doi:10.1080/21670811.2016.1248989

Meyer, K. M., & Tang, T. (2015). #socialjournalism: Local news media on Twitter. *The International Journal on Media Management*, 17(4), 241–257. doi:10.1080/14241277.2015.1107569

Molyneux, L., & Mourão, R. R. (2019). Political journalists' normalization of Twitter: Interaction and new affordances. *Journalism Studies*, 20(2), 248–266. doi:10.1080/1461670X.2017.1370978

Mong, A. (2018, March 12). Mission journal: In Poland, some journalists fear worst is yet to come. *Committee to Protect Journalists*. Retrieved from https://cpj.org/2018/03/mission-journal-in-poland-some-journalists-fear-wo/

Murray Svidronova, M., Kascakova, A., & Bambusekova, G. (2019). Social media in the presidential election campaign: Slovakia 2019. *Administration & Public Management Review*, 1(33), 181–195. Retrieved from. https://ramp.ase.ro/_data/files/articole/2019/33-11.pdf

Newman, N., Fletcher, R., Schulz, A., Andi, S., Robertson, C. T., & Nielsen, R. K. (2021). *Reuters Institute digital news report 2021*. Reuters Institute for the Study of Journalism.

Nuernbergk, C. (2016). Political journalists' interaction networks. *Journalism Practice*, *10*(7), 1–12. doi:10.1080/17512786.2016.1162669

Nuernbergk, C., & Conrad, J. (2016). Conversations and campaign dynamics in a hybrid media environment: Use of Twitter by members of the German Bundestag. *Social Media + Society*, *2*(1), 1–14. doi:10.1177/2056305116628888

Owen, D. (2014). New media and political campaigns. In K. Kenski & K. H. Jamieson (Eds.), *The oxford handbook of political communication theory and research* (pp. 823–836). New York: Oxford University Press. doi:10.1093/oxfordhb/9780199793471.013.016_update_001

Paatelainen, L., Kannasto, E., & Isotalus, P. (2022). Functions of hybrid media: How parties and their leaders use traditional media in their social media campaign communication. *Frontiers in Communication*, *287*, Retrieved from https://www.frontiersin.org/articles/10.3389/fcomm.2021.817285/full

Praet, S., Martens, D., & Van Aelst, P. (2021). Patterns of democracy? Social network analysis of parliamentary Twitter networks in 12 countries. *Online Social Networks and Media*, *24*, 100154. doi:10.1016/j.osnem.2021.100154

Rafaeli, S. (1988). Interactivity: From new media to communication. In R. P. Hawkins, J. M. Wiemann, & S. Pingree (Eds.), *Advancing communication science: Merging mass and interpersonal process* (pp. 110–134). Newbury Park, CA: Sage.

Rafaeli, S., & Sudweeks, F. (1997). *Networked interactivity*. University of Southern California. Retrieved from http://www.usc.edu/dept/annenberg/vol2/issue4/rafaeli.sudweeks.html

Rega, R. (2021). Social media news: A comparative analysis of the journalistic uses of Twitter. *Central European Journal of Communication*, *14*(29), 195–216. doi:10.51480/1899-5101.14.2(29).1

Revers, M. (2014). The Twitterization of news making: Transparency and journalistic professionalism. *Journal of Communication*, *64*(5), 1–21. doi:10.1111/jcom.12111

Robins, G. (2015). *Doing social network research*. Los Angeles: Sage.

Silva, B. C., & Proksch, S. O. (2021). Politicians unleashed? Political communication on Twitter and in parliament in Western Europe. *Political Science Research and Methods*, *10*(4), 1–17.

Štětka, V., Mackova, A., & Fialova, M. (2014). A winding road from "likes" to votes. The role of social media in the 2013 Czech presidential elections. In B. Pătruț & M. Pătruț (Eds.), *Social media in politics: Case studies on the political power of social media* (pp. 225–244). New York: Springer. doi:10.1007/978-3-319-04666-2_13

Stevens, J. (2010). Comparing multiple social networks using multiple dimensional calling. *Methodological Innovations Online*, *5*(1), 86–102. doi:10.4256/mio.2010.0012

Stier, S., Bleier, A., Lietz, H., & Strohmaier, M. (2018). Election campaigning on social media: Politicians, audiences, and the mediation of political communication on Facebook and Twitter. *Political Communication*, *35*(1), 50–74. doi:10.1080/10584609.2017.1334728

Van Dalen, A. (2021). Rethinking journalist–politician relations in the age of populism: How outsider politicians delegitimize mainstream journalists. *Journalism*, *22*(11), 2711–2728. doi:10.1177/1464884919887822

Van der Goot, E. S., Van der Meer, T. G., & Vliegenthart, R. (2021). Reporting on political acquaintances: Personal interactions between political journalists and politicians as a determinant of media coverage. *International Journal of Communication*, *15*, 23. Retrieved from file:///C:/Users/48695/Downloads/15313-51377-1-PB.pdf.

Vargo, C. J., Guo, L., McCombs, M., & Shaw, D. L. (2014). Network issue agendas on Twitter during the 2012 US presidential election. *Journal of Communication*, *64*(2), 296–316. doi:10.1111/jcom.12089

Vergeer, M., Hermans, L., & Sams, S. (2013). Online social networks and micro-blogging in political campaigning: The exploration of a new campaign tool and a new campaign style. *Party Politics*, *19*(3), 477–501. doi:10.1177/1354068811407580

Verweij, P. (2012). Twitter links between politicians and journalists. *Journalism Practice*, *6*(5–6), 680–691. doi:10.1080/17512786.2012.667272

Vesnic-Alujevic, L., Jurišić, J., & Bonacci, D. (2021). Changing sourcing practices: Journalists' use of Facebook in Croatia. *Journal of Applied Journalism & Media Studies*, *10*(3), 253–273. doi:10.1386/ajms_00034_1

Zhang, X., & Ho, J. C. (2022). Exploring the fragmentation of the representation of data-driven journalism in the Twittersphere: A network analytics approach. *Social Science Computer Review*, *40*(1), 42–60. Retrieved from. https://journals.sagepub.com/doi/10.1177/0894439320905522

The audience logic in election news reporting on Facebook: What drives audience engagement in transitional democracies of Albania and Kosovo?

Lindita Camaj, Erlis Çela, and Gjylie Rexha

ABSTRACT
This study provides insights on how journalists in the Western Balkans conceptualize and practice audience engagement during electoral campaigns. Taking a holistic approach, we first explore audience demand and news supply of strategic and negative election news on Facebook, then turn to news editors to explore what type of audience logic drives their reporting. Our data confirm previous findings about audience demand for strategic news but contradict the predominance of audience negativity bias in the context of Southeast Europe. These findings support generic trends in how social media audiences engage with political information, but also emphasize the importance of the socio-political context as a determinant of audience engagement with online news. Interview data identified an alignment between journalists' imagined readership preferences with the reality, yet reporting patterns on Facebook do not entirely follow engagement trends. Together, these findings suggest that journalism culture developed in this region is more nuanced than previously defined, while news editors embrace new technologies to serve the commercial needs and audience strengthening logics in parallel during electoral campaigns.

A long-debated question in literature explores if strategic game framing and negative reporting of electoral campaigns is detrimental or beneficial to democracy (Cushion & Thomas, 2018). Issue framing of political messages is favored because it increases voter knowledge and participation, while others associate strategy game frames with political malaise (Cappella & Jamieson, 1997). Yet, the predominance of strategic game framing in electoral coverage has become a standard feature of election news reporting across countries (Aelst, 2018) partially explained by the audience logic – journalists' presumption of public demand for strategic news (Cushion & Thomas, 2018). In this study, we explore if audiences in two transitional democracies of Southeast Europe indeed exhibit a preference for strategic game frame and negative election news and investigate what type the audience logic guides election news production on social media.

Specifically, this paper analyzes news media use of Facebook as a platform for campaign news reporting and user interaction during the 2019 parliamentary elections in Kosovo and 2021 parliamentary elections in Albania. The content analysis in this article examines three trends in election coverage on Facebook (Esser & Strömbäck, 2012): 1) media depoliticization, (2) personalization, and (3) negativity, and ties it to audience engagement via comments, shares, and reactions. Guided by the concept of audience logic (Landerer, 2013), in-depth interviews examine how journalists conceptualize audience engagement with campaign news on social media.

This study contributes to the literature in meaningful ways, theoretically and practically. With very few exceptions (Valenzuela, Piña, & Ramírez, 2017), most research has explored the "audience turn in journalism" either from the news production focus or from the audience's perspective (Swart, Groot Kormelink, Costera Meijer, & Broersma, 2022). This study builds on recent research that examines the interaction between news supply and demand on social media. We combine content analysis and news user data with in-depth interviews with news producers in order to explore the prevalence of "news gap" between what journalists and consumers of political news deem newsworthy (de León & Vermeer, 2022) in a non-Western context.

There is an increasing trend in journalists' use of social media for news construction and news dissemination, offering new potentials to create more diverse journalism (Humayun & Ferrucci, 2022). Overall audience engagement is perceived as a means to improve audience's trust in news media, deliver economic benefits, and strengthen journalism's democratic function in society (Singer et al., 2011). On the audience side, social media engagement is an indication of the high level of audience involvement with election news (Oeldorf-Hirsch & Sundar, 2015) that might lead to different patterns in voter learning, opinion formation, and participation. Against this backdrop, the current study aims to identify ways in which journalists can engage audiences with quality information during electoral campaigns that contributes to an informed and active voter. It is important to understand how digital media transformations in Southeast Europe have impacted audience conceptualization and engagement in journalism, especially if we consider the important role that the media have played in the Balkan's turbulent past and the more recent democratization developments (Kovacevic & Perisin, 2018).

Theoretical framework

The democratic value of audience engagement

The democratic relevance of audience engagement with election information is especially important if we consider them as acts of civic engagement (Dalton, 2017). Audience engagement with election news on social media can be understood as a continuum. Facebook affordances facilitate three main ways users can engage with news: liking, commenting and sharing, each of which carries different levels of participation (Larsson, 2015). Using the like/reaction button in relation to news posts is considered a light form of engagement, since it does not take much social capital and effort for this type of engagement. News commenting, on the other hand, is consider a superior form of engagement given that citizen discussions about politics are perceived as vital for deliberative democracy and can contribute to learning about issues and candidate positions during elections (Carpini, Cook, & Jacobs, 2004). Similarly, news sharing is a more involved practice of news engagement as it indicates news endorsement and can lead to high visibility of news posts (Kalsnes & Larsson, 2018). Popularity cues such as sharing and liking can influence people's attention to quality news (Dvir-Gvirsman, 2019) and can influence other people's engagement with the same quality news (Muddiman & Stroud, 2017).

This study is situated within the fast-growing literature that investigates how social media users engage with quality news while exploring how specific news content dimensions might determine different forms of engagement (Trilling, Tolochko, & Burscher, 2017). Most of this line of research is based in Western contexts, which limits our understanding of election news making and consuming across media systems, political cultures and levels of voter engagement (Cushion & Thomas, 2018). Comparative research emphasizes that country context is a significant predictor of news audiences' social media engagement (Ferrer-Conill et al., 2021; Salgado & Bobba, 2019) and journalists adoption of the audience-centric approach in news production (Andresen, Hoxha, & Godole, 2017).

This study is situated in the emerging democracies of Albania and Kosovo, in Southeast Europe. While these countries are similar in their level of development, language and culture, historical legacies, democratization, market openness, and media system (Peruško, Vozab, & Čuvalo, 2021), they also provide a specific context for exploring news reporting and audience engagement with election news. The post-socialist transformation of the media in Central and Eastern Europe (CEE) resulted in systems that are different from Western democracies in terms of political parallelism, media markets and journalism culture (Hallin & Mancini, 2004; Peruško, Čuvalo, & Vozab, 2020). Media in Southeast Europe countries have remarkably low levels of autonomy, while media in Albania and Kosovo face similar problems related to ownership concentration, political polarization, and clientelistic ties (Kovacevic & Perisin, 2018). These factors are determinant for journalism professional roles including media-related practices of audiences (Peruško, Vozab, & Čuvalo, 2021, p. 1). More specifically, clientelistic relationships observed in these countries (Camaj, 2016) are less likely to encourage audience-centric news reporting and more likely to focus on reporting that benefits media clients or owners, such as political attacks that discredit political opponents.

However, this region has also undergone heavy media commercialization (Harro-Loit & Saks, 2006) and digitalization that might impact journalists' attitudes toward their audiences. Facebook has more than 50% penetration in this region (Internet World Stats), while social media are the second most consumed news source in both countries, with more than half of the population in Albania (53%) and two-thirds of the population in Kosovo (65%) using these platforms as news gateways on a daily basis (SEENPM, 2021). In this context, journalists working for commercial media can't afford to ignore their audiences. In addition, previous research suggests that journalists in the Western Balkans consider their role as facilitators of democratic transitions (Andresen, Hoxha, & Godole, 2017), and this context might present new opportunities for digital news media to engage with their audiences during elections – a critical time in political transitions.

However, such developments need to be understood within broader concept of "digital mediascapes" that consider the important implications of the macro factors for journalism performance (Peruško, Čuvalo, & Vozab, 2020). Media systems in CEE are not monolithic as countries within this region took divergent development, economic and political trajectories during the formative years (Peruško, Vozab, & Čuvalo, 2021). The history of pluralism in Kosovo has developed in different circumstances from Albania. During the post-civil war period, Kosovo was under the international protectorate that dictated strict rules of campaigning and campaign coverage by the media which still affect current campaigns to this day. In Albania, the political system is dominated by two major parties which also have a strong influence on the media. Therefore, the political and media system in Albania is more polarized than in Kosovo. Hence, we are more likely to observe a heavier focus on political attacks and negativity in news reporting and audience engagement with this content in Albania than in Kosovo. Yet, corruption has been one of the main issues that has dominated both campaigns (Uberti, 2020); hence, we might expect heavy engagement with news posts that emphasize corruptive issues and candidate character. But, given the disputed political status and the volatility of political parties in Kosovo, we are more likely to find an issue-focused electorate.

Audience engagement with election campaign news

Research in political communication has identified core characteristics of election reporting that emphasize three coverage dimensions documented across cultures: : (1) depoliticization, (2) personalization, and (3) negativity (Esser & Strömbäck, 2012). Comparative research suggests a low level of substantial issue coverage and high emphasis on strategic game and negative coverage has become a standard feature of election news reporting across countries (Aelst, 2018; Cushion & Thomas, 2018), with a tendency to find such coverage more often in commercialized media systems (Strömbäck & Dimitrova, 2006), in competitive party systems and in countries with high political polarization (Banducci & Hanretty, 2014).

Media depoliticization. It is conceptualized as news coverage of elections that marginalizes "the core of politics – the substance, issues, ideologies, and linkages between real-world problems and proposed solutions" (Esser & Strömbäck, 2012, p. 318). Instead, election coverage predominantly concentrates on the process of political campaigns (Cappella & Jamieson, 1997) adopting a strategic game reporting style. Strategy framing refers to election reporting that focuses on candidates' motives and strategies used for winning elections, and game framing refers to news stories that emphasize who is winning or losing elections and often involve a language or war or games (Aalberg, Strömbäck, & de Vreese, 2012, p. 172). In this study, we operationalize two aspects of depolarization: issue coverage and strategy game framing.

Many studies have documented the association of the strategy game frame with the political malaise – voter cynicism, decrease substance-based knowledge and trust in the political process (see Zoizner, 2021 for an overview). However, some scholars argue that such coverage of politics has the potential to engage audiences with election news which can lead to higher interest in elections (Iyengar, Norpoth, & Hahn, 2004; Trussler &

Soroka, 2014). Yet, the evidence on audience's appetite for strategic game framed news in online spaces is inconsistent (Gonçalves, Pereira, & Torres da Silva, 2020; Kalsnes & Larsson, 2018). Offering a more nuanced perspective, recent studies suggest that strategic game framed news gets more exposure and clicks, yet issue-oriented news is more likely to generate comments and shares (Ørmen, 2019; Stroud & Muddiman, 2019). This literature suggests that content characteristics are linked to different types of engagement measures (Salgado & Bobba, 2019; Stroud & Muddiman, 2019). In other words, not all forms of news engagement are linked to all news characteristics. Thus, we pose the following question:

RQ1: *How do issue focused and strategic game framed posts affect user engagement (likes, comments and shares) with election news on media's Facebook pages?*

Personalization

We are also interested to examine the consequences of personalization of election coverage for audience engagement. In this study, we follow Esser and Strömbäck (2012) in differentiating "personalization" as a distinct category that emphasizes news coverage focus on individual politicians, and can include news on candidate personality traits, their performance, and personal lives at the expense of parties, ideologies, or policies. The rise of "candidate-centered politics" (Van Aelst, Sheafer, & Stanyer, 2012) is especially dominant on social media, where candidates adopt a more personalized communication style when discussing their professional, emotional, and private lives (Bene, 2017; Metz, Kruikemeier, & Lecheler, 2020). While these studies have explored audience interactivity with personalized information on candidates' social media pages, very little is known about how digital news audiences interact with personalized election information. The only study in this regard suggests that emphasis on candidates alone might lead to decreased selection of election news in digital spaces (Jang & Oh, 2016) but does not illuminate how this might translate into likes, comments, and shares. Hence, we pose the following research question:

RQ2: *How do personalized posts affect user engagement (likes, comments and shares) with election news on media's Facebook pages?*

Negativity

Previous research emphasizes that politics in general and election news more specifically have a bias toward negativity, confrontation and conflict (Esser & Strömbäck, 2012). There are two aspects to negative news coverage: the media-initiated negativity – initiated by journalists via news framing and media-disseminated negativity – triggered by news sources (Lengauer, Esser, & Berganza, 2012). In this study, we focus on media-disseminated negativity triggered by political candidates, to avoid collinearity with other dimensions of elections reporting given that some aspects of media-initiated negativity, such as conflict and drama, are captured in strategic game framing. Second, during election reporting we are less likely to encounter some aspects of media-initiated negativity, such as negative tone toward politicians and parties, given journalists tendency to avoid bias accusations.

There is a strong theoretical conceptualization for audience negativity bias in news selection that has been linked to evolutionary processes (Shoemaker, 1996) that predisposes audiences to be more responsive to negative than positive messages, cognitively, emotionally, and physically. The most compelling empirical evidence comes from a cross-national study from 17 countries that offers a comprehensive support for the negativity bias hypothesis, as people were more aroused by and were more attentive to negative news (Soroka, Fournier, & Nir, 2019). Yet, other studies doubt the inherent audience negativity bias, offering evidence that news that is framed as conflict is shared less on social media (Valenzuela, Piña, & Ramírez, 2017), while news coverage of politicians behaving with incivility discouraged interactions with online news (Muddiman, Pond-Cobb, & Matson, 2020). Thus, we pose the following research question:

RQ3: *How do negative posts affect user engagement (likes, comments, shares) with election news on media's Facebook pages?*

The audience logic in election news coverage

In this study, we are also interested to explore the extent to which audience logic drives election news reporting in the context of Southeast Europe. The predominance of the strategic game frame and negativity found in electoral coverage across countries has been largely explained by the media logic – professional orientations and news values that prioritize drama, negativity, and personal focus (Aalberg, Strömbäck, & de Vreese, 2012), the commercial objectives of news media, and the political logic (Cushion & Thomas, 2018; Strömbäck & Esser, 2014). The role of audiences has been largely ignored, although recent research emphasizes the need for the shift toward the "audience logic" in digital journalism at large (Blassnig & Esser, 2021) and election reporting specifically (Cushion & Thomas, 2018).

Literature distinguishes three different sub-logics that might explain the audience turn in digital journalism (see table 1). The "Audience logic" in election reporting style has been traditionally defined within the economically inspired theoretical model (Landerer, 2013), namely the market sub-logic. Within this approach, the news making process is driven by the commercial goals, and the audiences are perceived as consumers. Thus, news media are more likely to focus on what attracts the largest audiences, in order to maximize the distribution of their product (Esser, 2013). The market/commercial sub-logic, in turn, determines certain characteristics of news content, with emphasis on confrontation and dramatization aspects of news associated with the horserace frame, depolarization, personalization (Esser, 2013), conflict and negativity (Karidi, 2018). Strategic game frame of electoral coverage has been traditionally explained by journalists' assumption that there is a consumer demand for it, given that the conflict and the drama associated with horserace frame attracts audiences' attention making election news more exciting (Cushion & Thomas, 2018).

Yet, another perspective defines the audience logic within the normative sub-logic (Landerer, 2013) that prioritize social or public responsibility over market considerations. This "public logic," as Landerer (2013, p. 245) refers to it, aims to advance the public interest agenda by emphasizing issues of public interest. News reporting is driven by what citizens should know in order to make informed decisions in a democracy. While it is hard to define and empirically capture what is in public's interest, in the context of election coverage, journalists emphasize the importance and concern with substance and policy issues. As Cushion and Thomas (2018) claim "an lection news agenda – or logic – driven by issues could also better represent the public's voice and policy preferences during a campaign" (p.102). A major difference between the two logics is that "normative logic is supply-driven, market logic is demand-driven" (Landerer, 2013, p. 249).

Yet, a third perspective, the network media logic (Klinger & Svensson, 2015), takes into consideration the technical affordances of digital technologies and communication platforms that have been integrated into digital journalism as determinants of audience involvement in the news process. Social media enable interactive and personalized communication, as users willingly share news for free setting the news agenda for their own networks. In this media ecology, peer recommendation system and endorsements are more important factors than a selection from professional newsmakers. Consequently, the revolution in audience analytics provides the ability to quantify audience behaviors on social media and identify what topics drive more audience attention (Lee & Tandoc, 2017). Within the networked media logic, journalists have to consider and balance the shareworthiness of the stories along with their newsworthiness (Trilling, Tolochko, & Burscher, 2017). As

Table 1. Three sub logics of audience logic in election news production.

Audience Logic		
Market sub-logic	Normative sub-logic	Networked Media sub-logic
Audience as consumer	Audience as citizens	Empowered audiences
Attract largest audience	Advance public interest	Balance shareworthiness with newsworthiness
Focus on confrontation and dramatization	Focus on issues	Equal distribution of strategic game and issue frame

Blassing & Esser (2022, p.51) emphasize, "while the market-oriented commercial logic remains a constant force on political news coverage, a connection-strengthening audience logic has developed in parallel" (see Table 1).

The attitude that higher engagement equates higher ratings and thus potentially leads to lower quality of news has created tensions between journalists and management related to catering interesting news at the expense of important news (Belair-Gagnon & Holton, 2018). Yet, proponents of engaged journalism challenge the traditional journalistic notion that journalists know better than audiences themselves what information they need (Lawrence, Radcliffe, & Schmidt, 2018). Although the new technological affordances provide grounds for a theorized audience empowerment in the new media ecosystem, it is not clear how journalists' perception of their audience has changed, if at all. In this paper we explore to what degree have news media in Southeast Europe incorporated the audience logic and how this logic is shaping their coverage of elections. We are guided by the following questions:

RQ4a: *How do journalists in Albania and Kosovo perceive consumer demand for strategy game frames, personalized and negative news?*

RQ4b: *How does the audience logic impact news reporting of elections on Facebook?*

Methods

In this study, we focus on 12 major news organizations in Albania and Kosovo. Our list of most popular news outlets in digital spaces comes from data provided by Amazon's Alexa. Alexa's top website rankings are based on estimated daily time on site per visitor, estimated daily unique pageview per visitor, the percentage of traffic from search, and the total number of sites linked to the specific site. The list was cross-checked with data from local providers on audience reach of individual news outlets. Our sample of news organizations includes a mix of mainstream (national news broadcasters, and daily newspapers) and digital native news outlets, and represents an important part of Albanian news media outlets on the Internet (the list and profile of news organizations is provided in Table 1 in Appendix 1).

Content analysis

Sample

The content data for this study were collected using the CrowdTangle software, an open-source web tool that compiles engagement data for specified Facebook accounts by accessing the Facebook API. First, we collected all Facebook posts from 12 major news organizations posted during the last 10 days of the electoral campaign in respective countries. In Kosovo, Facebook posts were collected from September 25th to October 4th (election day was on October 6th, 2019), while in Albania, Facebook posts were collected from April 12 to 22 (election day was on April 25, 2020). From this sample, we selected only Facebook posts that specifically focused on election campaign coverage excluding the duplicates. The final media sample includes 6,749 election-related news posts from news organizations' Facebook pages: 6 outlets from Albania (Top Channel = 619; TV Klan = 393; ABC News = 507; Gazeta Panorama = 675; Balkan Web = 366; and Syri = 1024) and 6 news outlets form Kosovo (Gazeta Express = 449; Telegrafi = 209; Koha.com = 464; Klan Kosova = 1050; Gazeta Blic = 764, and RTK = 229).

Coding categories

Based on previous work, we developed a codebook which was used to manually code Facebook posts. The coding was done by one of the authors and a graduate student who were extensively trained to use the codebook with four different training sessions using different subsamples of $n = 30$ posts for each. After establishing satisfying intercoder reliability on a random sample of 10% of the Facebook posts (Cohen's Kappa ranged from .71 to 1.0.), they each proceeded to code independently.

We created two different binary categories to capture the concept of "depoliticization": we coded if Facebook posts mentioned issues (Kappa = .90), and if they discussed strategic game aspect of the election campaign (for example: strategies used to win voters over, who is ahead in the race, etc.; Kappa = .75). Strategy versus issue coverage was coded as separate dimensions in a way that the same article could be coded as both.

To capture "personalization" in news coverage, we coded if news posts discussed candidate character traits (for example: leadership, knowledge, morality, ect., Kappa = .78). Negativity in Facebook news posts was operationalized with a measure that captures candidate attacks as follows: we identified posts that quoted or paraphrased one of the candidates, and then we coded for the function of the candidate message: acclaims (discuss their policy achievements, plans, or their personal character), defense (defend their actions), or attacks (attack their political opponents' performance, policy or character) (Kappa =.73). This measurement was transformed into a dichotomous variable denoting candidate attacks.

In addition, this study coded for the following control variables that have been identified as important determinants of social media news engagement: type of news genre (news, analysis, editorial, interview, or sponsored programming) (Kappa =.80); the name of candidates (Kappa = 1) and the name of the party mentioned (Kappa = 1). In addition, we adopted the coding scheme from the Comparative Agendas Project (Baumgartner, Green-Pedersen, & Jones, 2006) in order to code for 10 most mentioned topics in Facebook posts (Kappa =.73). To account for the different intercepts between countries, we inserted a dummy variable with Kosovo serving as the reference category.

Audience engagement data included three categories: reactions (inclusive of all kinds: like, love, wow, haha, sad, and angry), comments, and shares. These data were collected by CrowdTangle and calculated by simply counting how many of each a post has. Engagements are measured at the per-post level, which is the primary unit of analysis.

In-depth Interviews

For the qualitative part of this study, we conducted semi-structured in-depth interviews with social media editors from the media sample ($N = 10$). We identified journalists who had strategic and operational responsibility to manage social media accounts of each news outlet. Out of twelve editors contacted, two did not respond to our request for the interview. Thus, our final sample includes social media editors from five news media in Albania (Top Channel, ABC News, Syri TV, Panorama, and BalkanWeb) and five news media in Kosovo (RTK, Koha, Klan Kosova, Express, Telegrafi). Interviews, conducted in person or over the Zoom, took place within a couple of months from election day. The interviews, which lasted between 45 minutes and an hour, were conducted in Albanian language by the authors, all native speakers, and included questions about motivations and strategies news organizations used to engage their audience during elections (see interview guide in appendix 2).

Data analysis and results

User engagement with election news on facebook

Tables 2 and 3 report descriptive analysis at the country level in terms of patterns of media coverage of election news on Facebook and audience engagement with election news. The preliminary examination of the data suggests that, across both countries, media coverage had a similar focus between strategic game frame and issue coverage, with a slightly higher emphasis on strategic game framing (58.1%) than issue coverage (42.9%). Much less focus was given to candidate traits or personality (9.1%), while less than 15% of the whole sample focused on candidate attacks. However, significant differences were observed between the two countries. Kosovo news media

Table 2. The share of election news coverage.

	Albania	Kosovo	Total	Chi Square
Issue coverage	36.9%	49.2%	42.9%	113.809***
Strategic game frame	52.1%	64.2%	58.1%	113.769***
Candidate Traits	7.6%	10.8%	9.1%	21.810***
Negativity	18.1%	5.6%	12.2%	247.456***
N	3165	3584	6749	

Percentages do not round up to 100, given that social media posts could be coded for multiple frames.

Table 3. Descriptive Statistics of Facebook Engagement.

	Reactions	Comments	Shares
Albania			
N	3,584	3,584	3,584
Mean	91.08	27.11	2.05
Std Dev.	342.469	105.483	11.666
Min	0	0	0
Max	8,918	4,749	293
Kosovo			
N	3165	3165	3165
Mean	68.36	56.01	3.52
Std Dev.	171.977	139.545	18.523
Min	0	0	0
Max	3,214	2,500	734

were more likely to emphasize issues and focus on strategic game framing and candidate personalities, while media in Albania were significantly more likely to focus on candidate attacks (see Table 2). When comparing audience engagement with election news across two countries, data on Table 3 suggest that overall Facebook posts of Albanian news media received higher audience reactions and comments, yet Kosovo media audiences generated more than twice the number of audience shares.

The first three research questions (RQ1, RQ2, and RQ3) asked how different patterns of election news coverage affect audiences' engagement on Facebook in the context of Albania and Kosovo elections. Given the hierarchical structure of the data – where Facebook posts are nested within news organizations – we estimate multilevel models that allow the intercepts to vary across news organizations (Gelman & Hill, 2006). Further, we use a negative binomial regression model to estimate our predicted relationships. The standard deviations of our dependent variables are higher than the means, indicating negative binomial regressions as the most appropriate approach (Gardner, Mulvey, & Shaw, 1995). Table 4 presents a mixed effects negative binomial regression model where the dependent variables are the rate of Facebook reactions, comments, and shares.

The results suggest that overall online news audiences were less likely to engage with Facebook posts that focus on issues compared to the posts that do not focus on issues. Issue coverage

Table 4. Multilevel Negative binomial regression with random intercepts predicting user engagement on Facebook.

	Reactions		Comments		Shares	
	b	SE	b	SE	b	SE
Election Coverage						
Issue coverage	−.385***	.072	−.507***	.090	−.375**	.127
Strategy game	.126**	.044	−.112*	.055	.121	.077
Candidate Traits	.246***	.062	.283***	.078	.007	.110
Negativity	−.163**	.057	−.128**	.072	−.242**	.103
Control Variables						
Story type (reference: *news story*)						
Analysis	−.239***	.066	.351***	.082	.142	.116
Editorial	.098	.452	.090	.569	.049	.773
Interviews	−.074	.047	.081	.059	.109	.083
Sponsored programing	1.425***	.119	1.477***	.148	1.535***	.202
Story Topics (*reference government operations*)						
Defense	.267	.182	−.137	.228	−.371	.323
Law & Crime	−.026	.092	−.009	.115	−.295	.164
International Affairs	−.179	.096	−.439***	.120	−.729***	.171
Economy	−.144	.115	−.085	.143	−.261	.206
Civil Rights	−.694***	.168	−1.077**	.211	−.859**	.310
Social Wealth fare	1.188***	.273	1.123***	.340	.666	.464
Health	.394**	.156	−.105	.195	−.455	.285
Education	−.673***	.132	−.868***	.165	−1.103***	.243
Immigration	.647**	.246	.562	.307	.740	.418
Campaign dates	.041***	.006	.030***	.008	.076***	.011
Albania (reference *Kosovo*)	−22.346***	2.77	−16.962***	4.69	−43.445***	6.64
Constant	2.013		3.135		5.523	
Random Effect variance	.502*	.253	.473*	.240		
Log-likelihood	40402.853		34156.387		46358.034	
Dispersion parameter						
N (FB posts)	6,747		6,748		6,748	

Cell entries are mixed effects coefficients where Facebook posts are level 1 and news organizations are level 2. If no reference category is mentioned, variables were coded as present or not present. Additional control variables include 1) names of specific candidates mentioned in the Facebook post and 2) names of specific parties mentioned in the Facebook post.
***$p < .001$. **$p < .01$. *$p < .05$.

was associated with a decrease in reactions (b=−.385, $p < .001$), comments (b=−.507, $p < .001$), and shares (b=−.375, $p < .01$). Yet, some issues were more likely to generate engagement than others. For example, Facebook posts that focused on social welfare, health, and immigration were significantly more likely to generate news user engagement than Facebook posts that focused on government operations.

Facebook posts that focused on strategic game frame generated a more nuanced engagement reflection. Posts that emphasized candidate strategies to win elections or the game aspect of the election race were associated with an increased number of user reactions (b = .246, $p < .001$), yet they were also associated with a decrease in the number of comments per post (b=−.112, $p < .05$).

Addressing RQ2, our data suggest that posts that emphasized candidate traits were associated with an increase in the number of reactions (b = .246, $p < .001$) and comments (b = .283, $p < .001$).

The third research question (RQ3) asked how audiences in Albania and Kosovo interact with negative election news. The results suggest that posts that emphasized candidate attacks had a consistent negative association with all three modes of engagement, as they decreased the number of reactions (b=−.163, $p < .01$), comments (b= −.128, $p < .01$), and shares (b=−.242, $p < .01$).

Analyzing the set of control variables, two relevant findings appeared: first, Kosovo media audiences were significantly more engaged with election news on Facebook than Albanian media audiences across all three measures of engagement. Second, audience engagement was significantly correlated with news story type. Compared to Facebook posts that focused on news stories, posts that provide news analysis were less likely to generate reactions and comments. However, Facebook posts that contained sponsored programing from live electoral events were more likely to generate higher number of reactions, comments, and shares than Facebook posts that reported campaign events. This last finding is not surprising, given that Facebook algorithms prioritize live video based on audiences' likelihood to interact more with video content (Salgado & Bobba, 2019).

The audience logic and election coverage on Facebook

The in-depth interviews conducted for this study focused on three main topics: (1) journalists' conceptualization of their social media audiences; (2) the decision-making process when posting election news on Facebook, and (3) the motivations for pursuing audience engagement. The analytical process was inductive, following a multilevel analytical coding scheme that allows for key themes and subthemes to emerge from the data (Corbin & Strauss, 2014). The data were synthesized into the following categories: market sub-logic approach, normative sub-logic, and networked media sub-logic approach. The quotes from the interviews incorporated in this analysis have been translated from Albanian language by the authors.

Market sub-logic

Interview-based data suggest that media in Albania and Kosovo perceive social media audiences predominantly as consumers of information. The prevailing attitude among social media editors interviewed for this study is that Facebook enables media to promote their brand and product with the intention to generate web traffic from Facebook audiences' clicks. From the editors' point of view, Facebook has the function of a virtual marketplace where news outlets compete for the attention of the audience, as summarized in the following quote:

> Facebook is the market, while we are market players to sell our products. In the big Facebook market, we try to encourage people to buy our products, in this case with the news (a male web editor from Kosovo).

In line with the audience-focused approach, editors acknowledge that they are oriented by audience interaction data on social media to understand the trend of news content consumption. Audience engagement data on Facebook is analyzed periodically. One of the interviewees admits that he receives monthly reports from the information technology department, which contain recommendations for news categories that need to be stimulated. High audience engagement with a specific story on Facebook is perceived as a measure that the story will provoke more interest, as summarized in the following quote by an editor at a news outlet in Albania: *"If a post provokes negative reactions, we think twice whether this topic should be addressed further or not. If we see that the audience is interested in it, we follow the story."*

In both countries, election news generated an increased audience interest and engagement on Facebook. The majority of the editors concur with the perception that social media audiences were mostly interested in news that focuses on polls, or the race aspect of elections, who's wining and losing, and they mostly engaged with news that focuses on politicians' personalities and drama, such as accusations of corruption or similar scandals. Therefore, many editors acknowledge their election reporting on Facebook is determined to a great degree by these trends. Here's how a social media editor from a television network in Albania explains their election reporting strategy:

> "At the beginning we prepared our readers by continually posting about the most contested races by county and then we built a poll for our social media sites. For example, the poll would ask 'Who will win Elbasan?' and we would list all the leading candidates ... our format was such that we placed the photo of the candidate from PS (Socialist Party) and the photo from PD (Democratic Party), with their names above their pictures and asked 'Who will win Elbasan?' or 'Who will win Tirana?' We adopted this strategy after the candidate lists were released. This strategy helped us increase audience interactivity on social media."

When discussing election stories of interest, several Kosovo editors emphasized the case of Ramush Haradinaj, a political candidate who would sing folk songs or give bombastic statements during media interviews as a spectacle that generated much media coverage and audience reactions on Facebook. This is how a male social media editor from Kosovo summarized: *"These spectacles had immense engagements. For example, a statement from Ramush Haradinaj saying "I'm not as stupid as I look" generated many laughs and its' effect was ten to fifteen times higher than a random news story on Facebook."*

Normative sub-logic. Although the "audience as consumers" approach prevailed, the analysis of the interviews also identified a group of editors that tend to adopt the normative perspective on audience conceptualization. While not denying the commercial aspect of social media, for some editors in Albania and Kosovo informing and educating audiences takes on a missionary nature. Below is how a social media editor summarizes their approach:

> We believe that the audience can be cultivated, educated. If we give the audience poor material, they will grow with that material. I think information is ultimately similar to food. If we give people, the right food they will grow up healthy, (a female editor at a television station in Albanian).

For this group of editors, the quality of news is primary, while they claim to avoiding falling prey of social media trends. As one editor from Kosovo puts it *"we don't measure (success) by likes, but we measure it by audience trust and loyalty."* Several editors emphasized two criteria that drove their election reporting: fairness and balance, and public interest manifested in political programs. The example below from a social media editor working for an online publication in Kosovo summarizes this approach:

> We set several parameters. We decided that if we post a story about a political party, we should post about other political parties as well, and not post two or three posts about the same party, so we show that we do not favor only one party. The second criteria was to determine if that information was relevant for the whole of Kosovo or only for one city or village ... it's very important to post if a politician discusses health insurance for all Kosovo, instead of posting about what a candidate said in a village about their election victory.

Yet, editors acknowledged tensions that emerge between their goal to focus on public interest and the necessity to follow social media trends when deciding what to post. Taking a paternalistic approach, they don't see much value in social media interactions and acknowledged Facebook posts that focused on party programs and policies received very little audience interactions. The prevailing view among this group of editors is that Facebook audiences tend to negatively influence the quality of news, and they do not necessarily reflect their whole audience. A few mentioned the high volume of engagement from partisan "trolls" in Albania, who were artificially trying to influence users' perception about support for their candidates. As the editor of one television news station in Albania claims, the aggressive comments of the audience on social media *"do not really show the reality of what people think."*

Network media sub-logic

Another smaller group of editors is mostly concerned with the affordances of social media that, in addition to content distribution and the financial prospect, allow also for two-way communication with their audiences. Here's how a social media editor for a multimedia news organization in Kosovo elaborates their approach:

> Currently, not only here but in the whole world, social media facilitate information distribution. This is one of the main reasons. The other reason is communication with our readers.... and of course we cannot sidetrack the financial aspect of this. But, as I said earlier, our readers are loyal and we don't have much oscillation in our readership, one day 10K and another 1K, this doesn't happen to us because they (audiences) are constant, (social media editor from Kosovo)

They conceptualize their audiences' interests as a mix of demand for quality as well as light news. At the same time, they acknowledge the need for balancing what audiences want and what they need, as emphasized in the following quote by a female social media editor from a television station in Albania: *"There is a strong relationship between those that give and those that receive the information. I strive to orient them, but the audience also orients me."*

Several editors emphasized that they pay attention to the comment section to gage public interest in issues they post on their Facebook pages. During election, there was a heightened interest from the audience to communicate with news media in different forms, sometimes commenting on news stories, other times sending information about political parties' activities in their own regions. Comments are perceived as an opportunity for the audience to engage in the networked public sphere where they can debate and express opinions about governance dissatisfaction or political preferences and some editors perceive comments as contributing to the quality of news. Some editors emphasized that their audiences are educated hence they demand quality news related to party platforms and programs. Yet, others also warned against perils of social media algorithms that favor content with certain type of engagement. Here's how a social media editor from Albania explains

> There is the principle that a news post that has many comments is more likely to also be shared on Facebook. Facebook favors news posts with high interactivity, and this was used as a public relations strategy by political parties. They created press offices and call centers that dealt only with this issue in order to increase the share of certain news posts (male editor from an online media in Albania).

This group of social media editors follows closely the changes to the Facebook algorithms in order to adapt as quickly without risking losing their audience. Consequently, editors try to find a balance between share-worthiness and news-worthiness for the news they post on Facebook. In such a situation, they need to make news selection according to the platforms and the profile of the audience that engages in these platforms. Overall, most editors interviewed for this study agreed that they are more likely to publish on Facebook news that generates more engagement, while stories they perceive as important and of interest to the public are published on the website of these media and Facebook serves as a gateway.

Discussions and conclusions

This study provides insights on how journalists in the Western Balkans conceptualize and practice audience engagement during electoral campaigns. Taking a holistic approach, we first explore audience demand and news supply of strategic and negative election news on Facebook, then turn to news editors to explore what type of audience logic drives their reporting.

One important takeaway lesson from this study is that strategic game framing does not erode political participation as previously feared. Similar to the Western context, our data confirm Albanian audiences' interest in strategic news (Gonçalves, Pereira, & Torres da Silva, 2020; Kalsnes & Larsson, 2018), as we found that strategic game framing was associated with higher levels of engagement with election news on Facebook, which might translate in increasing interests and participation in elections (Iyengar, Norpoth, & Hahn, 2004; Trussler & Soroka, 2014). Yet, our data also confirm previous studies that election news characteristics are not linked to all three forms of engagement in the same way (Salgado & Bobba, 2019). Strategic game framing of election news was associated with higher number of user reactions, yet it was likely to decrease user comments. These findings point out to two explanations. First, they relate to general patterns in digital news engagement that can be explained by audiences' predispositions. Supporting the "social media gap" hypothesis (Bright, 2016), our data suggest that in private audience might be clicking, reading and liking strategic game news, yet they are less likely to share or comment on it publicly given that this type of behavior has a higher social currency (Kalsnes & Larsson, 2018).

Second, the socio-political context is another crucial factor that determines engagement with online news. Political parties in both countries have mobilized their voter base on social media with the aim to create an opinion climate that favors them as frontrunners, potentially increasing the number of Facebook engagements with strategic game reporting. Moreover, we found that Facebook posts that emphasized candidate characteristics were more likely to generate higher user reactions and comments. These results suggest that news personalization has the potential to engage voters in news discussion that can contribute to voter learning and participation (Carpini, Cook, & Jacobs, 2004). Given that corruption has been one of the major problems that both Albania and Kosovo have faced in their transitional path (Uberti, 2020), it is not surprising to find that news audiences are interested to discuss candidate characteristics on social media. However, voter mobilization was more pronounced in Kosovo, where the challenger party Vetvendosje had a younger social media savvy base of supporters. This might explain our results, suggesting that Facebook audiences in Kosovo reacted, commented, and shared election news more than users in Albania.

In addition, our data contradict theoretical predictions that emphasize the predominance of negativity bias in the context of Southeast Europe. We found that news coverage that focuses on candidate attacks was limited across both countries, although we found it to be more prevalent in Albania than in Kosovo. Rather than being an editorial decision, it could be that there were more candidate attacks in Albania due to the higher levels of political polarization than in Kosovo. Hence, these cross-country differences suggest that the extent of audience engagement with negative campaigning might depend on systemic factors, given that political polarization and lower media independence are important factors that determine news consumptions (Tóth, Mihelj, Štětka, & Kondor, 2022).

However, at the same time editorial decisions on electoral reporting might be determined by audience analytics. Our data suggest that news coverage of politicians' attacks might discourage user interactions with online news. Both countries, Albania and Kosovo, are undergoing political transitions in addition to facing economic hardship, and in the case of Kosovo, disputed territorial integrity. Hence, it is not surprising that voters might be more drawn to engage with politicians who present solutions to the problems that face their nations, instead of engaging with politicians who accuse their opponents of failure (Muddiman, Pond-Cobb, & Matson, 2020). This, in turn, might have important implications for editorial decisions.

Indeed, we identified an alignment between journalists' imagined readership preferences with the reality (Robinson, 2019). In line with audience behavior, social media editors assume that their audiences prefer news that focuses on strategy game frames and politicians' performance and morality. Supporting previous research (Bullard, 2015), this study found that most news media in Albania and Kosovo are guided by the market sublogic in their use of social media to build their brand name and use Facebook as a gateway to their websites. Given the popularity of strategic game election news on social media (Ørmen, 2019), it is not surprising that news producers pay attention to audiences' social media engagement. These findings are not surprising when we consider high levels of media commercialization (Harro-Loit & Saks, 2006) and instrumentalization (Örnebring, 2012) in this region where news media are often used as tools for economic benefit of their owners rather than subscribe to audience focused outcomes.

Yet, the market logic does not entirely drive their news coverage of elections. Our interviews indicate that a smaller group of social media editors adopt the normative sub-logic taking a paternalistic role in educating their social media audiences while disregarding the value of audience engagement data. Hence, it is not surprising that a good amount of election news in both countries is issue focused, although such election reporting doesn't necessarily drive social media engagement. An even smaller minority of social media editors interviewed for this study are concerned with the affordances of social media that go beyond commercial nature and open opportunities for two-way communications with their audiences. They are not hesitant to promote content they deem valuable on Facebook, however also do not shy away from following audiences' preferences. Together these data show editors' need to comply with user preferences and Facebook's News Feed algorithm, while also adhering to traditional journalistic standards. Together, these findings suggest that the journalism culture developed in this region is more nuanced than previously defined (Örnebring, 2012; Roudakova, 2008), while news editors embrace new technologies to serve the commercial and audience strengthening logics in parallel (Blassing & Esser, 2021).

Like other research done in similar context, this study is limited in its scope and operationalization. These study results are limited to Facebook, which, while it is one of the most important platforms in the region studied here, might not be as widely used in other contexts. This study is also limited to examining audience behavior in the form of reactions, comments, and shares; nevertheless, as previous research has shown, news selection measured via clicks constitutes another important dimension of news engagement that is more private and thus might be driven by different reporting patterns. Finally, it is possible that, as some interviewed editors mentioned, some of the engagement with election news is not organic but rather driven by political actors and organizations who engage their partisans to generate engagement to enhance positive attributes of their preferred candidates. This is a valid concern that needs further examination.

Despite these limitations, this study helps understand the nature of consumer demand for election news as a central facet to understanding the nature of media content production. It shows that election reporting could be more sensitive to the democratic needs of citizens without replacing strategic game coverage with policy discussions. As Cushion and Thomas (2018, p. 102) argue, it can involve "slicing together issues and horserace reporting in ways that serve a public logic by exciting and informing the audience." Indeed, this study shows the reciprocity of the relationship between demand and supply in the context of election reporting on social media (Trussler & Soroka, 2014). Journalists can use these tools to identify consumer demand for news, but also engage the same tools to lead a shift in consumer behavior toward quality news.

Disclosure statement

No potential conflict of interest was reported by the author(s).

ORCID

Lindita Camaj http://orcid.org/0000-0002-5934-6159
Erlis Çela http://orcid.org/0000-0002-9202-2981

References

Aalberg, T., Strömbäck, J., & de Vreese, C. H. (2012). The framing of politics as strategy and game: A review of concepts, operationalizations and key findings. *Journalism*, 13 (2), 162–178. doi:10.1177/1464884911427799

Aelst, P. V. (2018). The whole world is watching: Comparing European and United States News Coverage of the U.S. 2008 and 2016 Elections. 23.

Andresen, K., Hoxha, A., & Godole, J. (2017). New roles for media in the Western Balkans: A study of transitional journalism. *Journalism Studies*, 18(5), 614–628. doi:10.1080/1461670X.2016.1268928

Banducci, S., & Hanretty, C. (2014). Comparative determinants of horse-race coverage. *European Political Science Review*, 6(4), 621–640. doi:10.1017/S1755773913000271

Baumgartner, F. R., Green-Pedersen, C., & Jones, B. D. (2006). Comparative studies of policy agendas. *Journal of European Public Policy*, 13(7), 959–974. doi:10.1080/13501760600923805

Belair-Gagnon, V., & Holton, A. E. (2018). Boundary work, interloper media, and analytics in newsrooms: An analysis of the roles of web analytics companies in news production. *Digital Journalism*, 6(4), 492–508. doi:10.1080/21670811.2018.1445001

Bene, M. (2017). Go viral on the Facebook! Interactions between candidates and followers on Facebook during the Hungarian general election campaign of 2014. *Information, Communication & Society*, 20(4), 513–529. doi:10.1080/1369118X.2016.1198411

Blassnig, S., & Esser, F. (2021). The "Audience Logic" in digital journalism: An exploration of shifting news logics across media types and time. *Journalism Studies*, 23(1), 1–22. doi:10.1080/1461670X.2021.2000339

Blassnig, S., & Esser, F. (2022). The "Audience Logic" in Digital Journalism: An Exploration of Shifting News Logics Across Media Types and Time. *Journalism Studies*, 23(1), 48–69. doi:10.1080/1461670X.2021.2000339

Bright, J. (2016). The social news gap: How news reading and news sharing diverge. *Journal of Communication*, 66(3), 343–365. doi:10.1111/jcom.12232

Bullard, S. B. (2015). Editors Use Social Media Mostly to Post Story Links. *Newspaper Research Journal*, 36(2), 170–183. doi:10.1177/0739532915587288

Camaj, L. (2016). Between a rock and a hard place: Consequences of media clientelism for journalist–politician power relationships in the Western Balkans. *Global Media and Communication*, 12(3), 229–246.3. doi:10.1177/1742766516675649

Cappella, J. N., & Jamieson, K. H. (1997). *Spiral of Cynicism: The press and the public good*. New York: Oxford University Press.

Carpini, M. X. D., Cook, F. L., & Jacobs, L. R. (2004). Public deliberation, discursive participation, and citizen engagement: A Review of the empirical literature. *Annual Review of Political Science*, 7(1), 315–344. doi:10.1146/annurev.polisci.7.121003.091630

Corbin, J., & Strauss, A. (2014). *Basics of Qualitative Research: Techniques and Procedures for Developing Grounded Theory*. Thousand Oaks, CA: SAGE Publications.

Cushion, S., & Thomas, R. (2018). *Reporting Elections: Rethinking the logic of campaign coverage*. Medfort, MA: Polity Press.

Dalton, R. J. (2017). *The participation gap: Social status and political inequality*. Oxford University Press.

de León, E., & Vermeer, S. (2022). The news sharing gap: Divergence in online political news publication and dissemination patterns across elections and countries. *Digital Journalism*, 11(2), 343–362. doi:10.1080/21670811.2022.2099920

Dvir-Gvirsman, S. (2019). I like what I see: Studying the influence of popularity cues on attention allocation and news selection. *Information, Communication & Society*, 22(2), 286–305. doi:10.1080/1369118X.2017.1379550

Esser, F. (2013). Mediatization as a Challenge: Media logic versus political logic. In H. Kriesi, S. Lavanex, F. Esser, J. Matthes, M. Bühlmann, & D. Bochsler (Eds.), *Democracy in the age of globalization and mediatization* (pp. 155–176). Basingstoke: Palgrave Macmillan. doi:10.1057/9781137299871_7.

Esser, F., & Strömbäck, J. (2012). Comparing news on national elections. In F. Esser, & T. Hanitzsch (Eds.), *Handbook of comparative communication research* (pp. 308–326). London: Routledge.

Ferrer-Conill, R., Karlsson, M., Haim, M., Kammer, A., Elgesem, D., & Sjøvaag, H. (2021). Toward 'Cultures of Engagement'? An exploratory comparison of engagement patterns on Facebook news posts. *New Media & Society*, 25(1), 95–118. doi:10.1177/14614448211009246

Gardner, W., Mulvey, E. P., & Shaw, E. C. (1995). Regression analyses of counts and rates: Poisson, overdispersed Poisson, and negative binomial models. *Psychological Bulletin*, 118(3), 392–404. doi:10.1037/0033-2909.118.3.392

Gelman, A., & Hill, J. (2006). *Data analysis using regression and multilevel/hierarchical models*. Cambridge University Press.

Gonçalves, J., Pereira, S., & Torres da Silva, M. (2020). How to report on elections? The effects of game, issue and negative coverage on reader engagement and incivility. *Journalism*, 23(6), 1266–1284. doi:10.1177/1464884920958367

Hallin, D., & Mancini, P. (2004). *Comparing media systems: Three models of media and politics*. Cambridge University Press.

Harro-Loit, H., & Saks, K. (2006). The diminishing border between advertising and journalism in Estonia. *Journalism Studies*, 7(2), 312–322. doi:10.1080/14616700500533635

Humayun, M. F., & Ferrucci, P. (2022). Understanding social media in journalism practice: A typology. *Digital Journalism*, 0(0), 1–24. doi:10.1080/21670811.2022.2086594

Iyengar, S., Norpoth, H., & Hahn, K. S. (2004). Consumer demand for election news: The horserace sells. *The Journal of Politics*, 66(1), 157–175. doi:10.1046/j.1468-2508.2004.00146.x

Jang, S. M., & Oh, Y. W. (2016). Getting attention online in election coverage: Audience selectivity in the 2012 US presidential election. *New Media & Society*, 18(10), 2271–2286. doi:10.1177/1461444815583491

Kalsnes, B., & Larsson, A. O. (2018). Understanding news sharing across social media: Detailing distribution on

Facebook and Twitter. *Journalism Studies*, *19*(11), 1669–1688. doi:10.1080/1461670X.2017.1297686

Karidi, M. (2018). News Media Logic on the Move?: In search of commercial media logic in German news. *Journalism Studies*, *19*(9), 1237–1256. doi:10.1080/1461670X.2016.1266281

Klinger, U., & Svensson, J. (2015). The emergence of network media logic in political communication: A theoretical approach. *New Media & Society*, *17*(8), 1241–1257. doi:10.1177/1461444814522952

Kovacevic, P., & Perisin, T. (2018). The potential of constructive journalism ideas in a croatian context. *Journalism Practice*, *12*(6), 747–763. doi:10.1080/17512786.2018.1472528

Landerer, N. (2013). Rethinking the Logics: A conceptual framework for the mediatization of politics. *Communication Theory*, *23*(3), 239–258. doi:10.1111/comt.12013

Larsson, A. O. (2015). Comparing to prepare: Suggesting ways to study social media today—and tomorrow. *Social Media + Society*, *1*(1), 2056305115578680. doi:10.1177/2056305115578680

Lawrence, R. G., Radcliffe, D., & Schmidt, T. R. (2018). Practicing Engagement: Participatory journalism in the Web 2.0 era. *Journalism Practice*, *12*(10), 1220–1240. doi:10.1080/17512786.2017.1391712

Lee, E.-J., & Tandoc, E. C., Jr. (2017). When news meets the audience: how audience feedback online affects news production and consumption. *Human Communication Research*, *43*(4), 436–449. doi:10.1111/hcre.12123

Lengauer, G., Esser, F., & Berganza, R. (2012). Negativity in political news: A review of concepts, operationalizations and key findings. *Journalism*, *13*(2), 179–202. doi:10.1177/1464884911427800

Metz, M., Kruikemeier, S., & Lecheler, S. (2020). Personalization of politics on Facebook: Examining the content and effects of professional, emotional and private self-personalization. *Information, Communication & Society*, *23*(10), 1481–1498. doi:10.1080/1369118X.2019.1581244

Muddiman, A., Pond-Cobb, J., & Matson, J. E. (2020). Negativity bias or Backlash: Interaction with civil and uncivil online political news content. *Communication Research*, *47*(6), 815–837. doi:10.1177/0093650216685625

Muddiman, A., & Stroud, N. J. (2017). News values, cognitive biases, and partisan incivility in comment sections: Uncivil comments. *Journal of Communication*, *67*(4), 586–609. doi:10.1111/jcom.12312

Oeldorf-Hirsch, A., & Sundar, S. S. (2015). Posting, commenting, and tagging: Effects of sharing news stories on Facebook. *Computers in Human Behavior*, *44*, 240–249. doi:10.1016/j.chb.2014.11.024

Ørmen, J. (2019). From consumer demand to user engagement: Comparing the popularity and virality of election coverage on the Internet. *The International Journal of Press/politics*, *24*(1), 49–68. doi:10.1177/1940161218809160

Örnebring, H. (2012). Clientelism, elites, and the media in Central and Eastern Europe. *The International Journal of Press/politics*, *17*(4), 497–515.

Peruško, Z., Čuvalo, A., & Vozab, D. (2020). Mediatization of journalism: Influence of the media system and media organization on journalistic practices in European digital mediascapes. *Journalism*, *21*(11), 1630–1654. doi:10.1177/1464884917743176

Peruško, Z., Vozab, D., & Čuvalo, A. (2021). *Comparing postsocialist media systems: The case of Southeast Europe*. Routledge & CRC Press. doi:10.4324/9780367226787

Robinson, J. G. (2019). *The audience in the mind's eye: How journalists imagine their readers*. doi:10.7916/d8-drvj-wj06

Roudakova, N. (2008). Media-Political Clientelism: Lessons from Anthropology' in Media. *Culture, & Society*, *30*(1), 41–59. doi:10.1177/01634437070843

Salgado, S., & Bobba, G. (2019). News on events and social media: A comparative analysis of Facebook users' reactions. *Journalism Studies*, *20*(15), 2258–2276. doi:10.1080/1461670X.2019.1586566

Shoemaker, P. J. (1996). Hardwired for News: Using biological and cultural evolution to explain the surveillance function. *Journal of Communication*, *46*(3), 32–47. doi:10.1111/j.1460-2466.1996.tb01487.x

Singer, J. B., Domingo, D., Heinonen, A., Hermida, A., Paulussen, S. ... Vujnovic, M. (2011). *Participatory Journalism: Guarding open gates at online newspapers*. John Wiley & Sons. doi:10.1002/9781444340747

Soroka, S., Fournier, P., & Nir, L. (2019). Cross-national evidence of a negativity bias in psychophysiological reactions to news. Proceedings of the National Academy of Sciences. PNAS. https://www.pnas.org/doi/abs/10.1073/pnas.1908369116

Strömbäck, J., & Dimitrova, D. V. (2006). Political and media systems matter: A comparison of election news coverage in Sweden and the United States. *Harvard International Journal of Press/politics*, *11*(4), 131–147. doi:10.1177/1081180X06293549

Strömbäck, J., & Esser, F. (2014). Mediatization of Politics: Towards a theoretical framework. In F. Esser & J. Strömbäck (Eds.), *Mediatization of Politics: Understanding the transformation of western democracies* (pp. 3–28). Palgrave Macmillan UK. doi:10.1057/9781137275844_1

Stroud, N. J., & Muddiman, A. (2019). Social media engagement with strategy- and issue-framed political news. *Journal of Communication*, *69*(5), 443–466. doi:10.1093/joc/jqz029

Swart, J., Groot Kormelink, T., Costera Meijer, I., & Broersma, M. (2022). Advancing a radical audience turn in journalism. fundamental dilemmas for journalism studies. *Fundamental Dilemmas for Journalism Studies Digital Journalism*, *10*(1), 8–22. doi:10.1080/21670811.2021.2024764

Tóth, F., Mihelj, S., Štětka, V., & Kondor, K. (2022). A media repertoires approach to selective exposure: News consumption and political polarization in Eastern Europe. *The*

International Journal of Press/politics, 1–25. doi:10.1177/19401612211072552

Trilling, D., Tolochko, P., & Burscher, B. (2017). From newsworthiness to shareworthiness: How to predict news sharing based on article characteristics. *Journalism & Mass Communication Quarterly*, *94*(1), 38–60. doi:10.1177/1077699016654682

Trussler, M., & Soroka, S. (2014). Consumer demand for cynical and negative news frames. *The International Journal of Press/politics*, *19*(3), 360–379. doi:10.1177/1940161214524832

Uberti, L. J. (2020). Bribes, rents and industrial firm performance in Albania and Kosovo. *Comparative Economic Studies*, *62*(2), 263–302. doi:10.1057/s41294-020-00112-5

Valenzuela, S., Piña, M., & Ramírez, J. (2017). Behavioral effects of framing on social media users: How conflict, economic, human interest, and morality frames drive news sharing. *Journal of Communication*, *67*(5), 803–826. doi:10.1111/jcom.12325

Van Aelst, P., Sheafer, T., & Stanyer, J. (2012). The personalization of mediated political communication: A review of concepts, operationalizations and key findings. *Journalism*, *13*(2), 203–220. doi:10.1177/1464884911427802

Zoizner, A. (2021). The consequences of strategic news coverage for democracy: A meta-analysis. *Communication Research*, *48*(1), 3–25. doi:10.1177/0093650218808691

🔓 OPEN ACCESS

One way or another? Discussion disagreement and attitudinal homogeneity on social networking sites as pathways to polarization in Czechia

Alena Macková, Martina Novotná, Lucie Čejková, and Lenka Hrbková

ABSTRACT
This study focuses on social networking sites and their role in partisan-based affective polarization and political antagonism. We examine the relationship by testing variables that indicate selective exposure to counter-attitudinal and pro-attitudinal information. The results from Czech survey data ($n = 2{,}792$) collected in 2020 show a positive relationship between both perceived discussion disagreement and attitudinal homogeneity of the network to political antagonism, and a positive relationship between the perceived attitudinal homogeneity of the network and affective polarization. The results thus question the existence of a single universal social media use pattern contributing to polarization.

Introduction

Many scholars argue that political polarization has been accelerated by ongoing changes within the political information environment, which has become increasingly information-rich and fragmented, and that recent changes have created wide opportunity structures for selective practices regarding media content (Prior, 2007; Skovsgaard, Shehata, & Strömbäck, 2016), especially on social media. However, the evidence that social media operate as a polarizing factor is still unclear and the results are mixed (Kubin & von Sikorski, 2021). Moreover, it seems there can be several plausible mechanisms through which different social media use patterns can contribute to polarization (Ali & Altawil, 2022; Nordbrandt, 2021; Törnberg, 2022).

In this paper, we address the relationship between polarization and the use of social networking sites (SNS). Building on the theory and research of selective exposure, and on the effects of social media use on political polarization, we extend the findings by a) distinguishing among the practices that are related to exposure to disagreement, providing examples of experience with negativity and conflict in cross-cutting discussions, and connecting selective exposure theory to the preference for pro-attitudinal exposure and a homogeneous information environment; b) testing the relationship with two different approaches to polarization, specifically partisan-based affective polarization and political antagonism; and c) focusing on the under-researched area of the Central and Eastern Europe region (CEE), namely Czechia.

Firstly, according to previous research, practices related to both types of exposure (pro- and counter-attitudinal) could possibly lead to different types of polarization (Garrett, 2009; Kubin & von Sikorski, 2021). Thus, on one side, we investigate the effects of perceived discussion disagreement and negativity (i.e., conflict) in cross-cutting discussions on SNS, and, on the other side, we investigate the effects of selective practices, like politically motivated unfriending (as an act of selective avoidance) and the attitudinal homogeneity of SNS.

Secondly, the available comparative research on the character of polarization and its possible sources reveals that the process of polarization substantially differs among countries and that the well-researched United States is, ostensibly, an outlier to some extent (Gidron, Adams, & Horne, 2020; Reiljan, 2020). It reveals that polarization is high in Western democracies with social inequality, high unemployment, and cultural divides (Gidron, Adams, & Horne, 2020). It is also

---

This is an Open Access article distributed under the terms of the Creative Commons Attribution License (http://creativecommons.org/licenses/by/4.0/), which permits unrestricted use, distribution, and reproduction in any medium, provided the original work is properly cited. The terms on which this article has been published allow the posting of the Accepted Manuscript in a repository by the author(s) or with their consent.

relatively strong in the regions of CEE and Southern Europe (Reiljan, 2020). Moreover, in the global context, it is associated with democratic backsliding (Orhan, 2022). Regarding the sources of polarization in individual media practices, findings from outside the U.S. are even more fragmented and ambiguous (Arguedas, Robertson, Fletcher, & Nielsen, 2022). Our study provides data on an under-researched CEE country, Czechia, where the character of polarization differs from the U.S. and several other contested countries: the nature of polarization in Czechia, with its multiparty system and proportional voting system (Gidron, Adams, & Horne, 2020; Reiljan, 2020), seems to be less associated with partisanship or ideologies.

Thirdly, because of the context-based differences in polarization among the countries and the nature of the polarization in Czechia (see Tóth, Mihelj, Štětka, & Kondor, 2022), we examine whether the perceived disagreement in discussions and/or political unfriending and network homogeneity are linked to affective polarization based on the voters' party sympathies. We also examine whether these practices are linked to political antagonism.

Theory and state of art

Affective political polarization

The recent dominant approach toward political polarization emphasizes the gaps in affect and sympathies to political parties rather than ideological divergence (Iyengar, Lelkes, Levendusky, Malhotra, & Westwood, 2019; Iyengar, Sood, & Lelkes, 2012). In the U.S., Democrats increasingly like the Democratic Party, and Democratic voters increasingly dislike the rival Republican party and its voters, and vice versa (Mason, 2018). Comparative research revealed that voters in European multiparty systems are also affectively polarized, especially in CEE and Southern Europe, where several countries face democratic backsliding (Reiljan, 2020; Orhan, 2022). Affective polarization in these countries, however, is more complex, because voters can like and hate multiple parties that are spread across the political space (Wagner, 2021) and, given the nature of party systems with multiple parties and coalitions, they are often affectively polarized toward blocks of parties with similar ideological profiles (Reiljan & Ryan, 2021).

Research suggests that affective polarization can lead to partisan prejudice (Iyengar & Westwood, 2015) and broad politically motivated biases against outparty supporters, even outside the realm of politics (Rudolph & Hetherington, 2021). Politically, affective polarization shapes the attitudes of the public toward policies (Druckman, Klar, Krupnikov, Levendusky, & Ryan, 2021) and democratic norms (Simonovits, McCoy, & Littvay, 2022).

From polarization to political antagonism

Polarization may exceed dislike and biases among different political camps and their supporters and escalate into a more pernicious form (McCoy & Somer, 2019). Research suggests that affective polarization does not automatically lead to partisan prejudice (Westwood, Peterson, & Lelkes, 2019); however, a more severe form of political antagonism (i.e., a form of political conflict in which people perceive their political outgroups as enemies and illegitimate elements of the polity) may emerge (Mouffe, 2011). Extremely polarized and antagonized individuals tend to dehumanize their opponents and perceive them as less civilized and lacking emotions. Antagonized individuals also behave in ways to deliberately upset their political outgroups and may even support or tolerate political violence (Kalmoe & Mason, 2019). This rejection of political opponents in the form of political antagonism may pose more of a threat to the functioning of democratic institutions (Simonovits, McCoy, & Littvay, 2022).

Affective polarization and politically driven hostilities seem to be associated, to a large extent, with the use of SNS (Lee, Rojas, & Yamamoto, 2022). Recent research suggests that SNS accelerates the sorting of individuals' identities, both political and other types. This leads to more polarization (Törnberg, 2022) because opinions on SNS become less important as opinions and become markers of identity (Törnberg, Andersson, Lindgren, Banisch, & Mahmoud, 2021). We explore the SNS practices that have the potential to contribute to both affective polarization toward political parties and affective polarization toward the antagonization of social conflict.

Polarization in Czechia

We test the effects of SNS use on polarization in the Czechia, which is a country with unstable and fragmented party system and shifting political cleavages. Comparative research reveals that, despite the party system fragmentation and voter volatility, Czechia scores high on the affective polarization of voters toward political parties (Orhan, 2022; Reiljan, 2020). However, the nature and sources of this polarization are unclear. While some issues have polarizing potential (e.g., immigration, development of the country after 1989), political attitudes are not clearly distributed around two opposing poles. Public opinion is fragmented into smaller groups regarding various issues (Buchtík, Eichler, Kopečný, Smejkalová, & Uhrová, 2021). The Czech public tends to convert political issues into culture wars between elites and ordinary people, which contributes to an identity-based form of political antagonism (Slačálek, 2021). Identities fueled by populist political actors play a more significant role compared to ideological preferences.

Socio-cultural identity-based conflict has become a dominant axis of electoral politics. Even economic issues, which dominated Czech politics after 1989, have become evaluated through the prism of identity (Vachudova, 2019). Two populist parties, the centrist ANO (Action of Dissatisfied Citizens) and the right-wing SPD (Freedom and Direct Democracy), have become important forces in Czech politics since 2017, which might contribute to group-based polarization by feeding cultural and identity-based conflicts. It suggests that Czech society is polarized, and that identities and politically defined groups are relevant, even though they are not necessarily based only upon a simple partisan divide.

SNS, selectivity, and polarization

Common fears that link the use of SNS with polarization are grounded in the theory of selective exposure (Mutz, 2006; Stroud, 2010), which is defined as the tendency for people to choose and prefer attitude-consistent information. This theory regained attention as the internet and SNS became increasingly important as a source of news and a space for interaction with others – and Czechia is not an exception in these trends. Whereas television plays an essential role as a source of news, longitudinal data show that the recent prevalence of online media and SNS is growing in importance (Macková, Novotná, Procházková, Macek, & Hrbková, 2021; Newman et al., 2021; Štětka, 2021). In general, the most popular SNS in Czechia is Facebook (70% of the citizens use Facebook). The usage of other SNS compared to Facebook is relatively low – with 11% users of Twitter and 28% users of Instagram (Newman et al., 2021). Furthermore, SNS have become an important space where citizens can be exposed to the opinions of others and where they can form an impression about the beliefs and attitudes of different groups in society by reading and participating in discussions. Yet, the willingness of Czechs to participate in online political discussions is similar to other countries (e.g., Duggan & Smith, 2016), which means relatively low (less than a third of Czech users indicated that they discussed politics on SNS in 2020). More importantly for our research, Czechs often reported unwillingness to engage in discussions with people with different opinions and they tended to avoid disagreement (Macková, Novotná, Procházková, Macek, & Hrbková, 2021). Although the international evidence for whether the overall selectivity is on the rise is mixed (Garrett et al., 2014), there is an agreement that the current high-choice information environment offers more opportunities than ever to select or to avoid information and news based on attitudes, opinions, and other preferences (Skovsgaard, Shehata, & Strömbäck, 2016).

Selectivity has often been assessed as party-based, and earlier studies based on the U.S. showed that engagement with partisan news and media can increase both ideological (Stroud, 2010) and affective polarization (Garrett et al., 2014; Iyengar, Sood, & Lelkes, 2012; Lelkes, Sood, & Iyengar, 2017). Studies which reflect countries outside the U.S. and emphasize more attitude-based selectivity are not as convincing in the effects on polarization (e.g. Trilling, van Klingeren, & Tsfati, 2017; Wojcieszak et al., 2021). Additionally, ideological selective exposure was often researched in countries with a more polarized media environment and with more opportunity structures for selective exposure (Skoric, Zhu, Koc-

Michalska, Boulianne, & Bimber, 2021; Steppat, Castro Herrero, & Esser, 2021). Compared to other countries (even in the CEE region), the Czech information environment and audiences are not very polarized, and the level of general selective exposure seems to be low because most of the dominant media is right-centrist and strong partisan media are absent (Fletcher, Cornia, & Nielsen, 2020; Tóth, Mihelj, Štětka, & Kondor, 2022). As a result, our study understands selectivity to be a more general concept that reaches beyond a strictly partisan-based practice, because the Czech partisan attachments are week.

Furthermore, Steppat, Castro Herrero, and Esser (2021) reveal that selective exposure is slightly more frequent among social media users than among the users of TV, radio, and newspapers. Still, recent evidence about the relationship between the use of SNS and polarization (Kubin & von Sikorski, 2021) is fragmented and the results vary (for the review, see Arguedas, Robertson, Fletcher, & Nielsen, 2022; Kubin & von Sikorski, 2021). For example, Cho, Ahmed, Kerum, Choi, and Lee (2018) used U.S. data to show that political expression on social media predicts both ideological and affective polarization, and Lee, Rojas, and Yamamoto (2022) found a positive relationship between social media news use and affective polarization in both the U.S. and Japan. On the other hand, other studies found only small or no effects of social media use (Ali & Altawil, 2022; Nordbrandt, 2021), and even a negligible depolarizing effect of social media use for news (Beam, Hutchens, & Hmielowski, 2018; Johnson, Neo, Heinen, Smits, & van Veen, 2020). Overall, the link between SNS use and polarization is mostly expressed by a concern with the creation of an ideologically homogeneous information environment (due to growing selectivity) or to a more hostile ideologically diverse environment (Flaxman, Goel, & Rao, 2016) – both, possibly, directly lead to polarization as a distinct mechanism. Due to these uncertain effects of general SNS use identified by previous research in Czechia, we investigate the effects of more clearly defined SNS practices (among SNS users).

Perceived discussion disagreement and negativity on SNS

Our first set of hypotheses is linked to the assumption that SNS can create an ideologically diverse information environment where users are often exposed to different content and views and where they may interact with those who hold dissimilar views. Additionally, users do not necessarily need to discuss politics to be exposed to counter-attitudinal content because they can just scroll through their the SNS feeds (Yang, Barnidge, & Rojas, 2017) and be exposed accidentally (see Weeks et al., 2017). The impacts of counter-attitudinal exposure on SNS can generally be twofold. On the one hand, prior research has shown that such exposure can increase tolerance to others and their opinions (Mutz, 2006) and depolarize attitudes (Westerwick, Johnson, & Knobloch-Westerwick, 2017). Contrary to the optimistic assumptions, counter-attitudinal exposure can increase perceived social distance, reinforce attitudes, and contribute to polarization (Duggan & Smith, 2016; Flaxman, Goel, & Rao, 2016; Iyengar, Sood, & Lelkes, 2012; Suhay, Bello-Pardo, & Maurer, 2018). Furthermore, some research shows no, poor, or mixed evidence (Lee, Choi, Kim, & Kim, 2014).

One of the main factors that contributes to polarization may not be primarily linked to counter-attitudinal exposure as such, but rather to the character of the content and of the interactions. Online discussions tend to be negative, uncivil, and offensive. Hostility is often used as a reaction to counter-attitudinal opinions (Vochocová, 2020) and can consequently lead to selective behavior (Goyanes, Borah, & Gil De Zúñiga, 2021). Many users find such interactions and exposure to disagreement to be stressful, and they get angry (Macková, Novotná, Procházková, Macek, & Hrbková, 2021). Negative language and hostile content can be problematic from the perspective of out-group beliefs (Hiaeshutter-Rice & Hawkins, 2022). As a result, such exposure can potentially shape behavior and attitudes (Weber, Viehmann, Ziegele, & Schemer, 2020; Winter & Krämer, 2016). It can generate anger and hostility, underline group differences (Druckman, Gubitz, Levendusky, & Lloyd, 2019), strengthen prior convictions and in-group attachments, and increase polarization

(Anderson, Yeo, Brossard, Scheufele, & Xenos, 2018; Hwang, Kim, & Huh, 2014).

The term negativity captures a range of forms of hostility in communication. Whereas some researchers define negativity as a part of incivility (see Hameleers et al., 2022), it is apparent that negativity is a broader concept and may occur in civil and uncivil ways contrary to incivility (see Otto et al., 2020). "Negativity" allows for the capture of a broader spectrum of adverse reactions that might be harmful. Counterarguments and "comment wars" are, from the point of view of discussion participants, mentioned as negative aspects of social-media discussions (Kruse et al., 2018). Both negative civil criticism and incivility need to be considered. Available data show that hateful comments and a negative tone, even if civil, affect people's attitudes and possibly shape intergroup polarization (Weber, Viehmann, Ziegele, & Schemer, 2020). This counters Brooks and Geer's (2007) argument that negativity is not as problematic as incivility.

We test the effect of perceived discussion disagreement, negativity, and conflict in discussions. We assume that the disagreement in discussions will be related to higher polarization. Moreover, we suppose that the effect will be stronger for users who are also exposed to negativity and conflict. Building on limited evidence, we assume that exposure to disagreement in (negative) cross-cutting discussions can be related to the perceived wider gap between political opponents, and to higher political antagonism.

H1a: Perceived discussion disagreement is linked to higher affective polarization.

H1b: Perceived discussion disagreement is linked to higher political antagonism.

H2a: The effect of perceived discussion disagreement on affective polarization will be stronger among users who have experienced negativity and conflict in discussions.

H2b: The effect of perceived discussion disagreement on political antagonism will be stronger among users who have experienced negativity and conflict in discussions.

Selective avoidance and attitudinal homogeneity on SNS

While SNS can expose citizens to diverse information and motivate them to engage in discussions with people who hold opposing views, they also allow them to establish a more homogeneous information environment through the practices of filtering and content curation on SNS (Skoric, Zhu, & Lin, 2018). Selective avoidance (e.g., content removal or politically motivated unfriending; Skoric, Zhu, Koc-Michalska, Bouliane, & Bimber, 2021; Zhu & Skoric, 2022) provides opportunities to avoid content shared by those with whom they politically disagree (Bode, 2016), and it can be seen as a reaction to the uncivil online environment of SNS (Goyanes, Borah, & Gil De Zúñiga, 2021). On the other hand, engagement with some degree of selective exposure does not necessarily imply engagement in the practices of selective avoidance (Garrett, 2009; Skoric, Zhu, & Lin, 2018; Yang, Barnidge, & Rojas, 2017; Zhu & Skoric, 2022). The use of this selective strategy (around a third of the respondents reported the usage of the unfriending function according to Barnidge, Peacock, Kim, Kim, & Xenos, 2022; Neely, 2021) is influenced by several factors, which may mitigate the final effects of unfriending on a diversity of content on SNS. Specifically, unfriending is more common for politically engaged users with higher exposure to political content, users with stronger political opinions, and those who are more exposed to disagreement (Bode, 2016; Duggan & Smith, 2016; Neely, 2021).

With the general tendency to prefer attitude-consistent content and news (Stroud, 2010) and the tendency to avoid attitude-discrepant or uncivil content (Garrett, 2009; Kim, Wang, Lee, & Kim, 2022), users of SNS can use strategies of selective avoidance to build a safer and ideologically homogeneous space. Thus, we can understand politically motivated unfriending as a strategy to prevent or reduce engagement with opposite viewpoints (Hwang, Kim, & Huh, 2014). However, Vaccari and Valeriani (2021) argue that it is very difficult to isolate oneself from disagreement. Apart from the active role of SNS users, there is the issue of accidental exposure to news (Vaccari & Valeriani, 2021) and the twofold role of SNS algorithms. The algorithms may break down the homogenous environment and bring up controversial content that gains more attention. Still, on the other side, algorithms contribute to creating a more homogeneous informational environment and they tend to produce "echo chambers." The common concerns connected to the dominance of online "echo chambers," as defined as bounded and enclosed media spaces (Jamieson & Cappella, 2008, p. 76), seem to be unfulfilled (Arguedas, Robertson, Fletcher, & Nielsen, 2022; Garrett, 2009; Vaccari & Valeriani, 2021). In Czechia, the media repertoires of citizens seem to also be relatively balanced (Tóth, Mihelj, Štětka, & Kondor, 2022). The same applies to online news media audiences (Fletcher, Cornia, & Nielsen, 2020) and SNS users (Macková, Novotná, Procházková, Macek, & Hrbková, 2021).

Despite the evidence that most citizens engage, to some degree, in counter-attitudinal exposure, worries about the implications of online selective exposure in terms of polarization remain, because one of the more conclusive findings of the literature on social media and polarization is the positive relationship between pro-attitudinal exposure and polarization (Kubin & von Sikorski, 2021). The information environment in which citizens mainly prefer pro-attitudinal exposure and where they are not much exposed to incongruent information, can magnify the distances among groups with different opinions and strengthen in-group positions and attitudes (Knobloch-Westerwick, Mothes, Johnson, Westerwick, & Donsbach, 2015). Consequently, we assume that politically motivated unfriending is a practice of selective avoidance, and that the level of perceived attitudinal homogeneity will be related both to higher affective polarization and to antagonization in society.

H3a: Politically motivated unfriending is linked to higher affective polarization.

H3b: Politically motivated unfriending is linked to higher political antagonism.

H4a: The perceived attitudinal homogeneity of the network is linked to higher affective polarization.

H4b: The perceived attitudinal homogeneity of the network is linked to higher political antagonism.

Political interest and polarization in high-choice media environment

As mentioned above, the current (online) media environment and SNS offer easier ways than ever before to select or avoid the news, content, and interactions based on individual preferences and characteristics. Nowadays, the role of individual characteristics in news consumption, and especially political interest, is becoming more significant (Skovsgaard, Shehata, & Strömbäck, 2016; Vaccari & Valeriani, 2021). A gap between politically interested and disinterested people is apparent (Prior, 2007, 2013). This might have consequences for political behavior and political attitudes, including polarization. While the current environment allows those with little interest in politics to avoid news or political discussions, it helps people with higher political interest to access political content to have political interactions (Kim, Guess, Nyhan, & Reifler, 2021). In the same vein, studies found that people who are more interested, politically sophisticated, or engaged in politics, are often exposed to more polarizing content (Westfall, Van Boven, Chambers, & Judd, 2015). More importantly, they hold more polarized opinions toward others (Ali & Altawil, 2022; Druckman, Klar, Krupnikov, Levendusky, & Ryan, 2021; Rekker & Harteveld, 2022). Nevertheless, the studies also imply that the relationship between political interest and social media practices is not straightforward. Building on this limited and mixed evidence, we focus on the relationship between political interest and polarization and hypothesize that, in the recent information environment (and in the case of SNS users), political interest is positively linked to affective polarization and to political antagonism.

H5a: Higher political interest is linked to higher affective polarization.

H5b: Higher political interest is linked to higher political antagonism.

Methodology

Data

We tested the set of hypotheses on the subsample of Czech SNS users ($n = 2,792$; 74.2%) from a survey of the adult population ($N = 3,763$) collected by Focus (Marketing & Social Research) agency in November-December 2020. The sample is based on quotas to represent the Czech 18+ population. It was compiled with a combination of computer-assisted web interviewing (65%) and computer-assisted personal interviewing (35%) by professionally trained interviewers. The original questionnaire covers selected political attitudes and values, polarization, attitudes about the media, and trust in detailed news reception practices. The practices used on SNS that were targeted by this paper represent a marginal and supplementary part of the questionnaire. The descriptive statistics and correlations for all of the variables for both the SNS users and the excluded non-SNS users are provided in Supplementary Materials (Table A1).

Measures

Affective polarization captures differences in the evaluations of political parties (Iyengar, Sood, & Lelkes, 2012). Respondents rated their sympathies for all of the political parties represented in the Chamber of Deputies on a 0–10 scale. To operationalize affective polarization in a multiparty system we used an index based on the spread of the party sympathies of individual respondents (Wagner, 2021). This approach recognizes that individuals can hold positive feelings toward more than one party and that a respondent who holds similar positive feelings for most or all of the parties is not affectively polarized. This type of operationalization emphasizes that high affective polarization results from the individual's different levels of party affect across the party spectrum. It also enables us to measure affective polarization for both undecided voters and nonvoters (for details and descriptive statistics see Supplementary Materials Table A1, Figure A1).

Political antagonism was measured as agreement with four statements (on a 5-point agreement scale that ranged from "totally disagree" to "absolutely agree"), which represented diverse domains that were affected by polarization: society, politics, media, and everyday life. Political antagonism includes the statements: "People whose opinions on important issues are opposite to mine can be dangerous for society;" "Politicians whose opinions on important issues are opposite to mine should not be in politics;" "It is not worth following media that have different opinions on important issues than I do;" and "It is not worth being friends with or talking to someone who has opinions that are opposite to mine on important issues" (Cronbach $\alpha = .82$).

Perceived discussion disagreement was measured with a statement (5-point scale that ranged from "completely disagree" to "totally agree"): "There are often discussions or comments on my network that I disagree with." The measure was inspired by a previous study by Lu, Heatherly, and Lee (2016).

Negativity and conflict in discussions was assessed by three items that looked at the perceived and initiated negativity: (1) "I have received a very negative reaction from a friend or from people who follow me on the social networking sites;" (2) "I fight in online discussions with people who have an opinion that is opposite mine;" and (3) "I add negative comments in discussions, including hostile or vulgar words, in answer to comments or posts shared by someone else." Respondents were asked for the frequency of the behavior on a 5-point scale that ranged from "never" to "very often." The score was computed as the mean of the values (Cronbach $\alpha = .84$). The measurement of experienced negativity was derived from the study by Rainie and Smith (2012). Using a broader concept of negativity, rather than only incivility, allows us to capture various attacks from two perspectives, perceived and initiated. As civility differs among the perception of the beholders (Herbst, 2010), this operationalization will enable users to put whatever they might evaluate as a negative reaction, or "fighting," into the concept.

To measure *politically motivated unfriending*, we asked if the users had ever unfriended someone (i.e., yes/no) for the following political reasons: 1) Did they share something you didn't agree with about politics or public affairs? 2) Did they argue with you or anyone you know about politics or public affairs? 3) Did they disagree with something you shared about politics or public affairs? And 4) Did they share posts about politics or public affairs too often? The score was computed as the sum of the values (Cronbach α = .79).

Level of perceived attitudinal homogeneity on SNS was measured as an agreement (5-point scale ranging from "completely disagree" to "totally agree") with the statement: "The vast majority of people on my social networking site have similar views as I do" (see Chen, Ai, & Guo, 2022).

Political interest was measured by the question "How interested are you in politics?" on an 11-point scale that ranged from "not interested at all" (0) to "very interested" (10). Control variables include gender, age, and education.

Analysis

We employed a hierarchical multiple regression analysis (IBM SPSS Statistics 27, 28) and a moderation analysis (PROCESS v4.2, Model 1; Hayes, 2022) to test the hypotheses. We began the analysis by exploring the variables and checking the assumptions.

After exploring descriptive statistics and correlations, we transformed the variable of politically motivated unfriending because it violated the assumption of normality (de Vaus, 2002). Thus, politically motivated unfriending (skewness = 1.756, SE = .049; kurtosis = 1.959, SE = .098) was recoded as follows: 0 – *never* (n = 1,729, 70.0%) and 1 – *at least once at some point* (n = 742, 30.0%).

In preparation for the moderation analysis, we calculated the mean-centered values of perceived discussion disagreement and negativity, and conflict in discussions, to avoid multicollinearity (Irwin & McClelland, 2001). Afterward, we computed the interaction of these two variables.

We tested two regression models with independent variables and the interaction as predictors. We also tested affective polarization and political antagonism as dependent variables. The independent variables were added in three blocks: (1) control variables; (2) study variables without interaction; and (3) interaction.

In both analyses, the assumption of the absence of multicollinearity was met. Correlations among variables (see Table A1 in Supplementary Materials), VIF, and tolerance had acceptable levels (de Vaus, 2002). We detected some multivariate violations of normality and slight issues with homoscedasticity. Nevertheless, due to having a large sample and having already adjusted one of the variables, we decided to proceed with the analysis. Some cases were removed from the analysis as outliers. After a listwise deletion of missing data, 1,924 cases were tested for affective polarization and 1,965 cases were tested for political antagonism.

Results

The results of a hierarchical regression analysis performed on the sample of interest for this study (i.e., SNS users) showed that political antagonism was better explained by the study variables than affective polarization (R^2 = .160 for political antagonism, R^2 = .120 for affective polarizations; for detailed results see Table 1).

As shown in Table 1, we did not find a relationship between perceived discussion disagreement and higher affective polarization (H1a; β = .006, p = .801), but those with higher political antagonism had more perceived discussion disagreement (H1b; β = .131, p < .001).

We also tested whether the effect of perceived discussion disagreement on affective polarization (H2a) and political antagonism (H2b) would be stronger for users who experienced more negativity and conflict in discussions. The interaction effect was insignificant for political antagonism (β = .013,

Table 1. Results of the hierarchical regression analysis.

<table>
<tr><th rowspan="3"></th><th colspan="9">Affective polarization</th><th colspan="9">Political antagonism</th></tr>
<tr><th colspan="3">Block 1</th><th colspan="3">Block 2</th><th colspan="3">Block 3</th><th colspan="3">Block 1</th><th colspan="3">Block 2</th><th colspan="3">Block 3</th></tr>
<tr><th>b (SE)</th><th>β</th><th>p</th><th>b (SE)</th><th>β</th><th>p</th><th>b (SE)</th><th>β</th><th>p</th><th>b (SE)</th><th>β</th><th>p</th><th>b (SE)</th><th>β</th><th>p</th><th>b (SE)</th><th>β</th><th>p</th></tr>
<tr><td>Gender</td><td>−0.093 (0.054)</td><td>−.039</td><td>.087</td><td>0.032 (0.054)</td><td>.014</td><td>.551</td><td>0.028 (0.054)</td><td>.012</td><td>.600</td><td>−0.021 (0.039)</td><td>−.012</td><td>.586</td><td>−0.004 (0.037)</td><td>−.003</td><td>.904</td><td>−0.004 (0.037)</td><td>−.002</td><td>.924</td></tr>
<tr><td>Age</td><td>0.014 (0.002)</td><td>**.197**</td><td>**<.001**</td><td>0.010 (0.002)</td><td>**.144**</td><td>**<.001**</td><td>0.010 (0.002)</td><td>**.143**</td><td>**<.001**</td><td>0.006 (0.001)</td><td>**.112**</td><td>**<.001**</td><td>0.007 (0.001)</td><td>**.128**</td><td>**<.001**</td><td>0.007 (0.001)</td><td>**.129**</td><td>**<.001**</td></tr>
<tr><td>Education</td><td>0.004 (0.030)</td><td>.003</td><td>.881</td><td>−0.043 (0.029)</td><td>−.032</td><td>.140</td><td>−0.043 (0.029)</td><td>−.032</td><td>.144</td><td>−0.119 (0.021)</td><td>**−.129**</td><td>**<.001**</td><td>−0.067 (0.020)</td><td>**−.072**</td><td>**.001**</td><td>−0.067 (0.020)</td><td>**−.072**</td><td>**.001**</td></tr>
<tr><td>Perceived discussion disagreement</td><td></td><td></td><td></td><td>0.020 (0.028)</td><td>.016</td><td>.470</td><td>0.007 (0.029)</td><td>.006</td><td>.801</td><td></td><td></td><td></td><td>0.114 (0.019)</td><td>**.128**</td><td>**<.001**</td><td>0.117 (0.020)</td><td>**.131**</td><td>**<.001**</td></tr>
<tr><td>Experienced negativity and conflict</td><td></td><td></td><td></td><td>−0.018 (0.037)</td><td>−.011</td><td>.636</td><td>−0.002 (0.038)</td><td>−.001</td><td>.959</td><td></td><td></td><td></td><td>0.282 (0.026)</td><td>**.242**</td><td>**<.001**</td><td>0.279 (0.026)</td><td>**.240**</td><td>**<.001**</td></tr>
<tr><td>Politically motivated unfriending</td><td></td><td></td><td></td><td>−0.148 (0.057)</td><td>**−.058**</td><td>**.010**</td><td>−0.153 (0.057)</td><td>**−.060**</td><td>**.008**</td><td></td><td></td><td></td><td>0.135 (0.040)</td><td>**.074**</td><td>**.001**</td><td>0.136 (0.040)</td><td>**.074**</td><td>**.001**</td></tr>
<tr><td>Level of attitudinal homogeneity</td><td></td><td></td><td></td><td>0.125 (0.029)</td><td>**.093**</td><td>**<.001**</td><td>0.131 (0.029)</td><td>**.098**</td><td>**<.001**</td><td></td><td></td><td></td><td>0.179 (0.020)</td><td>**.187**</td><td>**<.001**</td><td>0.178 (0.020)</td><td>**.186**</td><td>**<.001**</td></tr>
<tr><td>Political interest</td><td></td><td></td><td></td><td>0.122 (0.010)</td><td>**.270**</td><td>**<.001**</td><td>0.123 (0.010)</td><td>**.271**</td><td>**<.001**</td><td></td><td></td><td></td><td>−0.022 (0.007)</td><td>**−.069**</td><td>**.002**</td><td>−0.022 (0.007)</td><td>**−.069**</td><td>**.002**</td></tr>
<tr><td>Perceived discussion disagreement × Experienced negativity and conflict</td><td></td><td></td><td></td><td></td><td></td><td></td><td>−0.092 (0.040)</td><td>−.051</td><td>.023</td><td></td><td></td><td></td><td></td><td></td><td></td><td>0.017 (0.028)</td><td>.013</td><td>.535</td></tr>
<tr><td>R^2 (R^2 change)</td><td colspan="3">.044</td><td colspan="3">.118 (.074)</td><td colspan="3">.120 (.002)</td><td colspan="3">.030</td><td colspan="3">.160 (.130)</td><td colspan="3">.160 (.000)</td></tr>
<tr><td>F change</td><td colspan="3">29.114</td><td colspan="3">32.172</td><td colspan="3">5.164</td><td colspan="3">20.116</td><td colspan="3">60.568</td><td colspan="3">.385</td></tr>
<tr><td>p</td><td colspan="3"><.001</td><td colspan="3"><.001</td><td colspan="3">.023</td><td colspan="3"><.001</td><td colspan="3"><.001</td><td colspan="3">.535</td></tr>
</table>

Gender was coded as 0 – *male* and 1 – *female*. Politically motivated unfriending was coded as 0 – *never* and 1 – *at least once at some point*.

$p = .535$). In the case of affective polarization, the interaction effect was significant and negative, but with the weakest effect among the study variables (β = −.051, $p = .023$). Moreover, when testing for moderation using PROCESS (Model 1, 10000 bootstrap samples), the moderation model, $R^2 = .002$, $F(3, 2227) = 1.816$, $p = .142$ and all its terms, tested as insignificant.

We observed that those who performed politically motivated unfriending at least once at some point had higher levels of political antagonism (H3b; β = .074, $p = .001$). Interestingly, the opposite was true for affective polarization (H3a; β = −.060, $p = .008$). Both associations were among the weakest – but still significant – in the model.

For Hypotheses 4a and 4b, we expected that higher levels of the attitudinal homogeneity of the network would be linked to higher affective polarization and political antagonism, respectively. The analysis supported both hypotheses (β = .098, $p < .001$; β = .186, $p < .001$, respectively), with attitudinal homogeneity being the strongest predictor of political antagonism.

In the case of affective polarization, the relationship with political interest was the strongest and positive (β = .271, $p < .001$), meaning that SNS users with higher political interest are also more affectively polarized. Thus, we found support for Hypothesis 5a. But for political antagonism, the association was the opposite: weak and negative (β = −.069, $p = .002$; H5b).

Additionally, older SNS users scored higher in affective polarization (β = .143, $p < .001$) and political antagonism (β = .129, $p < .001$), and those with lower education were more politically antagonized (β = −.072, $p < .001$).

Discussion

The study examined the relationship between several SNS practices, political interest and partisan-based affective polarization and political antagonism. We consider the Czech case to be highly interesting and valuable because the countries in the CEE region are not in the spotlight of researchers. Importantly, comparative studies on polarization or the character of SNS use and its effects show the diversity in results and relevance of various contexts (Gidron, Adams, & Horne, 2020; Steppat, Castro Herrero, & Esser, 2021). Czechia represents a relatively young European democracy with a fragmented and unstable multiparty system and multiple populist parties who play roles in parliamentary politics. While populist political actors have been exploiting identity-based issues, such as immigration and EU, for voter mobilization (Slačálek, 2021), the political system has not been disrupted by the democratic backsliding that is typical for other countries in the region. Similarly, regarding the character of the media environment and its polarization, Czechia does not represent an extreme case, even when compared to other CEE countries (Tóth, Mihelj, Štětka, & Kondor, 2022).

This case study produced several important findings. Firstly, we found that the effects of SNS use differed in some respects for affective polarization and political antagonism. It confirms the need for deeper contextualization with a focus on a clear conceptualization of polarization in order to compare the effects of SNS use in different contexts (Johnson, Neo, Heinen, Smits, & van Veen, 2020; Kubin & von Sikorski, 2021). The only consistent and positive effect on both of the examined dependent variables was found in the case of the perceived attitudinal homogeneity of networks. This is in line with previous research that reported quite reliable results about the effects of the tendency for selectivity and pro-attitudinal exposure on polarization (Knobloch-Westerwick, Mothes, Johnson, Westerwick, & Donsbach, 2015; Kubin & von Sikorski, 2021). The reason for the stronger effect for the political antagonism compared to affective polarization may lie in the construction of the contested variable. Attitudinal homogeneity is assessed as the general agreement in views, and it is not focused on political attitudes or the ideological homogeneity of the network in the sense of the partisanship of friends or followed users. Following the argument about the tendency for pro-attitudinal exposure, we also found weak effects for political unfriending on both dependent variables. Interestingly, their directions are opposite. While political antagonism has a positive effect (similar to attitudinal homogeneity), affective polarization has a negative, albeit small, one. Political unfriending and political antagonism refer to actions that are motivated by counter-opinions, whereas affective polarization does not.

It seems that removing friends is connected to more extreme polarization and the active exclusion of "out-groups," which could potentially go further beyond friend removal and result in more serious conflicts. To sum up, political unfriending and attitudinal homogeneity are both connected with higher antagonism against "others." Regarding the opposite relation between political unfriending and affective polarization, it seems that other characteristics probably shape the homogeneous composition of the network, as following like-minded pages that align with the political affiliation and consequently result in affective polarization.

Compared to the tendency for pro-attitudinal exposure, the relationship between polarization and counter-attitudinal exposure was less straightforward in previous research. Consistent with our expectations, we found an effect of perceived disagreement in discussions, although this was only for political antagonism. Additionally, we did not find evidence for the moderating effect of experienced negativity and conflict, though we found that experienced and initiated negativity, or conflicting behavior, has an effect on political antagonism itself. For comparison, the research from the U.S. shows a positive relationship between negativity and perceived polarization (Anderson, Yeo, Brossard, Scheufele, & Xenos, 2018; Hwang, Kim, & Huh, 2014). These discrepancies may be caused by a combination of factors, such as the country-related context, the differences within the concept of polarization, and the capture of negativity via an experimental study (Anderson, Yeo, Brossard, Scheufele, & Xenos, 2018). Similarly, the operationalization of the concept in the study can also make a difference, because it specifically combines negativity and conflict. We suggest that future research focus on the survey data and that it should more delicately examine the concept of incivility and more harmful attacks, such as hate speech and intolerance. They should also target the differences among the effects of experienced negativity, initiated negativity, and incivility, which could imply different consequences for polarization.

We also tested the effect of political interest for the case of SNS users on affective polarization and political antagonism. We were interested if and how much political interest was associated with polarization in the current information environment (Prior, 2007, 2013). While we found a substantial positive effect for affective polarization based on the expression of sympathies or antipathies toward the voters of different parties (in line with expectations and previous research), the effect on political antagonism is surprisingly negative (albeit weak). We understand this crucial difference as being derived from the character and definition of antagonism, which is not necessarily related only to partisan identities, but also to the political issues and the orientation of the politics. As such, political antagonism, in contrast to the concept of affective polarization, is more likely for both people who are more alienated from politics and current affairs and people who are less interested and knowledgeable about politics (and who have lower education).

These results produce three important related ideas. First, it seems that the disagreement between scholars who tend to overestimate the influences of ostensibly contrasting SNS practices related to the fears of the effects of attitudinally homogeneous networks or cross-cutting exposure may be overstated. Our data show that both more ideologically homogeneous networks and perceived discussion disagreement are linked to higher political antagonism, but the effects are moderate or weak. Our second thought is related to political antagonism. We built this concept on the theories of group-based polarization and the antagonization of political conflicts (McCoy & Somer, 2019). According to our data, the practices on SNS that are related to making distinctions between "us" and "them"—like the filtering of friends on the network, engagement in cross-cutting distinctions, and conflict or negativity that often targets specific groups – is linked to the antagonization of society rather than to affective polarization toward political parties in Czechia. We assume that this is the reason that we also identified the effects on both sides of the practices – all of them generally reported the tendency to act in an antagonistic way, even when they were used by most SNS users to varying degrees. Our third limitation considers the way that the direction of the relationships were determined. Since we work with cross-sectional data, it is not advisable for our study to infer any causal effects and their directions (e.g., Spector, 2019). Such an approach can be found in studies that examine the effect of content exposure on polarization with experimental methods or panel data (e.g., Lee, Choi, Kim, & Kim, 2014; Lee, Rojas, & Yamamoto, 2022; Trilling, van Klingeren, & Tsfati, 2017). However, the selected SNS practices investigated in the present study could trigger antagonism and, we cannot rule out the possibility that political antagonism may be the cause, rather than the consequence, of such behavior. This reversed causal pattern would mean that SNS in Czechia simply provides antagonized groups with the space for the expression of polarized behavior.

Besides the issue of causal reasoning, the research has further limitations. Similar to several other studies (Lee, Choi, Kim, & Kim, 2014; Skoric, Zhu, Koc-Michalska, Boulianne, & Bimber, 2021) we rely on self-reported measures, which could be less reliable among different groups of users based on their reflexivity or self-perception. Furthermore, because *perceived discussion disagreement* and the perceived *level of attitudinal homogeneity on SNS* were measured by single items in the previous research studies, we suggest that future research implement multiple-item measurements to increase both reliability and validity. Also, our research assesses polarization as a state of public opinion rather than a process (McCoy & Somer, 2019). And, lastly, we do not differentiate among various SNS, though there is evidence that the effects of various SNS can differ (e.g., Yarchi, Baden, & Kligler-Vilenchik, 2021). Additionally, we admit that the use of SNS can be, for many citizens, only one part of their media repertoire (and we are not able to access the role of SNS algorithms). Despite these limitations, we believe that this research enlightens the understanding of SNS practices in Czechia (as the first study to examine the relationship between SNS use and the polarization within the country), but we also believe that it is a contextually interesting case for polarization research in general.

Disclosure statement

No potential conflict of interest was reported by the author(s).

Funding

The research was funded by the project Political polarization in the Czech Republic: The case of multi-party system (grant no. GA19-24724S) of the Czech Science Foundation.

ORCID

Alena Macková http://orcid.org/0000-0001-5967-5166
Martina Novotná http://orcid.org/0000-0001-5536-4790
Lenka Hrbková http://orcid.org/0000-0003-3755-3322

References

Ali, M., & Altawil, A. (2022). Affective polarization and political engagement in the United States: What factors matter? *Atlantic Journal of Communication*, 1–16. doi:10.1080/15456870.2022.2076856

Anderson, A. A., Yeo, S. K., Brossard, D., Scheufele, D. A., & Xenos, M. A. (2018). Toxic talk: How online incivility can undermine perceptions of media. *International Journal of Public Opinion Research*, 30(1), 156–168. doi:10.1093/ijpor/edw022

Arguedas, A. R., Robertson, C. T., Fletcher, R., & Nielsen, R. K. (2022). *Echo chambers, filter bubbles, and polarization: A literature review*. Oxford: Reuters Institute for the Study of Journalism.

Barnidge, M., Peacock, C., Kim, B., Kim, Y., & Xenos, M. A. (2022). Networks and selective avoidance: How social media networks influence unfriending and other avoidance behaviors. *Social Science Computer Review*, 089443932110696. doi:10.1177/08944393211069628

Beam, M. A., Hutchens, M. J., & Hmielowski, J. D. (2018). Facebook news and (de)polarization: Reinforcing spirals in the 2016 US election. *Information, Communication & Society, 21*(7), 940–958. doi:10.1080/1369118X.2018.1444783

Bode, L. (2016). Pruning the news feed: Unfriending and unfollowing political content on social media. *Research & Politics, 3*(3), 1–8. doi:10.1177/2053168016661873

Brooks, D. J., & Geer, J. G. (2007). Beyond negativity: The effects of incivility on the electorate. *American Journal of Political Science, 51*(1), 1–16. doi:10.1111/j.1540-5907.2007.00233.x

Buchtík, M., Eichler, P., Kopečný, O., Smejkalová, K., & Uhrová, J. (2021). *Jedna Společnost, Různé Světy*. One Society, Different Worlds. Praha: STEM, Masarykova demokratická akademie.

Chen, H. T., Ai, M., & Guo, J. (2022). The effect of cross-cutting exposure on attitude change: Examining the mediating role of response behaviors and the moderating role of openness to diversity and social network homogeneity. *Asian Journal of Communication, 32*(2), 93–110. doi:10.1080/01292986.2021.2022173

Cho, J., Ahmed, S., Kerum, H., Choi, Y. J., & Lee, J. H. (2018). Influencing myself: Self-reinforcement through online political expression. *Communication Research, 45*(1), 83–111. doi:10.1177/0093650216644020

de Vaus, D. (2002). *Analyzing social science data: 50 key problems in data analysis*. London: SAGE Publications.

Druckman, J. N., Gubitz, S. R., Levendusky, M. S., & Lloyd, A. M. (2019). How incivility on partisan media (de)polarizes the electorate. *The Journal of Politics, 81*(1), 291–295. doi:10.1086/699912

Druckman, J., Klar, S., Krupnikov, Y., Levendusky, M., & Ryan, J. (2021). How affective polarization shapes Americans' political beliefs: A study of response to the COVID-19 Pandemic. *Journal of Experimental Political Science, 8*(3), 223–234. doi:10.1017/XPS.2020.28

Duggan, M., & Smith, A. (2016). The political environment on social media. *Pew Research Center*. Retrieved from https://www.pewresearch.org/internet/2016/10/25/the-political-environment-on-social-media/.

Flaxman, S., Goel, S., & Rao, J. M. (2016). Filter bubbles, echo chambers, and online news consumption. *Public Opinion Quarterly, 80*(S1), 298–320. doi:10.1093/poq/nfw006

Fletcher, R., Cornia, A., & Nielsen, R. K. (2020). How polarized are online and offline news audiences? A comparative analysis of twelve countries. *The International Journal of Press/politics, 25*(2), 169–195. doi:10.1177/1940161219892768

Garrett, R. K. (2009). Echo chambers online?: Politically motivated selective exposure among Internet news users. *Journal of Computer-Mediated Communication, 14*(2), 265–285. doi:10.1111/j.1083-6101.2009.01440.x

Garrett, R. K., Gvirsman, S. D., Johnson, B. K., Tsfati, Y., Neo, R., & Dal, A. (2014). Implications of pro- and counter attitudinal information exposure for affective polarization. *Human Communication Research, 40*(3), 309–332. doi:10.1111/hcre.12028

Gidron, N., Adams, J., & Horne, W. (2020). *American affective polarization in comparative perspective*. Cambridge: Cambridge University Press.

Goyanes, M., Borah, P., & Gil De Zúñiga, H. (2021). Social media filtering and democracy: Effects of social media news use and uncivil political discussions on social media unfriending. *Computers in Human Behavior, 120*, 120. doi:10.1016/j.chb.2021.106759

Hameleers, M., van der Meer, T., & Vliegenthart, R. (2022). Civilized truths, hateful lies? Incivility and hate speech in false information – evidence from fact-checked statements in the US. *Information, Communication & Society, 25*(11), 1596–1613. doi:10.1080/1369118X.2021.1874038

Hayes, A. (2022). *Introduction to mediation, moderation, and conditional process analysis* (3rd ed.). Guilford Press.

Herbst, S. (2010). *Rude democracy: Civility and incivility in American politics*. Temple University Press.

Hiaeshutter-Rice, D., & Hawkins, I. (2022). The language of extremism on social media: An examination of posts, comments, and themes on reddit. *Frontiers in Political Science, 4*, 4. doi:10.3389/fpos.2022.805008

Hwang, H., Kim, Y., & Huh, C. U. (2014). Seeing is believing: Effects of uncivil online debate on political polarization and expectations of deliberation. *Journal of Broadcasting & Electronic Media, 58*(4), 621–633. doi:10.1080/08838151.2014.966365

Irwin, J. R., & McClelland, G. H. (2001). Misleading Heuristics and moderated multiple regression models. *Journal of Marketing Research, 38*(1), 100–109. doi:10.1509/jmkr.38.1.100.18835

Iyengar, S., Lelkes, Y., Levendusky, M., Malhotra, N., & Westwood, S. J. (2019). The origins and consequences of affective polarization in the United States. *Annual Review of Political Science, 22*(1), 129–146. doi:10.1146/annurev-polisci-051117-073034

Iyengar, S., Sood, G., & Lelkes, Y. (2012). Affect, not ideology: A social identity perspective on polarization. *Public Opinion Quarterly, 76*(3), 405–431. doi:10.1093/poq/nfs038

Iyengar, S., & Westwood, S. J. (2015). Fear and loathing across party lines: New evidence on group polarization. *American Journal of Political Science, 59*(3), 690–707. doi:10.1111/ajps.12152

Jamieson, K. H., & Cappella, J. N. (2008). *Echo chamber: Rush Limbaugh and the conservative media establishment*. New York: Oxford University Press.

Johnson, B. K., Neo, R. L., Heinen, M. E. M., Smits, L., & van Veen, C. (2020). Issues, involvement, and influence: Effects of selective exposure and sharing on polarization and participation. *Computers in Human Behavior, 104*, 1–12. doi:10.1016/j.chb.2019.09.031

Kalmoe, N., & Mason, L. (2019). *Lethal mass partisanship: Prevalence, correlates, & electoral consequences* [Paper presentation]. In American Political Science Association's Annual Meeting, Boston, MA. https://www.dropbox.com/s/bs618kn939gq0de/Kalmoe%20&%20Mason%20APSAVol.202018.

Kim, J. W., Guess, A., Nyhan, B., & Reifler, J. (2021). The distorting prism of social media: How self-selection and exposure to incivility fuel online comment toxicity. *Journal of Communication*, 71(6), 922–946. doi:10.1093/joc/jqab034

Kim, B., Wang, Y., Lee, J., & Kim, Y. (2022). Unfriending effects: Testing contrasting indirect-effects relationships between exposure to hate speech on political talk via social media unfriending. *Computers in Human Behavior*, 137, 107414. doi:10.1016/j.chb.2022.107414

Knobloch-Westerwick, S., Mothes, C., Johnson, B. K., Westerwick, A., & Donsbach, W. (2015). Political online information searching in Germany and the United States: Confirmation Bias, source credibility, and attitude impacts. *Journal of Communication*, 65(3), 489–511. doi:10.1111/jcom.12154

Kruse, L. M., Norris, D. R., & Flinchum, J. R. (2018). Social media as a public sphere? Politics on social Media. *The Sociological Quarterly*, 59(1), 62–84. doi:10.1080/00380253.2017.1383143

Kubin, E., & von Sikorski, C. (2021). The role of (social) media in political polarization: A systematic review. *Annals of the International Communication Association*, 45(3), 188–206. doi:10.1080/23808985.2021.1976070

Lee, J. K., Choi, J., Kim, C., & Kim, Y. (2014). Social media, network heterogeneity, and opinion polarization. *Journal of Communication*, 64(4), 702–722. doi:10.1111/jcom.12077

Lee, S., Rojas, H., & Yamamoto, M. (2022). Social Media, Messaging Apps, and affective polarization in the United States and Japan. *Mass Communication and Society*, 25(5), 673–697. doi:10.1080/15205436.2021.1953534

Lelkes, Y., Sood, G., & Iyengar, S. (2017). The hostile audience: The effect of access to broadband internet on partisan affect. *American Journal of Political Science*, 61(1), 5–20. doi:10.1111/ajps.12237

Lu, Y., Heatherly, K. A., & Lee, J. K. (2016). Cross-cutting exposure on social networking sites: The effects of SNS discussion disagreement on political participation. *Computers in Human Behavior*, 59, 74–81. doi:10.1016/j.chb.2016.01.030

Macková, A., Novotná, M., Procházková, K., Macek, J., & Hrbková, L. (2021). Češi na sítích, důvěra a polarizace v době pandemie. [Czechs on social networking sites, trust and polarization in pandemic]. Retrieved from https://www.researchgate.net/publication/352708609_Cesi_na_sitich_duvera_a_polarizace_v_dobe_pandemie_vyzkumna_zprava_2021

Mason, L. (2018). *Uncivil agreement: How politics became our identity*. University of Chicago Press.

McCoy, J., & Somer, M. (2019). Toward a theory of pernicious polarization and how it harms democracies: Comparative evidence and possible remedies. *The Annals of the American Academy of Political and Social Science*, 681(1), 234–271. doi:10.1177/0002716218818782

Mouffe, C. (2011). *On the political*. Routledge.

Mutz, D. C. (2006). *Hearing the other side: Deliberative versus participatory democracy*. New York, NY: Cambridge University Press.

Neely, S. R. (2021). Politically motivated avoidance in social networks: A study of Facebook and the 2020 Presidential election. *Social Media + Society*, 7(4), 205630512110554. doi:10.1177/20563051211055438

Newman, N., Fletcher, R., Schulz, A., Andi, S., Robertson, C. T., & Nielsen, R. K. (2021). *Reuters Institute Digital News Report 2021*. Oxford: Reuters Institute for the Study of Journalism.

Nordbrandt, M. (2021). Affective polarization in the digital age: Testing the direction of the relationship between social media and users' feelings for out-group parties. *New Media & Society*, 0(0), 146144482110443. doi:10.1177/14614448211044393

Orhan, Y. E. (2022). The relationship between affective polarization and democratic backsliding: Comparative evidence. *Democratization*, 29(4), 714–735. doi:10.1080/13510347.2021.2008912

Otto, L. P., Lecheler, S., & Schuck, A. R. (2020). Is context the key? The (non-)differential effects of mediated incivility in three European Countries. *Political Communication*, 37(1), 88–107. doi:10.1080/10584609.2019.1663324

Prior, M. (2007). *Post-broadcast democracy: How media choice increases inequality in political involvement and polarizes elections*. New York: Cambridge University Press.

Prior, M. (2013). Media and political polarization. *Annual Review of Political Science*, 16(1), 101–127. doi:10.1146/annurev-polisci-100711-135242

Rainie, L., & Smith, A. (2012). Politics on Social Networking Sites. *Pew Research Centre*. Retrieved from 14 April 2023 https://www.pewresearch.org/internet/2012/09/04/politics-on-social-networking-sites/

Reiljan, A. (2020). 'Fear and loathing across party lines' (also) in Europe: Affective polarisation in European party systems. *European Journal of Political Research*, 59(2), 376–396. doi:10.1111/1475-6765.12351

Reiljan, A., & Ryan, A. (2021). Ideological tripolarization, partisan tribalism and institutional trust: The foundations of affective polarization in the Swedish multiparty system. *Scandinavian Political Studies*, 44(2), 195–219. doi:10.1111/1467-9477.12194

Rekker, R., & Harteveld, E. (2022, Oct). Understanding factual belief polarization: The role of trust, political sophistication, and affective polarization. *Acta Politica*, 20, 1–28. doi:10.1057/s41269-022-00265-4

Rudolph, T. J., & Hetherington, M. J. (2021). Affective polarization in political and nonpolitical settings. *International Journal of Public Opinion Research*, 33(3), 591–606. doi:10.1093/ijpor/edaa040

Simonovits, G., McCoy, J., & Littvay, L. (2022). Democratic hypocrisy and out-group threat: Explaining citizen support for democratic erosion. *The Journal of Politics*, 84(3). doi:10.1086/719009

Skoric, M. M., Zhu, Q., Koc-Michalska, K., Boulianne, S., & Bimber, B. (2021). Selective avoidance on social media: A comparative study of Western Democracies. *Social Science Computer Review, 40*(5), 1–18. doi:10.1177/08944393211005468

Skoric, M. M., Zhu, Q., & Lin, J. H. T. (2018). What predicts selective avoidance on social media? A study of political unfriending in Hong Kong and Taiwan. *The American Behavioral Scientist, 62*(8), 1097–1115. doi:10.1177/0002764218764251

Skovsgaard, M., Shehata, A., & Strömbäck, J. (2016). Opportunity structures for selective exposure. Investigating selective exposure and learning in Swedish Election Campaigns using panel survey data. *The International Journal of Press/politics, 21*(4), 527–546. doi:10.1177/1940161216658157

Slačálek, O. (2021). Czech republic: Populism without culture wars? In P. Barša, Z. Hesová, & O. Slačálek (Eds.), *Central Europe culture wars: Beyond post-communism and populism* (pp. 158–202). Prague: Humanitas.

Spector, P. E. (2019). Do not cross me: Optimizing the use of cross-sectional designs. *Journal of Business and Psychology, 34*(2), 125–137. doi:10.1007/s10869-018-09613-8

Steppat, D., Castro Herrero, L., & Esser, F. (2021). Selective exposure in different political information environments– How media fragmentation and polarization shape congruent news use. *European Journal of Communication, 37*(1), 82–102. doi:10.1177/02673231211012141

Štětka, V. (2021). Czech Republic. Reuters Institute Digital News Report 2021. Reuters Institute for the Study of Journalism. Retrieved from https://reutersinstitute.politics.ox.ac.uk/digital-news-report/2021/czech-republic

Stroud, N. J. (2010). Polarization and partisan selective exposure. *Journal of Communication, 60*(3), 556–576. doi:10.1111/j.1460-2466.2010.01497.x

Suhay, E., Bello-Pardo, E., & Maurer, B. (2018). The polarizing effects of online partisan criticism: Evidence from two experiments. *The International Journal of Press/politics, 23*(1), 95–115. doi:10.1177/1940161217740697

Törnberg, P. (2022). How digital media drive affective polarization through partisan sorting. *Proceedings of the National Academy of Sciences, 119*(42), e2207159119. doi:10.1073/pnas.2207159119

Törnberg, P., Andersson, C., Lindgren, K., Banisch, S., & Mahmoud, A. B. (2021). Modeling the emergence of affective polarization in the social media society. *PLoS One, 16*(10), e0258259. doi:10.1371/journal.pone.0258259

Tóth, F., Mihelj, S., Štětka, V., & Kondor, K. (2022). A media repertoires approach to selective exposure: News consumption and political polarization in Eastern Europe. *The International Journal of Press/politics*, 1–25. doi:10.1177/19401612211072552

Trilling, D., van Klingeren, M., & Tsfati, Y. (2017). Selective exposure, political polarization, and possible mediators: Evidence from the Netherlands. *International Journal of Public Opinion Research, 29*(2), 189–213.

Vaccari, C., & Valeriani, A. (2021). *Outside the bubble: Social media and political participation in Western Democracies.* Oxford: Oxford University Press.

Vachudova, M. A. (2019). From competition to polarization in Central Europe: How populists change party systems and the European Union. *Polity, 51*(4), 689–706. doi:10.1086/705704

Vochocová, L. (2020). 'Frustrated women invite the immigrants to Europe': Intersection of (xeno-) racism and sexism in online discussions on gender aspects of immigration. *European Journal of Cultural Studies, 24*(1), 333–349. doi:10.1177/1367549420973207

Wagner, M. (2021). Affective polarization in multiparty systems. *Electoral Studies, 69*, 102199. doi:10.1016/j.electstud.2020.102199

Weber, M., Viehmann, C., Ziegele, M., & Schemer, C. (2020). Online hate does not stay online – how implicit and explicit attitudes mediate the effect of civil negativity and hate in user comments on prosocial behavior. *Computers in Human Behavior, 104*, 106192. doi:10.1016/j.chb.2019.106192

Weeks, B. E., Lane, D. S., Kim, D. H., Lee, S. S. & Kwak, N. (2017). Incidental Exposure, Selective Exposure, and Political Information Sharing: Integrating Online Exposure Patterns and Expression on Social Media. *Journal of Computer-Mediated Communication, 22*(6), 363–379. doi:10.1111/jcc4.12199

Westerwick, A., Johnson, B. K., & Knobloch-Westerwick, S. (2017). Confirmation biases in selective exposure to political online information: Source bias vs. content bias. *Communication Monographs, 84*(3), 343–364. doi:10.1080/03637751.2016.1272761

Westfall, J., Van Boven, L., Chambers, J. R., & Judd, C. M. (2015). Perceiving political polarization in the United States: Party identity strength and attitude extremity exacerbate the perceived Partisan divide. *Perspectives on Psychological Science, 10*(2), 145–158. doi:10.1177/1745691615569849

Westwood, S. J., Peterson, E., & Lelkes, Y. (2019). Are there still limits on partisan prejudice? *Public Opinion Quarterly, 83*(3), 584–597. doi:10.1093/poq/nfz034

Winter, S., & Krämer, N. C. (2016). Who's right: The author or the audience? Effects of user comments and ratings on the perception of online science articles. *Communications, 41*(3). doi:10.1515/commun-2016-0008

Wojcieszak, M., de Leeuw, S., Menchen-Trevino, E., Lee, S., Huang-Isherwood, K. M., & Weeks, B. (2021). No polarization from partisan news: Over-time evidence from trace data. *The International Journal of Press/politics*, 1–26. doi:10.1177/19401612211047194

Yang, J., Barnidge, M., & Rojas, H. (2017). The politics of "unfriending": User filtration in response to political disagreement on social media. *Computers in Human Behavior, 70*, 22–29. doi:10.1016/j.chb.2016.12.079

Yarchi, M., Baden, C., & Kligler-Vilenchik, N. (2021). Political polarization on the digital sphere: A cross-platform, over-time analysis of interactional, positional, and affective polarization on social Media. *Political Communication, 38*(1–2), 98–139. doi:10.1080/10584609.2020.1785067

Zhu, Q., & Skoric, M. M. (2022). Political implications of disconnection on social media: A study of politically motivated unfriending. *New Media & Society, 24*(12), 2659–2679.

Soros's soldiers, slackers, and pioneers with no expertise? Discursive exclusion of environmental youth activists from the digital public sphere in Hungary and Czechia

Lenka Vochocová, Jana Rosenfeldová, Anna Vancsó, and Annamária Neag

ABSTRACT
Our paper fills the gap in research on online public representations of politically active youth by focusing on the discursive representations of Fridays for Future, a youth-led climate movement, in user generated content in Czechia and Hungary. By employing the childism approach, we aim to contribute to a better understanding of the exclusion of youth from the public sphere. Our qualitative analysis identified two exclusionary strategies: 1) normative roles attributed to youth; 2) labeling youth for allegedly holding aberrant values. We stress both similarities and differences in the two countries of Central and Eastern Europe, reflecting this region's historico-political features.

Introduction

Children's active citizenship remains controversial in many contemporary democracies and the position of children and youth in political participation is still a matter of symbolic contestation (Pickard, 2019). Youth activists gained special attention in many of the Central and Eastern European countries (CEE), the focus of our study, in the late 1980s as "harbingers of historic events"– they acted as a mobilizing force against the socialist or communist totalitarian rule (Tymowski, 1994, p. 115). Approximately in the same historical period, academics in the West started to be concerned with what they labeled the crisis of democracy, explained as a decline of trust in traditional parliamentary systems among citizens, mainly the younger generations (Coleman & Blumler, 2009).

However, the rapid development of digital technologies was perceived by some as a mobilizing tool, as it promised to provide young citizens with new tools to facilitate their political participation and involvement in social movements (Dahlgren, 2005). But online spaces also provide adult citizens with the opportunity to produce competing discourses on youth political participation and even completely deny the political action of youth (Alexander, Petray, & McDowall, 2022; Von Zabern & Tulloch, 2021).

The online sphere thus represents a natural space for young digital natives to express themselves politically but is also heavily populated by adults and their discursive power. Given this dynamic character of the online environment, and reflecting on the lack of similar studies, we find it useful to address the intergenerational contestation in the online sphere outlined above by focusing on the strategies employed by adults to exclude youth[1] from political participation. To theoretically grasp the issue, we combine three research traditions from the field of political communication.

Firstly, we build upon theories of political-discursive inclusion (Ferree, Gamson, Gerhards, & Rucht, 2002); more specifically, studies explaining historical patterns of discursive exclusion of marginalized groups from the public sphere (women, people of color) and showing similarities between these patterns and the strategies of excluding youth from public participation (Kulynych, 2001). The approach of "childism" (Wall, 2019) serves as an overarching conceptual framework to understand the normative assumptions related to the role of youth in political matters.

Secondly, to better understand the online space as a sphere where youth and adults contest their views, we borrow from theories of online deliberative expression or "e-expression" as a recent form of civic digital participation (Casteltrione, 2015;

Gibson & Cantijoch, 2013), playing an important role in the negotiation of the public issues, but also in the polarization of public opinion (Szabo, Kmetty, & Molnár, 2021).

Thirdly, as part of our interpretive context in the discussion part of this paper, we reflect on recent concerns about the growing anti-liberal tendencies in Europe, namely in the CEE region (Bustikova & Guasti, 2017), as a useful frame helping us understand the dominant aspects of citizen representations of the youth activism.

To study the means of exclusion of politically active youth from participation, we focus on the case of Fridays for Future's (FFF) climate-change oriented civic activities. The emergence of the movement is linked to Swedish climate activist Greta Thunberg, who began protesting outside the Swedish Parliament in August 2018 as a then 15-year-old, demanding that politicians take stronger action against further global warming. Through her regular Friday "School Strike for Climate," she inspired young people worldwide to join the FFF movement, whose largest global strike, held on 20 September 2019, was attended by 4 million people in 155 countries (Fridays for Future, 2021). FFF was selected as it provides young citizens in the CEE countries an opportunity to join political action, influencing both the global political sphere and the domestic political culture. It also represents one of the strongest global civic movements led by youth and relies extensively on digital communication tools to engage with the public.

We are specifically focusing on distinct forms of exclusion of political actors related to age. Social protests tend to be represented negatively in the mediated public sphere, irrespective of the age of the activists, a pattern widely described in the literature as a protest paradigm (Gil-Lopez, 2021; McLeod & Hertog, 1999). Our aim is to demonstrate how, beyond those well-described tendencies to represent climate activism as problematic or related to specific ideologies (Castillo Esparcia & López Gómez, 2021), age becomes another significant intersecting characteristic in the discursive exclusion from political participation.

Our study is based on the analysis of user-generated content published in the comment section of mainstream online daily news and weeklies in Czechia and Hungary in 2019 and 2021, when the main public activities of FFF in the region took part. Those two countries share the post-socialist, post-transformation historical context of the CEE region. Both adopted the representative approach to the public sphere in the 1990s with its low support for citizens' public political participation (Ferree, Gamson, Gerhards, & Rucht, 2002). Moreover, the two countries share the recent trend visible mainly in the CEE region, described as the proliferation of anti-liberal stances in politics and among citizens (Bustikova & Guasti, 2017). It creates a specific political environment promoting conservative values, including those related to civic and, specifically, youth political participation. However, the level of anti-liberalism in the two countries differs significantly, as do their transformation trajectories, current political representation and media environments. The Hungarian media landscape is rather bipolar than plural (as in the case of the Czech Republic, where media are also independent from direct political influence), with increased ownership concentration and active governmental influence over the media market (Bátorfy & Urbán, 2020). Whereas in the Czech context, anti-communism related to the country's past still resonates in the public debates, the Christian-conservative ideology dominates the political discourse in Hungary. Due to these specifics and the fact that the two countries differ significantly in some of our key empirical findings, this country comparison contributes to our theoretical understanding of the importance of the underlying historical, political and cultural reasons for such differences.

Childism in the context of exclusion of various actors from the public sphere

Different approaches to the public sphere connect the inclusion of actors with distinct normative expectations. The usual starting point in thinking about inclusivity in the public sphere is the seminal work of Habermas (1989), who formulated the ideal of the modern public sphere with its proclaimed, yet widely criticized inclusivity (McLaughlin, 1999). However, in addition to the Habermasian discursive model, Ferree et al. offer three other models of the public sphere in modern democracies – liberal representative, participatory representative and constructionist (Ferree, Gamson, Gerhards, & Rucht, 2002). Each of the four models conceptualizes participation in the public sphere differently, but three of them can be considered inclusionary, supporting the highest possible "participation of citizens in the public decisions that affect their lives" (ibid, 295). On the contrary, representative liberal theory prefers low public participation. It models a system based on "passive, quiescent" citizens, "limited in their political participation in a well-functioning, party-led democracy" (Ferree, Gamson, Gerhards, & Rucht, 2002, p. 291).

Neither Ferree, Gamson, Gerhards, and Rucht (2002) nor the models they describe mention specifically youth as civic or political actors. Despite this, we find their typology highly suitable for the theoretical context of our two national cases. It clearly explains the tendency of the representative liberal theory to exclude citizens from active participation in the public sphere, whereas the participatory liberal and discursive models would embrace popular inclusion (ibid, 300) "approximating a general will" (ibid, 295) and the constructionist theory would even "privilege the voices of those who are marginalized in society, since they can offer the 'double vision' of those who are 'outsiders within' the system" (ibid, 307).

Czech and Hungarian politics have followed the model of representative democracy during their transformation into democratic systems and have not included many participatory elements since then. The skepticism of the representative liberal theory about the possible contribution of "ordinary citizens" in policy issues can thus provide us with a better understanding of the civic arguments excluding a specific group of citizens, the youth, from political participation. As Ferree et al. summarize, the representative liberal theory suggests that citizens do not need to participate in public political debates and "public life is actually better off if they don't" as "ordinary citizens are poorly informed and have no serious interest in public affairs and are generally ill-equipped for political participation," mainly because they lack the expertise necessary for decision making (Ferree, Gamson, Gerhards, & Rucht, 2002, pp. 290–291).

Apart from excluding non-expert, "ordinary" citizens from political decision-making, the representative liberal theory also refuses passion and emotions in public deliberation. Unlike in participatory theories, emotionality and rationality "are defined as inherently contradictory" in the representative tradition, rationality represents a norm and, as a result, "all impassioned appeals" are considered suspect (Ferree, Gamson, Gerhards, & Rucht, 2002, p. 294). Although we share the concerns of those afraid that the ill-informed, emotion-driven participation can be very problematic (ibid, 298), in the context of this research we are more concerned, in accordance with the constructionist theory introduced by Ferree et al., with how the refusal of emotions can be mobilized to bar non-established actors from public participation.

Historically, labeling groups of actors (such as women, people from ethnic minorities etc.) as emotional, rather than rational, has been used to exclude them from public and political participation or citizenship as such (Kulynych, 2001). According to Kulynych (2001), the same tendency occurs with youth and their political identity. In the context of deliberative democracy, Kulynych believes that youth "offer a unique social perspective that must be included in public deliberation that seeks the most just solutions to common problems" (Kulynych, 2001, p. 232). However, she concludes, the possibility to identify as political actors is not available to youth and the exclusion of the underaged is even one of the constitutive aspects of the public sphere. It is based, among others, on the discursive construction and cultural understanding of the distinction between public and private and the positioning of youth in the latter. This, together with arguments that "[p]olitical rights apply to mature individuals only, not to people in all stages of their development," that youth are in a dependent position or that their capacity for rationality is weak, is a clear argumentation pattern which bears "a remarkable similarity to many of the arguments against the provision of citizenship rights to women and slaves" (Kulynych, 2001, pp. 234–235).

In this vein, we embrace, for our argument, Wall's (2019) concept of "childism" as an apt critique of the "deeply engrained adultism" (Wall, 2019, p. 1). Childism has its roots in childhood studies, and it is comparable to movements such as feminism or ableism that aim to critically assess societal contexts. By building on post-structuralism but moving forward to what Wall (2019) calls reconstructionism, childism aims not only to understand and include children's experiences, but also to critique adultism in society and academic research as well (Wall, 2019, p. 10).

In this paper, we use childism as a lens to understand and perhaps also challenge deep-seated normative assumptions of the role children and youth should play in political matters in the CEE region. We also follow childism's stress on the arbitrary definition of the exclusion criteria by actors who are privileged in participation – adult online discussants in our case. Furthermore, through the lens of childism, we tend to understand parallels between the exclusion of youth from politics and the historical (and to some extent still ongoing) exclusion of women and other groups, especially through strategies related to the exclusion of emotions from political participation and the emphasis on expertise.

The negative portrayal of youth activism in media

Existing literature on media discourses on youth activism describes various ways of excluding young activists from political participation and undermining their political agency (Alexander, Petray, & McDowall, 2022; Bergmann & Ossewaarde, 2020; Von Zabern & Tulloch, 2021).

Alexander, Petray, and McDowall (2022) summarize some of these strategies within "anticipatory narratives," suggesting that children are not yet prepared to intervene in the adult world, and should therefore follow "model obedience and conformity" (p. 7) and develop appropriately into adults before being awarded political agency. First, there is a consensus across studies on the high importance of the "skipping school" theme, specifically in the media coverage of recent FFF activities organized during Friday school hours. Von Zabern and Tulloch (2021) refer to a "truancy frame," Mayes and Hartup (2021) identify a "rebellious truants" frame, and Bergmann and Ossewaarde (2020) claim that the media compare strikers to "absentees." The media raise the issue of compulsory education (Bergmann & Ossewaarde, 2020; Huttunen & Albrecht, 2021) and construct young strikers as "deviant rule-breakers who would benefit more from formal education than activism" (Alexander, Petray, & McDowall, 2022, p. 107). The media thus reframe the FFF actions as a political-educational issue (Von Zabern & Tulloch, 2021, p. 41) and create "the pseudo conflict within the conflict: voices debating whether it is ok for children to strike instead of attending school" (Jacobsson, 2021, p. 488).

Second, young activists are often represented as insufficiently competent or educated to be considered valid political actors. Mayes and Hartup (2021, p. 1) identified a frame of "ignorant zealots," Bergmann and Ossewaarde (2020) suggest that the German media represent young activists as "pupils" and "dreamers," and Jacobsson (2021) refers to the infantilization of their protests. In this way, the media again reframe the debate toward "the youthfulness of the activists" (Bergmann & Ossewaarde, 2020, pp. 272–273), promoting their subordination and creating "an inferior position for them based on their alleged ignorance."

Lastly, Huttunen and Albrecht (2021) identified "the sustainable lifestyle frame" in the Finnish media, recommending that youth protestors be individually responsible or, in more negative terms, ridiculing and blaming them for their hypocrisy. "Lifestyle choices were not only seen as a possible way to create political change but rather as something [...] they should do before they could even have a say in more traditional arenas of politics" (Huttunen & Albrecht, 2021, p. 51).

Apart from what Alexander, Petray, and McDowall (2022) summarize as "anticipatory narratives," they also identified "protectionist narratives," emphasizing the need to protect children from adult issues. According to them, and following the protectionist nature of childhood, child activists are often presented as being exploited by adults for their political agenda (Von Zabern & Tulloch, 2021). In their comparative study, Bosi, Lavizzari, and Voli (2020, p. 620) found similar portrayals of young people in center-right and center-left newspapers, suggesting that "the social construction of the concept of youth dominates in the adult world, regardless of any political differences." Therefore, it seems that children and youth are considered a homogeneous group, with childhood being "the primary factor affecting political participation" (Alexander, Petray, & McDowall, 2022, p. 108).

This paper aims to expand academic knowledge on how politically active youth are excluded in public discourse by examining citizens' perspectives as expressed in online news media comment sections. A review of existing literature shows that research has so far focused on portraying young protesters in news media (Bergmann & Ossewaarde, 2020; Von Zabern & Tulloch, 2021) and Twitter (Huttunen & Albrecht, 2020), while studies examining representations of youth activism in user-generated content are still lacking. We consider interactive online platforms (news comment sections, social network site discussions) an important part of the public and political debate as they provide citizens with the opportunity to express their opinions and exchange ideas (Nagar, 2011). This user-generated content can complement or even contest journalistic discourses (Rowe, 2015), providing an opportunity to observe the mechanisms of exclusion of young activists from political participation.

Methodology

Research questions

We follow the theoretical approaches summarized above, informing us that a) youth interests and concerns are discursively neglected in various ways, including in relation to issues of high importance to them, such as the future of the climate; b) interactive online platforms play an important role in the public debate on political issues (Nagar, 2011) and may complement or even contest journalistic discourses (Rowe, 2015). Thus, to compensate for the lack of research combining these two perspectives and to contribute specifically to the theories of exclusion of various actors from the public sphere, we formulate the following research question:

RQ1: *What strategies do online discussants employ and what arguments do they offer to exclude FFF activist youth from the public sphere?*

To identify both similar patterns and differences in the civic approach to FFF activities in the two CEE countries analyzed, Hungary and Czechia, we formulated the following research question leading our comparative analysis:

RQ2: *What are the differences and similarities in the patterns of discussants' representations of the FFF movement in Hungary and Czechia?*

Data collection and analysis procedures

This article draws on an analysis of user-generated content published in the comment section of mainstream online daily news and weeklies or their Facebook pages in Czechia and Hungary in 2019 and 2021. Our research sample was obtained through a multistage procedure. By using Sentione's social listening tool and predefined keywords ("Fridays for Future," "FFF," "Greta Thunberg," "climate strike," "strike for climate") in respective languages, we searched for all content in three two-month periods, when the main public activities of FFF in the region took part. These were March-April 2019 (the first Global Climate Strike on March 15), September-October 2019 (Global Week for Climate Action), and March-April 2021 (online Global Climate Strike).

In the second step, we selected a diverse sample of media for each country, considering their online circulation range and their diversity in terms of editorial style and political leaning. We combined mainstream dailies and weeklies, alternative media platforms with interest in environmental issues, and popular tabloids in each country. Since some online news websites do not allow discussions or invite readers to comment on their articles on Facebook, we included both online news websites and news portals' Facebook pages. In total, we selected 14 media outlets, seven from Czechia and seven from Hungary. We identified the five most commented articles or Facebook posts for each medium in each of the three selected periods. The research sample consisted of the comments related to the selected articles. In determining the final size of our sample, we followed the logic of theoretical saturation (Strauss & Corbin, 1998). For each country, we started reading the first 30 comments related to each selected article. Given that the main theoretical context of our study lies in the exclusion of various groups of actors from political participation, only comments which are clearly contributing to the exclusion of youth from the political debate on the climate crisis were analyzed- i.e., those which question the activities of youth or deny youth the right to participate in the topic politically.[2] We continued until the saturation point was reached (1200 comments in Czechia and 900 comments in Hungary[3]).

We analyzed the comments applying the first two coding procedures from grounded theory – open and axial coding (Strauss & Corbin, 1998) to inductively explore ways of excluding youth and children from public or political participation. We were led by the theoretical approaches outlined above as concepts increasing our theoretical sensitivity (Strauss & Corbin, 1998). In this way, we could also systematically compare the two countries and see the structure of the categories and their relations. As we did not find major differences in the means of exclusion in the comments related to various media outlets within the countries, beyond the style and rhetorical devices used, we focus on comparing the country differences in exclusionary strategies, not the negligible differences within the national user-generated content.

Results

Brief results summary

Online discussants in both countries exclude youth from the public sphere in two general ways (see Figure 1). First, they do so by *referring to normative roles* attributed to youth in society, by denying youth the expert, experienced and rational position allegedly necessary for political participation (a pattern similar to the exclusion of women or racial groups in history- see Kulynych, 2001, for comparison). Second, they exclude youth from political participation by *referring to aberrant values* allegedly held by youth and thus exclude them using various labeling strategies reflecting broader ideological trends in the region, mainly anti-liberalism (Bustikova & Guasti, 2017). Whereas the first general category (roles) highlights differences related to age (different roles attributed to adults and youth), the second one, employing value-based labeling, consists of strategies polarizing the society along ideological lines and relates mainly to the allegedly different *values* held by the striking youth. These values contested by the discussants in our sample are mainly related to liberalism and are refuted in the discussants' clearly anti-liberal discourse.

Some of the labels identified in our material (in our second general category) relate to a more

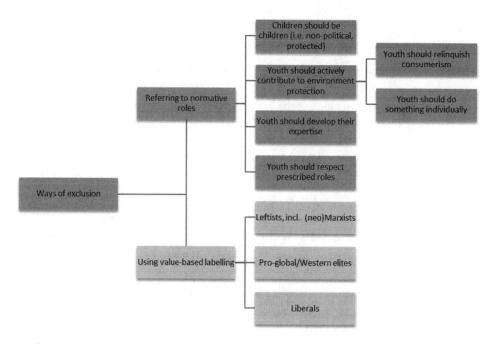

Figure 1. Strategies of exclusion.

general refusal of climate activism as "leftist" or "liberal" and may stem from negative perceptions of activism as such (Castillo Esparcia & López Gómez, 2021; McLeod & Hertog, 1999). However, age or age-related characteristics (naive, dependent, manipulated due to their immaturity etc.) are, with a few minor exceptions, stressed in these cases as another discriminatory characteristic preventing the FFF activists from being accepted as relevant political actors.

In the following sections, we describe the categories sketched above and their subcategories in detail and focus on key differences in our national samples.[4]

"Plant trees, reduce consumption and study instead of yelling in the streets:" normative roles attributed to the striking youth

The first general category represents a set of normative expectations related to the *roles* of youth in society (what they are and are not supposed to do). Young activists are represented as those who should a) be children in the first place and let the adults protect them, b) protect the environment through their individual environmentally friendly activity rather than through direct collective action, c) develop their rationality and expertise, i.e., study. These three types of activities are represented as the only proper ones for youth who aim to save the planet. Striking or other political activity is, on the contrary, represented as inappropriate. Arguments in this category contribute to a clear polarization of the societies along the axis of age (different roles attributed to adults and youth).

Asking youth to focus on being children instead of being involved in political action

Comments in the first subcategory recommend youth to *"enjoy childhood instead of interfering in such things"* (CZ), to *"be kids and enjoy life"* (HU) or express their concerns about youth losing their childhood. In the Hungarian data, this concern with youth enjoying the careless phase of life builds upon the construction of childhood as in need of adult protection, stressing that protecting youth from entering the political arena should be the responsibility of their parents. We can thus witness a strategy excluding youth from public participation, which is, however, masked as their protection – a pattern which can be found in the history of exclusion of women and other marginalized groups from the public sphere.

> *"She [Greta] looks like my daughter. If she was my kid, I would not let her carry the problems of the world on her shoulders at this young age! (HU)*

Allowing youth to enter the public sphere is represented by the Hungarian discussants as a direct attempt to destroy family ties and strong family relations, since, according to this conservative perspective, politically active youth show little respect for adults and older generations and sometimes even argue against them in their attempts to save the planet:

> *"Here, even preschoolers are fighting against their parents. This is a new kind of Crusade ... Here, their own people, their own grandparents are their enemies ... "* (HU)

Asking youth to be active in direct environmental protection, not in politics

The second category related to prescribed roles is divided into two subcategories delimiting youth to specific desired activities (instead of protesting): giving up consumerism to save the environment and doing something for the planet individually. The theme of youth giving up technology, traveling, comfort and consumption is very strong in the comments and represents a typical call for individual responsibility in relation to the climate crisis discourse. These comments can be read as a sign of an intergenerational conflict in terms of who really is responsible for the climate crisis. However, given the overall climate awareness of the striking youth, we tend to interpret this tendency to teach them about necessary private action for the climate as a strategy to shift attention away from their political demands for systematic changes and toward their own alleged contribution to the climate crisis:

> *"What these kids can do for the environment: [...]to go to school on foot for one or two kilometers and save fuel this way; [...] to save electricity, to reduce the temperature at home and warm themselves up with movement or work ... "* (CZ)

"They replace [their phone] each year with the latest model. And drive their daddy's diesel . . . " (HU)

In relation to this strategy, youth are typically called hypocritical for being part of the consumer society and contributing to it strongly. Thus, their alleged lifestyle is represented as in conflict with what they demonstrate for or against:

"On the one hand, the young destroyers of the environment protest, on the other, they are not willing to give up all the 'achievements' of the modern world, which cause the destruction of the environment." (CZ)

"The main problem lies in the consumer society, but she [Greta Thunberg] doesn't mention it, why? Because she is also part of it!" (HU)

The recommendation that youth replace striking or political activity with direct pro-environmental activities is a strong pattern in the data. Whereas we consider private action an important part of politics,[5] what is noteworthy in our data is that the call for private action is used to exclude youth from publicly visible political action (striking). Most comments in this category ask the youth to do something for the planet individually or "start with themselves" *instead of* participating in a strike. Thus, private political activity is not represented as a necessary complement to a public one, but as its desired replacement, the only appropriate type of political activity for youth. Youth are asked to *"go plant trees instead of striking"* (CZ), to *"clean the ocean"* (CZ) or to *"collect garbage"* (HU). As one of the commenters suggests: *"There are plenty of things that can be done, in short: we won't save the planet by striking"* (CZ).

Asking youth to study and become experts instead of being politically active

Arguments in this subcategory develop a distinction between experience, expertise and rationality as attributes of adulthood and the lack of these qualities on the side of youth. This duality represents the strongest accent in comments in both countries. Youth involved in the FFF movement are dominantly represented as immature, naïve, ill-informed, and unrealistic (attributes acting as causes) and therefore not suitable for political activity (restricted roles as a consequence).

The discussants also simply refer to the striking youth as "stupid," "demented dunces" or of "low IQ," very frequently exploiting the Asperger syndrome diagnosis of Greta Thunberg, the leader of the FFF movement, who is openly labeled as "a mongoloid child," "mentally retarded" etc. But, more typically, reason is represented in the comments as a deserved target, as something those immatures can achieve in the future if they stick to their appropriate roles now. Some discussants even stress that non-reasonable children can be perceived as being at a developmental stage which can be overcome with age *("Hopefully they will grow out of this." CZ).*

Therefore, in direct relation to expertise as a necessary quality in political decision making that the youth are allegedly lacking, youth are asked to focus on developing their expertise, i.e., to study ("for the future"). A clear dichotomy between the strike, the symbol of the FFF movement, and work or studying, is constructed mainly in the Czech public discourse and is used as a strong strategy delimiting youth in their allegedly appropriate space and public activities. Work/studies and political activity (striking) are constructed by Czechs as mutually exclusive, as if the youth can't do both:

"These wannabe activists, who only keep demanding, alerting, and demonstrating, but will never do anything on their own and still think how they are saving the world, make me feel sick." (CZ)

"Only if you go out to demonstrate on holidays, I will believe that you take it seriously . . . .:(((((" (HU)

Studying, as the appropriate activity for youth, is offered by the discussants as a solution to the problems the youth are demonstrating for. By studying, the discussants suggest, youth can become experts (preferably in *"math, physics and other natural sciences"*) who *"can graduate in some reasonable field and then help develop some stable, clean source of energy"* (CZ). As one discussant puts it, *"they can reverse the unfavorable development by learning rather than stupid striking"* (CZ).

A clear normative message stressing that political interests are not suitable for youth and that the interest in politics conflicts with the interest in the studies is a prominent part of our data, mainly in its Czech part. Discussants stress that youth should normally have *"different interests than some demonstrations"*, that *"children can be interested in anything as long as they do so after their classes"*, that *"they shouldn't want to rule the world"* or that *"politics doesn't belong in the classroom!"* (CZ).

Labelling youth for allegedly deviating from normatively prescribed roles

Labeling strategies often serve the discussants in the Hungarian and Czech online public sphere as a supporting strategy in excluding youth from the public sphere. When they attribute youth roles other than political ones in society (i.e., "appropriate" roles), they also label youth for deviating from the prescribed normative roles. They are thus typically labeled as spoiled, lazy truants or slackers because they allegedly prefer going to demonstrations instead of studying or working to save the planet. This perspective mainly dominates the Czech online discussions in which people label the demonstrating youth as *"spoiled clowns who just want to skip school"*, *"bored brats"*, *"stupid truants"* or *"millennials from the age of abundance"*. Czech debates on the FFF are virtually flooded with this strategy, together with another one labeling striking youth as hypocritical (or *"eco-hypocritical"*) because they consume too much and thus, paradoxically, *"demonstrate against the climate destruction which they fairly contribute to"*.

Manipulated puppets of the leftists, the liberals, and the globalized West: value-based labeling employed to exclude youth from the public sphere

Labels used against the environmentally engaged youth in this value-based category show a prevalence of anti-liberal stances among the discussants in both countries and, more specifically, anti-Western and anti-global stances in Hungary and anti-Leftist stances in Czechia (RQ2). In this category, we can see how a general refusal of activism (McLeod & Hertog, 1999) and specifically climate activism (Castillo Esparcia & López Gómez, 2021) intersects with more specific stress on age-related characteristics of FFF, mainly that they are easily influenced/manipulated and thus represent the youth offshoot of the rejected ideologies (such as the pioneers of the communist/socialist regimes in the Czech case or "puppets" of liberals in case of Hungary). Thus, although the rejection of activism, left-wing ideologies and/or liberalism as such is probably a decisive motive for the publication of comments summarized in this category, they also contain argumentation typical for adultism, i.e., belittling of youth and their role in society.

All labels share one similar tendency: they refer to the FFF movement as bearers of aberrant values and as *"manipulated youth"* or, more expressively, *"stupefied brainwashed youth"* or simply the *"puppets"* of various actors. Among these actors who allegedly exploit youth are the environmental activists and NGOs (or *"eco-terrorists"* – CZ), climate-oriented political parties (or *"climate mafia"* as one of the Czech discussants puts it), the scientists publishing alarming findings related to the climate crisis (or *"alarmists"* - CZ), some teachers, the media or "the Internet" in general. In the Hungarian discussions, young activists are labeled as *"soldiers of Soros"* or *"liberal-fascists"* manipulated by globalized liberal elite groups led by financier George Soros. This last labeling strategy is strongly embedded in the national political system in which the opposition – similarly to the youth- is represented as guided by these global actors. Labeling politically active youth as puppets of other political actors' interests is a strategy aimed at disparaging them as valuable participants in the political debate. It is also clearly linked to stereotypical representations of youth as dependent actors needing protection, as described in the previous subchapter.

In the Czech context, FFF activists are frequently represented as leftists or complicit with the Left (*"a true leftist"*, *"neo-Marxists,"* the *"communists of the 21st century"*). A prominent part of the comments creates a clear connecting line between the activities of FFF activists and the socialist past of Czechoslovakia, comparing young climate activists to *"the enthusiastic pioneers and Komsomols in the [communist] parades"*. Some discussants consider the youth environmental movement *"a certain form of a socialist dictatorship"* aiming at controlling people's activities. As one comment states, *"communism has not succeeded, hence they are trying with ecology now"*. These discussants perceive the ecological movement as *"a green totality replacing* *the brown or red one"*, suggesting a link not only between environmentalism and socialism/communism, but also Nazism.

Some discussants clearly refer to the "puppets" label by suggesting that the striking youth are organized (as well as paid) by political forces aiming at reestablishing socialism or communism in Europe and elsewhere:

"I wonder who is in charge of this Maoist cultural revolution" (CZ)

It is necessary to read these comparisons in the context of the socialist history of Czechoslovakia and the whole region, which can explain the negative attitudes of the Czech discussants toward anything reminding them of socialism/communism. It is obvious that they tend to understand the efforts of the striking youth as an attempt to reduce individual freedoms (restrictions related to consumption etc.), which the discussants perceive as the achievement of capitalism (as opposed to communism or socialism) and thus react very sensitively to it:

"Rather than a strike for the climate, this protest should be called a strike against capitalism." (CZ)

The Hungarian data offer a very different picture (RQ2), although the two countries share similar histories related to socialism or communism. Hungarian discussants focus on a much more recent "enemy" and the one situated in a different part of the world – in the West. FFF activists are represented as liberal, a "group of liberal-fascists" allegedly guided by "global forces." The connecting line between these global actors is the "liberal ideology," the destruction of "normal values," and businessman George Soros. Comments in this category represent a combination of anti-Western, anti-liberal and anti-globalist values and claim to stand for traditional values and normality when *"the globalist left-liberal politics are in agony due to their own worldview and value crisis."* Since FFF is a global movement, it is perceived as necessarily depending on those values:

"These kids are just Soros's soldiers!" (HU)

Despite the above-mentioned national differences, we can witness a similar tendency in both countries to anti-liberalism or illiberal discourse in excluding youth. The discussants in both countries relate the FFF to vulnerable groups that are typical targets of anti-liberal Othering among the non-negligible part of the public in the CEE countries, such as ethnic minorities, gender and sexual minorities (LGBTQ+) and their advocates, typically nonprofit organizations or, more generally, liberal cosmopolitan educated people. Conservatism is a common feature of these anti-liberal moods, including the refusal of feminism and the promotion of patriarchal values.

Online discussants discredit the gender or sexual identity of the striking youth based on their alleged "abnormality" or an aberration from what the discussants perceive as a norm. They openly mock young activists for allegedly not conforming to normative masculinity or femininity and hereby distract attention from their political activity to their appearance or gender performance:

"Is there a male or female in the picture?" - "Something in-between." - "You mean the third gender which is so fashionable these days? Well, at least it [sic] is not going to reproduce." (CZ)

Sexist attacks on the appearance of female activists are very common in our data (*"the beauties set out in the streets"* - ironically, CZ), so is homophobia (*"what a faggot!"* - CZ; *"climate activism is the new 'buzulás' [derogatory term for the sexual relationship between gay men]"* (HU). This type of comments builds upon traditional conservative norms and creates the image of youth activists as endangering these norms and weakening the values cherished by the older generations. To deal with this perceived danger, the discussants often target Greta Thunberg, the most visible representative of the FFF movement, with openly sexist comments challenging her sexual attractivity or even suggesting that she should be disciplined by having sexual intercourse with men (instead of leading a global climate movement):

"She [Greta Thunberg] would need to get f... ed properly by some ginger guy so that she starts dealing with other stuff." - "I wonder who would volunteer in the case of this intelligent beauty [irony]. (CZ)

Intersectional attacks combining various discriminatory labels and thoughts are also typical for some of the anti-liberal comments. In some cases, sexism is combined with xenophobia in a reminder of the relatively recent immigration from Muslim countries to Europe:

> *"She [Greta Thunberg] should be finally given some pleasure by an immigrant of whom there are plenty in Sweden these days."* (CZ)

In Hungary, attacks against "liberal-fascists" in the comments on FFF are frequent and mainly refer to what the discussants perceive as the exclusion of "normality" by liberal ideology. "normality" is often interpreted through the prism of Christian values praising traditional roles in the family, including children's position, also as a counterpole to immigrants or Muslims represented as threatening this "normality." The strength of the Christian position in the Hungarian comments (a clear Hungarian characteristic of the data, RQ2) is demonstrated in the frequent labeling of Greta Thunberg with derogatory Biblical metaphors. She is called *"the daughter of Satan"* or *"the messenger of the Apocalypse"*, labels demonstrating the fight between the good and the evil, where the latter is represented by Greta Thunberg.

Institutions perceived as liberal (the media, the nonprofits) are a frequent target in the negative comments as well. They are represented mainly as those who support FFF uncritically, calling for more restrictions on individual freedoms in the name of the climate-crisis solution, and are thus perceived as a danger to the values of freedom and human rights, as *"eco-terrorist nonprofits"* (CZ) or *"dangerous [...] media supporting that Greta and company"* (CZ).

Discussion and conclusions

Our main finding answering the first research question reveals that online discussants (or the "online public") in Hungary and Czechia employ two basic sets of strategies to exclude youth from the public sphere. First, they attribute the youth roles represented as appropriate for them while simultaneously denying them political activity. Second, they represent the youth as irrelevant political actors by labeling young activists as bearers of aberrant values and/or manipulated by other actors discredited for their political views.

Concerning the role-based exclusion, one of the most dominant discussant arguments in favor of exclusion of youth from political participation in both countries is the lack of knowledge and expertise. This stress on the expert or rational position allegedly necessary for political participation represents a well-known argument for excluding other groups in history, mainly women or racial groups (Kulynych, 2001). It also corresponds with the "anticipatory narratives" observed in Australian media coverage, which imply that children are not yet prepared to intervene in the adult world (Alexander, Petray, & McDowall, 2022). Czech discussants offer a solution to this "problem" by enhancing the role of education and massively criticizing the fact that FFF activists skip school to protest in the streets. This strategy is similar to the "truancy frame" described by many scholars studying media representations of FFF (Bergmann & Ossewaarde, 2020; Von Zabern & Tulloch, 2021). However, the Hungarian discussants deviate from this common European strategy of exclusion. They stress the necessary protection of the allegedly naive and easily manipulated youth and focus on the responsibility of parents and adults in their protection. This narrative can be traced back to one of Hungary's most dominant governmental narratives, the protection of families, which has its roots in the so-called Christian-conservative ideology gaining strength in Hungary. Czechs, on the other hand, strongly emphasize the individual environmental action of youth. Huttunen and Albrecht (2021) identified a similar tendency in the Finnish media coverage of FFF and labeled it as a "sustainable lifestyle frame." In relation to the Czech data, we interpret the stress on individual pro-environmental action and mainly the simultaneous rejection of collective political action as a result of the dominance of the neoliberal ideology among the political leadership in the early democratic years after the Velvet Revolution. It is evident that many Czech discussants associate the FFF activities with the collectivist ideology of socialism and position themselves against this ideology, not only by labeling the youth as "pioneers" or "neo-Marxists" but also by pointing out individual responsibility as a key feature of capitalism and the neo-liberal ideology.

Concerning value-based exclusion in Hungary, the reminder of the socialist times is not present, having been replaced with other concerns, such as the influence of global, Western-liberal forces allegedly aiming to undermine nation-states and conservative norms often represented by Christian values. The current Hungarian government has a specific approach to climate change, called "conservative green politics," which includes criticism of globalization and the global character of the left-liberal approach to environmental issues (Antal, 2021, p. 221). Thus, the FFF movement is represented as suspicious because it stresses the importance of global action. Moreover, the Hungarian comments generally represent demonstrations as going hand in hand with leftist ideologies, in stark contrast to the conservative approach stressing the importance of the state in protecting its citizens.

Despite the national differences, we identified a strong common pattern in the analyzed comments in both countries, which differs from previous studies on media representations of young environmental activists. These comments strongly associate the activities of FFF with global liberal movements, which, according to them, threaten the status quo. The environmental activities of young people are thus related to other global movements, such as feminism and LGBTQ+, solidarity movements and the liberal Left, liberal media and nonprofit organizations promoting multiculturalism, gender issues etc. These actors and institutions are represented as either dangerous (shaking the "taken-for-granted") or ridiculous by the commenters in both countries and strictly refused. We interpret these tendencies not only as strategies aimed at excluding young people from the public sphere (because they are allegedly manipulated by these liberal "ideologies," which makes them appear immature, weak, and dependent) but also as symptoms of the growing anti-liberal tendencies in Europe, namely in the region of Central and East Europe (Bustikova & Guasti, 2017). As we illustrate with our empirical data, these moods are firmly embedded in the history and current political influence in the analyzed countries and can be considered an indicator of strongly polarized societies in which different generational approaches to the climate crisis and its possible solutions are becoming a new axis of division.

As concerns the theoretical contribution of our study, we consider our empirical findings a contribution to childism studies as our data help us reveal and unmask specific strategies of exclusion used against publicly active children and youth, mainly the well-known stress on the importance of "reason" and "expertise." These exclusionary tendencies are similar to the exclusion of other groups whose position in society was historically marginalized and normatively constructed as dependent (as in the case of women – cf. Wall, 2019). Reason and expertise also represent the building blocks of modern societies, typical for some of the (exclusionary) approaches to the public sphere (Ferree, Gamson, Gerhards, & Rucht, 2002). Our data thus reveal that particular approaches to public participation (those favoring rationality and expertise, as well as individual, private actions over collective or global ones) and exclusionary ideologies masked as protectionism dominate the public representations of FFF in Hungary and Czechia.

Furthermore, our identification of the specific Hungarian and Czech features of these more general tendencies, mainly the anti-liberal (both HU and CZ), anti-Western and anti-global (HU) and anti-Leftist (CZ) stances, the Christian-conservative stress on family and children protection (HU) or the reminiscence (and refusal) of the socialist past and its collectivity (CZ) help us interpret, in a theoretical way, the importance of more detailed knowledge of the particular historical-political context influencing public acceptance (or refusal) of non-traditional political actors. Our results are partly at odds with what Alexander, Petray, and McDowall (2022) claim, that childhood is a major factor influencing the political participation of children and youth. Our analysis shows that young climate activists are denied relevant political positions not just because they are young. The form of their protest, a publicly exposed, collective, global action calling for a complex, systemic reaction to the climate crisis, seems to be an even more critical burden. It challenges some deep-seated normative beliefs which differ in the two countries. In Hungary, the Christian-conservative ideology directs citizens to take private, family-oriented actions instead of collective ones, whereas in the Czech case, it is rather the neoliberal transformation trajectory that renounces anything that recalls socialist collectivism. The continuing reckoning with the communist era among the Czechs affects the negative association of youth activists with the pioneers, whereas the ideological leaning of the Hungarian political representation likely influences the public ideology refusing the current (Western) global elites.

There are, of course, certain limits to our study. The main limitation results from the specific sample selection. Our findings do not represent general public opinion, rather, they only relate to active contributors to online discussion sections of the news media. Moreover, we focused solely on comments negative toward the movement, i.e., on the exclusionary discourse. Although FFF refusal represents the dominant approach in online civic comments, our research design does not allow us to understand the complex civic online discourse on FFF, including the supportive voices. Furthermore, we are fully aware that FFF represent a specific form of a youth-led movement and that public perception of other youth political activities, especially related to different issues, can be very different. The last two limits also open space for a hope that both the specific topic (environmental activism) and the analyzed online environment influence the representations of youth political actors and that reactions in other online environments may counterbalance the disappointing findings presented in our study. Our data from related research on mainstream media representations of FFF (Vochocová & Rosenfeldová, forthcoming) indicate that the media perspective on youth activism is more welcoming than the related users' discourse. Given the variety of online spaces dedicated to users' political discussions, it is also likely that online spaces beyond our sample, such as various third spaces and niche discussion forums, provide more supportive representation of active youth citizens.

Notes

1. By using the term "youth" we generally refer to under-aged populations, i.e., children and youth under 18, those without the right to vote in the two countries under scrutiny. We keep the term "child/children" only where it stems directly from the empirical data, i.e., in quotations or categories named using the language of the empirical material – "in vivo codes" (Strauss & Corbin, 1998).
2. Our study is qualitative in nature, but the frequency analysis we conducted on a smaller sample shows that exclusionary comments were prevalent in the data. Their proportion ranged between 80–90% in both countries if we take only comments dealing with the FFF as a base. Across all comments, this proportion was 45% in Hungary and 65% in the Czech Republic, indicating that unrelated debates and attacks on other actors, especially politicians, are more prevalent in Hungarian discussions.
3. The variety of representations of FFF youth activists was generally smaller in the Hungarian data (a lower number of specific categories of representations was identified), there were also generally fewer comments related to the articles, hence the saturation moment was identified earlier than in the Czech case, where the data were more diverse as concerns various representations.
4. To meet ethical standards, we did not use authors' names when citing comments in our paper; furthermore, translating the citations into English makes it basically impossible to link individual comments to discussants' identities.
5. In this context, Bennett (1998) refers to lifestyle politics, typical especially for the younger generations, wherein the declining interest in conventional politics is replaced by the tendency of individuals to see political meanings in their everyday lifestyle choices.

Disclosure statement

No potential conflict of interest was reported by the authors.

Funding

This work was supported by Charles University under Grant number: PRIMUS/21/HUM/003

ORCID

Lenka Vochocová http://orcid.org/0000-0001-9873-4536
Jana Rosenfeldová http://orcid.org/0000-0002-2015-3798
Anna Vancsó http://orcid.org/0000-0001-7783-6963
Annamária Neag http://orcid.org/0000-0003-3395-4006

References

Alexander, N., Petray, T., & McDowall, A. (2022). More learning, less activism: Narratives of childhood in Australian media representations of the school strike for climate. *Australian Journal of Environmental Education*, 38(1), 96–111. doi:10.1017/aee.2021.28

Antal, A. (2021). Authoritarian populism, environmentalism and exceptional governance in Hungary. *Politologický časopis-Czech Journal of Political Science*, 28(3), 209–228. doi:10.5817/PC2021-3-209

Bátorfy, A., & Urbán, Á. (2020). State advertising as an instrument of transformation of the media market in Hungary. *East European Politics*, 36(1), 44–65. doi:10.1080/21599165.2019.1662398

Bennett, W. L. (1998). The uncivic culture: Communication, identity, and the rise of lifestyle politics. *PS: Political Science & Politics*, 31(4), 741–776. doi:10.1017/S1049096500053270

Bergmann, Z., & Ossewaarde, R. (2020). Youth climate activists meet environmental governance: Ageist depictions of the FFF movement and Greta Thunberg in German newspaper coverage. *Journal of Multicultural Discourses*, 15(3), 267–290. doi:10.1080/17447143.2020.1745211

Bosi, L., Lavizzari, A., & Voli, S. (2020). Representation of youth in the public debate in Greece, Italy, and Spain: Does the political leaning of newspapers have any effect? *American Behavioral Scientist*, 64(5), 620–637. doi:10.1177/0002764219885437

Bustikova, L., & Guasti, P. (2017). The illiberal turn or swerve in Central Europe? *Politics & Governance*, 5(4), 166–176. doi:10.17645/pag.v5i4.1156

Casteltrione, I. (2015). The internet, social networking web sites and political participation research: Assumptions and contradictory evidence. *First Monday*, 20(3). doi:10.5210/fm.v20i3.5462

Castillo Esparcia, A., & López Gómez, S. (2021). Public opinion about climate change in United States, partisan view and media coverage of the 2019 United Nations climate change conference (COP 25) in Madrid. *Sustainability*, 13(7), 1–19. doi:10.3390/su13073926

Coleman, S., & Blumler, J. G. (2009). *The internet and democratic citizenship: Theory, practice and policy (communication, society, and politics)*. Cambridge; New York: Cambridge University Press.

Dahlgren, P. (2005). The internet, public spheres, and political communication: Dispersion and deliberation. *Political Communication*, 22(2), 147–162. doi:10.1080/10584600590933160

Ferree, M. M., Gamson, W. A., Gerhards, J., & Rucht, D. (2002). Four models of the public sphere in modern democracies. *Theory and Society*, 31(3), 289–324. doi:10.1023/A:1016284431021

Fridays for Future. (2021). List of countries. https://fridaysforfuture.org/what-we-do/strike-statistics/list-of-countries/

Gibson, R., & Cantijoch, M. (2013). Conceptualizing and measuring participation in the age of the internet: Is online political engagement really different to offline? *The Journal of Politics*, 75(3), 701–716. doi:10.1017/S0022381613000431

Gil-Lopez, T. (2021). Mainstream protest reporting in the contemporary media environment: Exploring (in)stability and adherence to protest paradigm from 1998 to 2017. *Journalism & Mass Communication Quarterly*, 98(3), 692–724. doi:10.1177/1077699020984783

Habermas, J. (1989). *The structural transformation of the public sphere. An inquiry into a category of bourgeois society*. Cambridge: MIT Press.

Huttunen, J., & Albrecht, E. (2021). The framing of environmental citizenship and youth participation in the Fridays for future movement in Finland. *Fennia - International Journal of Geography*, 199(1), 46–60. doi:10.11143/fennia.102480

Huttunen, J., & Albrecht, E. (2021). The framing of environmental citizenship and youth participation in the Fridays for Future Movement in Finland. *Fennia - International Journal of Geography*, 199(1), 46–60. doi:10.11143/fennia.102480

Jacobsson, D. (2021). Young vs old? Truancy or new radical politics? Journalistic discourses about social protests in relation to the climate crisis. *Critical Discourse Studies*, 18(4), 481–497. doi:10.1080/17405904.2020.1752758

Kulynych, J. (2001). No playing in the public sphere: Democratic theory and the exclusion of children. *Social Theory and Practice*, 27(2), 231–264. doi:10.5840/soctheorpract200127211

Mayes, E., & Hartup, M. E. (2021). News coverage of the school strike for climate movement in Australia: The politics of representing young strikers' emotions. *Journal of Youth Studies (Online)*, 1–23. doi:10.1080/13676261.2021.1929887

McLaughlin, L. (1999). Beyond "separate spheres": Feminism and the cultural studies/political economy debate. *Journal of Communication Inquiry*, 23(4), 327–354. doi:10.1177/0196859999023004003

McLeod, D. M., & Hertog, J. K. (1999). Social control, social change and the mass media's role in the regulation of protest groups. In D. Demers (Ed.), *Mass media, social control, and social change: A macrosocial perspective* (pp. 305–330). Phoenix: Marquette Books.

Nagar, N. (2011). *The loud public: The case of user comments in online news media*. (Doctoral dissertation). University at Albany, State University of New York.

Pickard, S. (2019). *Politics, protest and young people*. London: Palgrave Macmillan UK. doi:10.1057/978-1-137-57788-7

Rowe, I. (2015). Deliberation 2.0: Comparing the deliberative quality of online news user comments across platforms. *Journal of Broadcasting & Electronic Media, 59*(4), 539–555. doi:10.1080/08838151.2015.1093482

Strauss, A., & Corbin, J. (1998). *Basics of qualitative research techniques and procedures for developing grounded theory* (2nd ed.). London: Sage Publications.

Szabo, G., Kmetty, Z., & Molnár, E. K. (2021). Politics and incivility in the online comments: What is beyond the norm-violation approach? *International Journal of Communication, 15*(2), 1659–1684.

Tymowski, A. W. (1994). Youth activism in the East European transformation. *Communist and Post-Communist Studies, 27*(2), 115–124. doi:10.1016/0967-067X(94)90019-1

Vochocová, L., & Rosenfeldová, J. (forthcoming). Are generations really divided by climate? Preference for conflict in Fridays for future media coverage. *Journalism Practice*

Von Zabern, L., & Tulloch, C. D. (2021). Rebel with a cause: The framing of climate change and intergenerational justice in the German press treatment of the Fridays for future protest. *Media, Culture & Society, 43*(1), 23–47. doi:10.1177/0163443720960923

Wall, J. (2019). From childhood studies to childism: Reconstructing the scholarly and social imaginations. *Children's Geographies*. doi:10.1080/14733285.2019.1668912

Like, share, comment, and repeat: Far-right messages, emotions, and amplification in social media

Larissa Doroshenko and Fangjing Tu

ABSTRACT
Investigating the role of emotions in online political engagement, we show that far-right parties receive more amplification online than centrist parties because their messages produce stronger emotional reactions. Using a 2 × 3 mixed design survey experiment (N = 303), which compared far-right and centrist messages about three campaign issues in Ukraine, we demonstrate that nationalist appeals evoked hope and enthusiasm, which resulted in more likes and shares. However, far-rights were only successful when addressing their traditional issues, such as national language policy. We conclude with advice on how other parties can harness emotional appeals to encourage political participation when facing competition from far-right parties.

Starting from the message of hope spreading through emerging social networks in 2008 (Katz, Barris, & Jain, 2013) to the fear of Russian interference and election fraud in 2020 (Goethals, 2021), the role of emotions on social media in election campaigns can hardly be overestimated. While social media foster political engagement and occasionally boost underdog candidates (Larsson & Moe, 2014), they also promote nationalist and xenophobic messages of far-right parties, which spread there unfiltered by mainstream media gatekeepers (Ernst, Esser, Blassnig, & Engesser, 2019). Recent evidence suggests that strong emotions contained in such messages make them viral: news content expressing anger, anxiety, and enthusiasm is found to be shared disproportionally more (Hasell, 2020). Such online amplification of messages creates an impression that many people support far-right ideas, increasing vote shares (Di Grazia, McKelvey, Bollen, & Rojas, 2013) and undermining liberal democracy.

While the importance of emotions in political decision-making and participation has been extensively studied (e.g., Marcus, Neuman, & MacKuen, 2000; Valentino, Gregorowicz, & Groenendyk, 2009), the role of emotions in political engagement on social media has only recently come into the attention of scholars. Studies point out that partisan media contain emotional content, which in turn facilitates sharing of this information on social networks (Hasell, 2020; Hasell & Weeks, 2016). Little is known, however, about the mechanism behind this sharing behavior and about other ways of message amplification on social media, such as likes and comments (Gan, Lee, & Li, 2017). Similarly, scholars focused on how xenophobic messages of far-right parties affect people's attitudes and behaviors (e.g., Bos, Van Der Brug, & De Vreese, 2013; Hameleers & Schmuck, 2017), but the influence of these messages on social media engagement and message amplification remains understudied (for an exception, see Ernst et al., 2019). To connect these two research veins and address existing research gaps, this study focuses on far-right social media posts and analyzes how emotions evoked by these messages prompt users to engage and amplify these posts on social media. Popularity of nationalist politicians and parties during Presidential and Parliamentary elections in post-Euromaidan Ukraine provides a suitable case for this research. Unlike recent research that examined the effects of far-right messages on users' reactions using digital trace and content analyses (e.g., Jacobs, Sandberg, & Spierings, 2020; Lilleker & Balaban, 2021), our work explores the psychological mechanism of engaging with these messages through four distinct emotions by using an experimental design.

This method also allows to account for participants' sociodemographic characteristics, political orientation, baseline emotional status, and their habits of social media use.

By conducting this study, we make several important contributions. First, we *differentiate among social media amplification activities*, investigating the role of emotions on likes, shares, and comments, which all have various stakes in social media ecology. Second, we *differentiate emotional reactions*, adopting a discrete approach to emotional response and studying the role of anger, anxiety, hope, and enthusiasm on each social media activity separately. Third, we *differentiate among popular electoral issues* studying not only those pertinent to far-right parties, such as national identity, but also explore whether these parties can compete on other mainstream issues, such as fighting corruption and establishing the rule of law. Fourth, we *investigate an understudied yet strategically important Eastern European region*, recognizing that most of the previous research about the role of emotions and far-right parties was conducted in Western democracies, making their findings contingent on and limited to the region.

To make these contributions, we conducted a 2 × 3 mixed design survey experiment (N = 303), assessing emotional response of participants after reading far-right or mainstream parties' messages, as well as willingness to engage with these messages on social media using expressive activities of liking, sharing, and commenting. Results demonstrate that people are more willing to engage with far-right messages on social media through liking and sharing, compared to posts by mainstream politicians. People also experienced stronger enthusiasm and hope in response to far-right messages, and these two emotions inclined them to engage in all social media expressive activities. Anger and anxiety only made people more likely to comment and share social media messages. We also show that political issues are not created equal: far-right parties fail to attract as much attention posting about issues that are traditionally discussed by all parties, while "pet" issues of national language and identity indeed gain more engagement from social media users. Discussion of how these findings can help both scholars and politicians to engage people in positive emotions and pro-democratic behavior on social media concludes this paper.

Emotions as a major partisan tool of far-rights

Far-rights, unlike center-right parties, share a core ideological focus on nationalism (Mudde, 2002), which involves exclusion of national, ethnic, or sexual minorities (Krämer, 2014). To distance themselves from the traditional political core, far-rights also share "anti-system" (Ignazi, 2003) or anti-establishment views, which often go as far as expressing radical and extremist positions. Far-right ideology is often paired with populism because nationalism resonates with people-centrism and exclusion of outgroups, which are defining features of this thin ideology (Ernst et al., 2019), while anti-system views align well with anti-elitism of populism (Marx, 2020). Political gains of far-right parties worldwide undermine values of liberal democracy by igniting xenophobia and intolerance, but this destructive impact is especially devastating for developing democracies, such as Ukraine. Previous research focused on legislative, economic, demographic (Givens, 2005), and media factors (Aalberg, Esser, Reinemann, Strömbäck, & de Vreese, 2017) that contribute toward the popularity of these parties. We focus on emotional appeals of far-rights' messages, which make them more viral on social media, ultimately boosting offline popularity.

Nationalism of far-right parties praises virtues of the people, perceived as a monolithic entity (Ernst et al., 2019), and enhances one's national identity, which promotes feelings of national pride, enthusiasm, and hopes for a better future (Widmann, 2021). Pride is a reaction toward receiving credit for a valued object or an achievement, either personal or group with whom one identifies (Lazarus, 1991). By emphasizing achievements and values of the people in their messages, far-right parties are well positioned to elicit pride. Enthusiasm and hope are reactions to appraisals of importance, goal congruence, and future expectations (Chadwick, 2015; Wirz, 2018), which are evoked in far-right messages appealing to unanimity of the people and their desires, as well as by describing collective bright future under these parties' leadership.

Anti-elitism of far-rights and portrayal of politics as a struggle between good and evil also contribute toward emotions of anger, fear, and anxiety. Blaming elites is cognitively easy, uses more emotional content, which in turn increases the persuasive effect of the message (Cassell, 2021). Anger is elicited when an adverse situation is created by others (Smith & Ellsworth, 1985), so by constructing a general culprit for socio-economic problems, far-rights' anti-elite rhetoric externalizes responsibility for people's situation and reinvigorates anger about it (Marx, 2020). Anger is a more enjoyable collective emotion in the face of an adverse situation than depression and shame, making it more attractive for both politicians and people alike. Fear and anxiety, on the other hand, are reactions to uncertain existential threats (Lazarus, 1991), and far-right parties evoke these emotions by depicting people as powerless at the mercy of the corrupt elites who do not protect them (Wirz, 2018).

Populist parties, which often include far-rights, use significantly more emotional appeals than mainstream ones, increasing anger and disgust along with joy and pride in their tweets (Widmann, 2021). In the study conducted among Western democracies, emotions of joy, pride, hope, and enthusiasm accompanied tweets about the nation and the populist leader, while anger and disgust were related to opponents, outgroups, and anti-system messages (Widmann, 2021). Scholars have also documented increasing emotionality of partisan news compared to mainstream coverage (Hasell & Weeks, 2016; Wojcieszak, Bimber, Feldman, & Stroud, 2016).

Thus, when far-right parties post their partisan appeals on social media, we can expect people to have stronger reactions toward such messages compared to more balanced political expressions. Hence, we formulate the following hypothesis:

Message type effect

H1: People are more likely to experience stronger emotions in response to far-right rather than non-far-right messages on social media platforms.

Likes, shares, and comments: social media expressive activities as an amplification mechanism

Empirical research has distinguished different forms of online expressive engagement ranging from forwarding political information to commenting on news online (Gibson & Cantijoch, 2013; Rojas & Puig-i-Abril, 2009). Translating these forms of online political engagement into social media, we get activities such as liking political posts, sharing political content on the wall or in a private message, and commenting on other users' posts. These social media expressive activities, however, are not created equal. To click like is a low-cost engagement activity (Gerodimos & Justinussen, 2015), while sharing already requires a more active practice of distribution (John, 2013) which suggests to their network that something is worth reading (Heiss, Schmuck, & Matthes, 2019). Commenting additionally signals interest in discussion and provides an opportunity for it (Heiss et al., 2019).

When users like, share, or comment on social media posts, they amplify these messages across social networks. Amplification in this context is understood as the contribution of social media publics to the attention paid to a message by elevating other users' perceptions of the message's worthiness and significance (Zhang, Wells, Wang, & Rohe, 2018). Such amplification has the potential to spread political information via weak ties to users who may not have discovered this information otherwise (Gil de Zúñiga & Valenzuela, 2011), as well as increase credibility and trust in the information if it was shared by peers rather than politicians themselves (Sterrett et al., 2019). Amplification of social media messages also spills over to traditional media outlets who perceive widely liked, shared, and commented messages as news- and trustworthy (Zhang et al., 2018). The more successful politicians are at mobilizing users to engage with their messages, the farther their political appeals travel in the hybrid media system.

Previous research discovered that emotional content facilitates news sharing online (Hasell, 2020), making it plausible that emotional appeals of far-right parties also get more shares on social media. In addition, social identity theory suggests that individuals derive self-images from their membership of and attachment to social groups (Tajfel, 1974).

Through nativism and anti-elitism, far-right parties accentuate in-group and out-group identities, creating a perception that the people are experiencing an in-group deprivation, no longer served by the elite, and the elites are viewed as an out-group threat. This segmentation between in-group and out-group identities has a mobilizing effect and triggers collective action (Hameleers et al., 2018), and social media expressive activities are a form of collective action.

Finally, far-right parties provoke greater social media engagement by using less cognitively demanding elements (Cassell, 2021). Research has shown that heuristics shortcuts help individuals process complex information and make political decisions (Berger & Milkman, 2012). This is particularly the case on social media, where users developed limited attention span, less cognitive load, and stronger tendency to rely on heuristics to process information. Far-right messages used cognitive simplicity content, allowing people to engage and react to the information more easily and intuitively. Research has also shown that partisan tweets are shared more widely, and populist politicians induce greater users' reactions (Hasell, 2020; Jost, Maurer, & Hassler, 2020) and engagements on social media (Blassnig & Wirz, 2019; Bobba, 2019) than mainstream political leaders. Summing up the ways these appeals can be amplified by users, we propose the following set of hypotheses:

Message type effect

H2a: People are more likely to amplify far-right rather than non-far-right messages on social media platforms with liking, sharing, and commenting.

H2b: People are more likely to amplify far-right rather than non-far-right messages on social media platforms with liking compared to sharing and commenting.

Anger, anxiety, hope, and enthusiasm: emotions and their role in social media amplification

The very concept of social media expressive activities implies that these technological features exist for showing users' feelings, impressions, and thoughts. Increased attention to the role of emotions in motivating political engagement (Marcus et al., 2000) suggests that emotions must also be at play when using social media for political purposes. Affective intelligence theory, the first framework to systematically explain the role of emotions in information processing and political participation, organizes all emotions into two systems – the surveillance and the disposition (Marcus et al., 2000). Emotions from the surveillance system make people more attentive and alert toward changes in the environment, as well as interrupt a person's reliance on existing habits and mental shortcuts. Emotions in the second system activate automatic routine reactions toward the environment, which are guided by personal dispositions.

To investigate the link between cognition and emotions, as well as differentiate discrete emotions from two systems, scholars have turned to cognitive appraisal theory. It suggests that emotions result from subjective evaluations of the world and that individuals take deliberate actions to cope with these emotions (Lazarus, 1991). To better understand how various emotions influence social media expressive activities, we utilize cognitive appraisal theory and its discrete approach to emotions, rather than focusing on the systems of emotions as a whole.

Anger is triggered by a threat to core beliefs under circumstances of certainty, motivating a reliance on partisanship cues (Marcus, Neuman, MacKuen, Wolak, & Keele, 2006), risk-seeking behavior (Lerner & Keltner, 200), and support for far-rights (Marcus, Valentino, Vasilopoulos, & Foucault, 2019). Anger also can lead to an increase in political efficacy when an angry individual participates in politics (Valentino et al., 2009). *Anxiety*, in turn, is caused by novel threats in the environment, making individuals more alert and cautious. Anxious people search for additional information, pay attention to political campaigns (Marcus et al., 2000), and are less likely to rely only on their partisan attachments (Marcus et al., 2006). As a result, anxiety triggers risk avoidance and suppresses participation (Huddy, Feldman, & Cassese, 2007). However, more recent studies found that anxiety is positively associated with less costly forms of participation, such as talking about voting and wearing a button (Valentino, Brader, Groenendyk, Gregorowicz, & Hutchings, 2011).

Positive emotions also stimulate political participation and engagement. Both enthusiasm and hope belong to the disposition system, stemming from individual existing attitudes. Just like anger, *enthusiasm* leads people to take action in order to achieve or preserve goals (Valentino et al., 2011). Enthusiastic individuals act to continue their success, which increases their efficacy and motivates further engagement. Thus, enthusiasm is linked to a higher likelihood of voter turnout (Marcus & MacKuen, 1993), campaign activism (Gerstlé & Nai, 2019), and reinforcement of existing partisan habits (Brader, 2006). *Hope* is akin to enthusiasm in the sense that it boosts efficacy and motivates for action (Valentino et al., 2011), and it supports the intent to participate civically and politically (Albanesi et al., 2016). Scholars suggest that political messages designed to invoke hope tend to both galvanize and sustain people's engagement in politics (Jenkins, 2018).

Summarizing the role of discrete emotions in traditional political engagement, we translate this knowledge to the digital realm and propose the following hypothesis and a research question:

Emotional effect

H3: Anger (H3a), enthusiasm (H3b), and hope (H3c) stimulate expressive activities of liking, sharing, and commenting.

RQ1: Does anxiety stimulate or inhibit expressive activities of liking, sharing, and commenting?

As emotions are evoked by messages and emotions facilitate expressive activities, we can expect that a mediation mechanism is also at play. Differential susceptibility to media effects model (Valkenburg & Peter, 2013) proposes that emotional responses mediate the relationship between media use and political outcomes. Emotions contribute toward persuasiveness of populist messages (Wirz, 2018): the more anger or hope people felt, the more persuaded they were by political posters. Emotions also mediate the relationship between media use and political participation (Namkoong, Fung, & Scheufele, 2012). Political engagement after cross-cutting news exposure was mediated by anger (Wojcieszak et al., 2016) and information provoking high-arousal emotions is more likely to be read and shared (Berger & Milkman, 2012; Hasell & Weeks, 2016). In line with these findings, we suggest that anger, enthusiasm, or hope triggered by far-right messages should mediate people's willingness to amplify them through social media expressive activities. Since we do not have a theoretical ground to talk about how discrete emotions work as multiple mediators or how they may interfere with each other in one model, we hypothesize the mediation effect of each emotion separately:

Mediation

H4: Anger (H4a), enthusiasm (H4b), and hope (H4c) respectively mediate the effect of far-right messages on the expressive activities of liking, sharing, and commenting.

Not all issues are created equal: raise of far-right parties in post-Euromaidan Ukraine

Far-right parties thrive by using emotional language when discussing issues of immigration, national identity, and anti-elitism toward political establishment (Hameleers et al., 2018; Hameleers & Schmuck, 2017). When competing in national elections, however, these parties also need to address other pressing issues in society. Very few studies compared effectiveness of far-right messages across various electoral issues (e.g., Ernst et al., 2019) and virtually none examined which issues promoted by these parties on social media get the most attention and amplification from users. Thus, it remains to be seen whether playing on emotions or addressing issues that fall out of their competency help far-right parties to gain traction among online social networks.

The Ukrainian post-Euromaidan Presidential and Parliamentary elections provide a unique opportunity to understand the success of several far-right actors who were competing for voters' attention. The Euromaidan revolution, which overthrew the pro-Russian government, brought to prominence three far-right parties: *Svoboda* (Freedom), *Radykalna*

Partyja Oleha Lyashko (the Radical Party of Oleh Lyahsko), and *Pravy Sector* (the Right Sector). Social media provided these parties with a megaphone for spreading their ideas and connecting like-minded individuals during street protests (Onuch, 2015). The momentum gained on social media during Euromaidan carried these parties into the following elections when politicians continued using these platforms to discuss political issues (Doroshenko et al., 2019). Over a hundred people were killed in the streets of Kyiv, hundreds dislocated Ukrainians as a result of the first land takeover in Europe since WWII, thousands of killed soldiers and civilians in Donbass – all of these traumatic events made those elections ripe for strong emotions both within society but also among parties' campaign appeals. These circumstances created a fertile ground for nativism, which, as we discussed earlier, is one of the main rhetorical tools used by far-right parties to elicit emotions and political engagement among voters. Like in Western Europe, nationalism was used by Ukrainian far-right parties to justify positions on many socio-economic issues, such as form of governance, land ownership, or minority language policies. Anti-system and anti-elitist views also allowed these parties to distance themselves from a "corrupt" political establishment, which led toward annexation and military conflict, imitating rhetorical strategies of other far-right parties who blamed centrist politicians for influx of immigrants and economic hardships in the EU (Schmuck & Matthes, 2017).

In this study, we compare three major issues of the 2014 election cycles in Ukraine, where some favored the far-right agenda, while others put them on par with other mainstream moderate political actors. The issue of corruption has besieged post-Communist countries for decades, and Ukraine is no exception (Wallace & Latcheva, 2006). Virtually all parties acknowledged that this is an important predicament on the way to more effective governance, but they provided different solutions. Far-right parties suggested to their followers a solution that might not be as effective in the long term, but which surely provoked a lot of strong emotions among constituencies: a "trash bucket challenge," which involved literal throwing officials who were suspected of corruption into garbage bins.[1] Many political parties also discussed a future form of governance as the situation in Donbass aggravated, and local authorities demanded more autonomy from Kyiv. However, approaches to this new issue were very different, ranging from ideas of decentralization to full-blown federalization (Norris, Martinez-Vasquez, & Norregaard, 2000). Far-right parties halted any negotiations about federalization, insisting that the country retains its current form of governance at all costs (Marlin, 2016). Similarly, in discussions about the status of the Russian language, far-rights rendered this issue as non-negotiable and insisted that only Ukrainian could be the official language. While other parties were also not keen on the idea of federalization, such a firm stand on the issue of national language became crucial for the popularity of far-rights and served as a pretense for Crimea annexation to save Russian-speakers from Ukrainian nationalists in Kyiv (Biersack & O'Lear, 2014).

Recognizing the importance of these campaign issues, we seek to observe whether some are more likely to produce stronger emotional reaction and engagement from social media users, as well as whether far-right parties are more successful with their "traditional" issues connected with national identity, we pose the following research question:

Message-issue interaction effect

RQ2: Which issue receives a higher level of amplification through liking, sharing, and commenting?

Methods

Participants

To examine our hypotheses, we conducted a 2 × 3 mixed design survey experiment. To conduct the multilevel mediation analyses for our study, power analysis suggested that a total sample size of 298 is needed to achieve statistical power of .80 with a small effect size (Pan, Liu, Miao, & Yuan, 2018). We recruited a sample of 303 students from one of the largest universities in Kyiv, Ukraine (M age = 19.3 years (SD = 2.3), 60.7% female). The subjects were predominantly undergraduate students who were paid for their voluntary participation. And, 87.5% of young Ukrainians used social media on a regular basis (Friedrich Ebert Stiftung, 2020), making them suitable subjects for studying the role of emotions in social media expressive activities.

It is important to keep in mind that this study's participants are more educated and have higher socio-economic status than the country's population. However, our goal is not to generalize findings to Ukrainians at large, but rather to understand the emotional mechanism behind social media amplification of emotional partisan messages, which was documented before by content analysis and survey studies (e.g., Hasell, 2020; Hasell & Weeks, 2016). Previous research studying the use of convenient samples in social sciences confirmed that treatment effects found in population samples are replicated in convenience samples. False negatives, false positives, and significantly different effect sizes are rarely, if ever, found in convenience samples; this is particularly true for student samples (Mullinix, Leeper, Druckman, & Freese, 2015).

Recognizing that our sample is not generalizable, we nevertheless wanted to ensure that our participants do not possess characteristics, such as political preferences or use of Ukrainian language, that would interfere with stimuli of the study. The geographical location and good reputation of the university enabled us to get participants from all regions of the country, including more pro-Ukrainian West (22% of participants), traditionally favoring far-right nationalist parties, and pro-Russian South-East (21.4%), which traditionally opposes them (for a detailed breakdown by oblast, see Online Appendix). The voting preferences for three far-right parties among our participants, Ukrainian students, and Ukrainian voters at large are comparable, confirming that our sample was close to the Ukrainian population at least in terms of their voting preferences for far-right parties (see Online Appendix). Since national language was one of the divisive issues exploited by far-right parties, we also checked how often participants used Ukrainian language at home, at work, and with friends: this variable was normally distributed with about half of respondents using both languages and a quarter sticking exclusively to Russian or Ukrainian (see Online Appendix).

The experiment used a 2 × 3 mixed design, where the between-subjects factor was the message type (far-right vs. not far-right/moderate), and the within-subject factor was the issue discussed (corruption, the form of governance, and national language). Participants completed the survey experiment on library computers in a controlled, quiet environment. Each participant started with a questionnaire that asked about their social media use, political preferences, and engagement in civic life. Then, participants were randomly assigned to one of the two conditions where they either received three far-right social media posts or three moderate social media posts, one post for each issue (corruption, the form of governance, and national language).

Participants were exposed to one of the three social media posts at a time, keeping the order of posts random. After exposure to each post, participants indicated on a 7-point scale (1 = not at all, 7 = very much) how much these social media posts make them feel enthusiastic (M = 3.02, SD = 2.17), hopeful (M = 3.17, SD = 2.23), angry (M = 2.34, SD = 1.93), and anxious (M = 3.13, SD = 2.09). The order of these distinct emotions appeared in random order. Immediately after, participants were asked how likely (1 = very unlikely, 7 = very likely) they were to engage in the following expressive activities with each post: like (M = 3.07, SD = 2.38), share (M = 1.63, SD = 2.05), and leave a comment (M = 2.23, SD = 2.16).

A between-condition randomization check on all control variables such as age, gender, socio-economic status, social media use, and ideology performed at the outset of the analysis revealed successful randomization (gender $F(1,301) = .005$, $p > .05$; age $F(1, 300) = .010$, $p > .05$; education $F(1, 301) = 1.151$, $p > .05$; income $F(1,301) = .82$, $p > .05$; ideology $F(1,301) = .183$, $p > .05$; social media use $F(1, 301) = .429$, $p > .05$).

Stimulus

Social media posts were selected from Twitter through a multistep procedure, which was part of a larger project designed to understand the discursive characteristics of far-right messages on social media. We selected 12 tweets for the pretest, six far-right partisan and six moderate tweets, with two tweets per issue in each of these two categories. After removing authorship identifiers from these tweets, we asked a small sample of pretest participants (N = 48) to rate their willingness to engage in social media expressive activities with these 12 posts. Based on the pretest results, we selected six tweets that generated a higher level of reported engagement, while maintaining the initial balance between issues and far-right strategies (see Online Appendix for statistical results of this pretest procedure and a full set of stimulus materials).

Analysis

We analyzed the data via multilevel modeling, which is commonly used to analyze nested data, a repeated-measure design produces. Multilevel modeling offers more flexibility than mixed-design ANOVA in at least four aspects. First, it allows estimating random effects, which account for variance among individuals. Therefore, the findings generated from multilevel modeling are extendable to a wider population. Second, multilevel modeling allows for relaxing certain assumptions with different approaches to assessing standard errors. For example, research has shown that when sphericity assumptions are not met, multilevel modeling can achieve greater power in detecting fixed effects than ANOVA models (Quené & van den Bergh, 2004). It also does not need to make assumptions about the structure of the residual variances and covariances. Third, it allows examining the main effects and interactions of categorical and continuous independent variables simultaneously. Finally, it handles missing data without causing additional complications (Hoffman & Rovine, 2007).

For each dependent variable, we conducted two sets of analyses. First, we estimated a baseline model. It involved message type, issues, and the interaction between the two as predictors via multilevel modeling using restricted maximum likelihood estimation (REML) and random intercepts. Second, to test the mediation hypotheses, we used multilevel mediation analysis (Rockwood & Hayes, 2017). These multilevel analyses allowed us to examine the between-subjects effects of message type, the within-subject effects of messages across three issues, and cross-level interactions between message type and issues.

We started by testing the within-subject differences on each dependent variable. The intraclass correlations for three expressive activities were 0.43, 0.5, and 0.21, respectively, indicating that 43%, 50%, and 21% of the variance could be explained by differences at the individual level (level-2), while the remaining variance should be explained by differences within individuals or at the issue level (level-1). We created two dummy variables for corruption and state language issues, leaving out governance as the reference group. These two issue variables and all the dependent variables were at level-1. The message type variable, far-right, and moderate message, was at level-2. All variables were standardized prior to the analysis.

Results

We start by estimating a series of multilevel random intercepts models fit by restricted maximum likelihood estimation (REML) to address the first set of hypotheses. Message type hypothesis predicted that people are likely to experience stronger emotions in response to far-right messages. Results in Table 1 show that far-right messages evoked greater enthusiasm and hope but less anger. There was no difference in the level of anxiety that the two types of messages stimulated. Thus, H1 was partially supported. Further, we hypothesized that people tend to amplify far-right posts with likes, shares, and comments (H2a) and that likes would be the more likely way of social media engagement (H2b). Results in Table 1 demonstrate that far-right messages were more likely to be liked and shared than non-far-right messages, but the effect of far-right messages on people's inclination to leave a comment was nonsignificant. These results partially supported H2a and support H2b.

Then, we examine whether anger (H3a), enthusiasm (H3b), and hope (H3c) stimulate expressive social media activities, while the role of anxiety requires more exploration (RQ1). We conducted multilevel mediation analyses with message type as the main predictor, emotions as a mediator, and expressive activities as outcomes. The results are presented in Table 2. Each model included only one emotion as the mediator and one expressive activity as the outcome variable. To allow examining the mediating role of each discrete emotion in

Table 1. The Effect of Far-right Messages and Issues on Expressive Activities

	Enthusiasm	Hope	Anger	Anxiety	Comment	Like	Share
Issue-level (level-1) fixed effects							
Language issue[a]	−.170*	−.198**	.482***	.016	.221***	−.139	.070
	(.071)	(.072)	(.072)	(.068)	(.057)	(.072)	(.061)
Corruption issue[a]	−.181*	.022	.227**	−.065	.029	−.061	−.057
	(.071)	(.072)	(.072)	(.068)	(.057)	(.072)	(.061)
Individual-level (level-2) fixed effects							
Far-right messages[b]	.242**	.396***	−.230**	.044	.034	.434***	.256**
	(.079)	(.075)	(.075)	(.084)	(.094)	(.075)	(.089)
Variance of random effects							
Intercept	.227***	.166***	.162***	.300***	.506***	.167***	.416***
	(.476)	(.407)	(.402)	(.556)	(.721)	(.408)	(.645)
Chi-squared test (df = 3)	17.379	37.897	52.463	1.860	30.38	221.81	68.756
	$p < .000$	$p < .000$	$p < .000$	$p > .05$	$p < .000$	$p < .000$	$p < .000$

N = 909. [2] [a]Reference category is exposure to non-far-right messages. *$p < .05$, **$p < .01$, ***$p < .001$.

Table 2. Estimates of Multilevel Mediation Model of Expressive activities

	Comment β(SE)	Like β(SE)	Share β(SE)
Enthusiasm model			
Direct effect of far-right message DV	−.037 (.044)	.153*** (.032)	.056 (.039)
Enthusiasm DVs	.443*** (.063)	.527*** (.046)	.589*** (.055)
Indirect effect: far-right message Enthusiasm DVs	.054** (.017)	.064*** (.018)	.071*** (.021)
Hope model			
Direct effect of far-right message DV	−.073 (.050)	.102** (.032)	.012 (.041)
Hope DV	.453*** (.067)	.576*** (.047)	.584*** (.060)
Indirect effect: far-right message Hope DV	.090*** (.020)	.114** (.021)	.116*** (.022)
Anger model			
Direct effect of far-right message DV	.055 (.046)	.227*** (.038)	.153*** (.045)
Anger DV	.325*** (.070)	.089 (.058)	.215** (.068)
Indirect effect: far-right message Anger DV	−.037** (.013)	−.010 (.008)	−.024* (.011)
Anxiety model			
Direct effect of far-right message DV	.012 (.045)	.216*** (.038)	.123** (.043)
Anxiety DV	.263*** (.063)	.065 (.051)	.223*** (.060)
Indirect effect: far-right message Anxiety DV	.006 (.009)	.001 (.003)	.005 (.008)

Notes: Multilevel mediation analysis. Grouped by participants. Estimates are restricted maximum likelihood estimates (REML). In each model, one emotion and one expressive activity are included. Message type is the main predictor, emotion is the mediator, and expressive activity is the ultimate outcome. *$p < .01$, **$p < .001$, ***$p < .000$.

the most parsimonious model, we decided not to include all emotions in the same model. The direct effects of emotional reactions on dependent variables in Table 2 supported H3b and H3c: hope and enthusiasm increased all three expressive activities. Results partially supported H3a since anger stimulated commenting and sharing, but not liking, which was not surprising because liking a message is an endorsement typically associated with positive emotions. Similar to anger, anxiety also provoked commenting and sharing, but not liking. The magnitude of these effects was smaller compared to the effects of enthusiasm and hope.

These results give the possibility to examine the mediating effects of emotions on expressive activities (H4). In Table 2, the indirect effects of the far-right message on expressive activities through hope and enthusiasm were positive and statistically significant. These positive meditations were mainly contributed by the significant lags from far-right messages to enthusiasm or hope, as well as from hope or enthusiasm to all expressive activities. However, the indirect effect of far-right messages on expressive activities via anger was negative. These negative indirect effects suggest that participants were angrier at non-far-right messages and more likely to comment and share these non-far-right messages, possibly leaving a negative comment along with the shared message. Lastly, the nonsignificant results in the anxiety model showed that anxiety did not mediate the effect of far-right messages on expressive activities. These results largely supported our mediation hypotheses H4a, H4b, and H4c.

To address the RQ2 about interaction effects between the message type and the discussed issue, we included cross-level interaction terms in our multilevel models. The results are numerically presented in Table 3 and visually plotted in Figure 1. Far-right message about a future form of governance, which was used as a comparison issue in the model, was more successful in being amplified through all expressive activities compared to non-far-right message addressing the same issue. On the contrary, far-right messages about fighting corruption produced a lower desire to engage in all expressive activities compared to a non-far-right message about corruption. When it came to the "pet" issue of Ukrainian far-right parties – state language policy – people who read far-right messages were more inclined to like it but were reluctant to comment on it than the non-far-right post.

Table 3. The Interaction Effect of Far-right Messages and Issues on Expressive Activities

	Comment	Like	Share
Issue-level (level-1) fixed effects			
Language issue[a]	.353***	−.454***	−.019
	(.080)	(.088)	(.083)
Corruption issue[a]	.224**	.524***	.280***
	(.080)	(.088)	(.083)
Individual-level (level-2) fixed effects			
Far-right messages[b]	.254*	.615***	.422***
	(.114)	(.104)	(.112)
Cross-level interactions			
Language issue × Far-right messages	−.264*	.628***	.177
	(.113)	(.124)	(.117)
Corruption issue × Far-right messages	−.392***	−1.168***	−.674***
	(.117)	(.124)	(.117)
Variance of random effects			
Intercept	.509***	.235***	.432***
	(.713)	(.485)	(.657)
Chi-squared test (df = 5)	30.38	221.81	68.756
	$p < .000$	$p < .000$	$p < .000$

N = 909. [2]. [a]Reference category is the issue of future form of governance. [b]Reference category is exposure to non-far-right messages. *$p < .05$; **$p < .01$; ***$p < .001$.

Table 4 further explores the interaction effects of issues and far-right messages on emotions. Far-right message about the future form of governance, which was used as a reference category, stimulated anger, while message about language policy reduced it. The effects of anxiety revealed the same pattern. In addition to anger, far-right message about future form of governance also bolstered enthusiasm and hope, but these two emotions were even more pronounced when people encountered the post about one state language. In contrast, far-right messages about corruption suppressed enthusiasm and hope. These results further detailed our RQ2, suggesting that far-right messages were not created equal, and their effect depended on the issue they addressed. In sum, when far-right parties in Ukraine advocated for one state language and unitarian form of governance, they invoked higher levels of enthusiasm and hope, as well as positive amplification in social media through liking, sharing, and commenting. However, these parties were unsuccessful when addressing issues discussed across the political spectrum, such as the fight against corruption in Ukraine. That is, people felt less enthusiastic and less engaged with far-right messages on corruption and were more likely to amplify moderate posts about corruption.

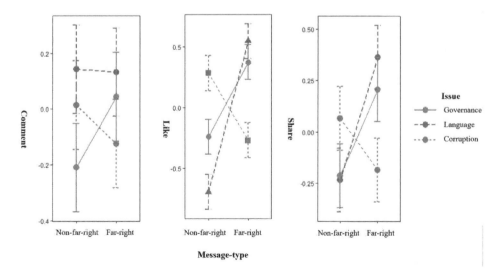

Figure 1. Interaction effect of Far-right messages and the discussed issues on expressive activities.

Table 4. The Effect of Far-Right Messages and Issues on Emotions

	Anger	Anxiety	Enthusiasm	Hope
Issue-level (level-1) fixed effects				
Language issue[a]	1.203*** (.090)	.532*** (.089)	−.588*** (.088)	−.676*** (.092)
Corruption issue[a]	.223* (.090)	−.111 (.089)	.238*** (.088)	.300** (.092)
Individual-level (level-2) fixed effects				
Far-right messages[b]	.246** (.105)	.356** (.111)	.242** (.107)	.262* (.106)
Cross-level interactions				
Language issue × Far-right messages	−1.438*** (.128)	−1.028*** (.126)	.833*** (.124)	.954*** (.131)
Corruption issue × Far-right messages	.009 (.128)	.092 (.126)	−.833*** (.124)	−.553*** (.131)
Variance of random effects				
Intercept	.219*** (.468)	.340*** (.583)	.284*** (.532)	.213*** (.462)
Chi-squared test (df = 5)	203.18 p < .000	93.153 p < .000	176.02 p < .000	161.62 p < .000

N = 909. [2]. [a]Reference category is the issue of future form of governance. [b]Reference category is exposure to non-far-right messages. *p < .05, **p < .01, ***p < .001

Conclusion and discussion

This experiment examined emotional reactions toward far-right messages about three different political issues and the role emotions play in amplification of such messages with social media expressive activities. We found that participants experienced enthusiasm and hope when they encountered far-right messages and were more likely to like and share those posts. Specifically, by evoking enthusiasm and hope, far-right messages received more likes, shares, and comments than centrist, middle-of-the-road posts. These findings support previous research, which demonstrated that enthusiasm led to higher voter turnout and campaign activism (Brader, 2006; Marcus & MacKuen, 1993), and suggest that these effects also exist for online political engagement. Similarly, our results demonstrate that anger stimulates sharing and commenting on a post, confirming that this emotion increases political engagement, both offline and online (Valentino et al., 2009). Our finding that anxiety increased inclination to comment also clarifies previous studies, which demonstrated that anxiety was positively associated with less costly forms of participation (Valentino et al., 2011). While anxiety might suppress political participation offline, it can still play a role in people's overall less costly political engagement online.

Many previous studies focused on the effect of negative campaigning and negative emotions elicited by far-right parties (Marx, 2020; Widmann, 2021; Wirz, 2018), and our study showed that positive emotions – enthusiasm and hope – are also an essential driver of far-rights' popularity. This observation is in line with findings about politicians' social media communication during election campaigns in Western democracies: more positive and enthusiasm-based campaigns increase media attention, as well as help to capture the attention of the public online and transform it into better electoral outcomes (Gerstlé & Nai, 2019). Our research shows that far-right parties are also capable of harnessing these positive emotions, alongside personal attacks and fear appeals, and that scholars need to pay attention to both ends of the emotional spectrum. Tendency to produce messages evoking enthusiasm and hope over those with anger and anxiety also depend on circumstances of the campaign: in post-Euromaidan Ukraine, nativist rhetoric helped far-right parties to promote feelings of hope, enthusiasm, and pride in the face of an external threat. Following Russian invasion of Ukraine, it is very likely that issues of national language and culture would become central not only to far-right parties, which lost their support in the second post-Euromaidan elections in 2020, but also all mainstream parties. At the same time, in other countries, perceived threat also comes from within, such as influx of immigrants or economic downturn, prompting far-right parties there to employ anti-elitist and anti-system rhetoric that resonates more with anger, fear, and anxiety. Future research should compare far-right messages overtime to better document this shift based on the geopolitical and socioeconomic circumstances.

Additionally, in this study, we tested whether the effects of far-right messages differ by issues they discuss. In line with previous research on partisan issue ownership (Tresch, Lefevere, & Walgrave, 2015; Walgrave & de Swert, 2004), we revealed that far-right parties can create online buzz when dealing with issues they traditionally 'owned' or dominated. However, when these parties discuss other issues, extensively addressed by other political parties before, the simplistic and exclusionary style of far-rights backfires. In our study, participants were more likely to amplify far-right messages about state language and future form of governance, issues pertinent to the far-right agenda in Ukraine, compared to the commonly addressed issue of corruption. These findings are good news because they suggest people are more likely to recognize the irrationality of far-right appeals when they are used in the discussion of topics that are well addressed by other political leaders. While it is hard to "steal" an issue from another party, mainstream politicians will benefit in long-term perspective if they start extensively discussing issues traditionally owned by far-rights such as immigration, asylum, crime and security, religion and morality (Gerstlé & Nai, 2019).

Our study also has a few shortcomings. First, it relies on a convenience sample of undergraduate students. Although our sample was geographically and ideologically diverse, and the voting preference of our participants was comparable to the general Ukrainian population, it was, nevertheless, more educated and not nationally representative. Different samples are still needed in future studies to assess the generalizability of our findings. Second, we did not measure why participants became angry, or whether comments they wanted to leave were meant to agree or disagree with the stimuli message. However, regardless of the comments' nature, such expressive activity still amplifies messages on social media. Just like in traditional outlets, any publicity is good publicity. Future research should create a more realistic setting where subjects would be dealing with software that closely mimics a social media environment and tracks real actions of subjects rather than the intentions of committing these actions.

Despite these limitations, this study has demonstrated that far-right messages are more likely to "go viral" on social media and that individual emotional reactions play an important role in spreading such messages. When people experience enthusiasm and hope as they read uplifting patriotic messages of far-right parties, they are more likely to endorse and amplify these posts. At the same time, far-right actors seem to be successful only when they are addressing issues that they "own," suggesting that if the online discussion is turned toward mainstream issues that are extensively addressed by other parties, far-right ideas might not be as appealing anymore. This conclusion should inspire political leaders to employ positive emotions, such as hope and enthusiasm, to engage with voters and motivate them for political participation online and offline. Examples from Barack Obama in the U.S. to Volodymyr Zelensky in Ukraine demonstrate that such messages are motivating and appeal especially to younger generations on social media.

Note

1. Oliphant, Roland. 2014. Up to a Dozen Ukraine Officials Dumped in Wheelie Bins. *The Telegraph*. https://www.telegraph.co.uk/news/worldnews/europe/ukraine/11145381/Up-to-a-dozen-Ukraine-officials-dumped-in-wheelie-binshtml.
2. Mixed-effect models with clustering by participants estimated via restricted maximum likelihood estimation (REML). For the variance of theintercept, a likelihood ratio test was used to compare the models with and without the random intercept. Nested model testing procedure was followed. TheChi-squared test shows the difference in deviance of two models: the one with the predictors vs. the one with the random intercept.

Acknowledgment

The authors would like to thank Zhongdang Pan for his support, guidance, and advice throughout all stages of this project. Our special gratitude also goes to Mykhailo Shumylo, Roksolana Hanyk-Pospolitak, Sergiy Kyselov, and Larysa Chovnyuk for their help with organizing data collection at the National University of "Kyiv-Mohyla Academy." This data collection also would not be possible without generous financial support of the Open Society Foundation and the Center for Russia, Eastern Europe, and Central Asia at the University of Wisconsin-Madison.

Disclosure statement

No potential conflict of interest was reported by the author(s).

Funding

This work was supported by the Open Society Foundations [Grant Number IN2016-27974].

ORCID

Larissa Doroshenko http://orcid.org/0000-0001-6763-628X

References

Aalberg, T., Esser, F., Reinemann, C., Strömbäck, J., & de Vreese, C. (2017). *Populist political communication in Europe*. New York, NY: Routledge.

Albanesi, C., Mazzoni, D., Cicognani, E., & Zani, B. (2016). Discriminatory contexts, emotions and civic/political engagement among native Italians and migrants. *Journal of Community & Applied Social Psychology*, 26(2), 179–186. doi:10.1002/casp.2245

Berger, J., & Milkman, K. L. (2012). What makes online content viral? *Journal of Marketing Research*, 49(2), 192–205. doi:10.1509/jmr.10.0353

Biersack, J., & O'Lear, S. (2014). The geopolitics of Russia's annexation of Crimea: narratives, identity, silences, and energy. *Eurasian Geography and Economics*, 55(3), 247–269. doi:10.1080/15387216.2014.985241

Blassnig, S., & Wirz, D. S. (2019). Populist and popular: An experiment on the drivers of user reactions to populist posts on Facebook. *Social Media+Society*, 5(4), 1–12. doi:10.1177/2056305119890062

Bobba, G. (2019). Social media populism: features and 'likeability' of lega nord communication on facebook. *European Political Science*, 18(1), 11–23. doi:10.1057/s41304-017-0141-8

Bos, L., Van Der Brug, W., & De Vreese, C. H. (2013). An experimental test of the impact of style and rhetoric on the perception of right-wing populist and mainstream party leaders. *Acta Politica*, 48(2), 192–208. doi:10.1057/ap.2012.27

Brader, T. (2006). *Campaigning for hearts and minds: How emotional appeals in political ads work*. Chicago, IL: University of Chicago Press.

Cassell, K. J. (2021). When "following" the leader inspires action: Individuals' receptivity to discursive frame elements on social media. *Political Communication*, 38(5), 581–603. doi:10.1080/10584609.2020.1829761

Chadwick, A. (2015). Toward a theory of persuasive hope: Effects of cognitive appraisals, hope appeals, and hope in the context of climate change. *Health Communication*, 30(6), 598–611. doi:10.1080/10410236.2014.916777

Di Grazia, J., McKelvey, K., Bollen, J., & Rojas, F. (2013). More tweets, more votes: Social media as a quantitative indicator of political behavior. *PLoS One*, 8(11), e79449. doi:10.1371/journal.pone.0079449

Doroshenko, L., Schneider, T., Kofanov, D., Xenos, M. A., Scheufele, D. A., & Brossard, D. (2019). Ukrainian nationalist parties and connective action: An analysis of electoral campaigning and social media sentiments. *Information, Communication & Society*, 22(10), 1376–1395. doi:10.1080/1369118X.2018.1426777

Ernst, N., Esser, F., Blassnig, S., & Engesser, S. (2019). Favorable opportunity structures for populist communication: Comparing different types of politicians and issues in social media, television and the press. *The International Journal of Press/Politics*, 24(2), 165–188. doi:10.1177/1940161218819430

Friedrich Ebert Stiftung. (2020). *Young worlds? Political and social views of young people in Russia, Ukraine and Belarus*. Berlin, Germany: Department for Central and Eastern Europe.

Gan, C., Lee, F. L., & Li, Y. (2017). Social media use, political affect, and participation among university students in urban China. *Telematics and Informatics*, 34(7), 936–947. doi:10.1016/j.tele.2017.04.002

Gerodimos, R., & Justinussen, J. (2015). Obama's 2012 Facebook campaign: Political communication in the age of the like button. *Journal of Information Technology & Politics*, 12(2), 113–132. doi:10.1080/19331681.2014.982266

Gerstlé, J., & Nai, A. (2019). Negativity, emotionality and populist rhetoric in election campaigns worldwide, and their effects on media attention and electoral success. *European Journal of Communication*, 34(4), 410–444. doi:10.1177/0267323119861875

Gibson, R., & Cantijoch, M. (2013). Conceptualizing and measuring participation in the age of the internet: Is online political engagement really different to offline? *The Journal of Politics*, 75(3), 701–716. doi:10.1017/S0022381613000431

Gil de Zúñiga, H., & Valenzuela, S. (2011). The mediating path to a stronger citizenship: Online and offline networks, weak ties, and civic engagement. *Communication Research*, 38(3), 397–421. doi:10.1177/0093650210384984

Givens, T. E. (2005). *Voting radical right in Western Europe*. New York, NY: Cambridge University Press.

Goethals, G. R. (2021). The 2020 election and its aftermath: Love, lies, and ensorceling leadership. *Leadership*, 17(2), 240–250. doi:10.1177/1742715021994352

Hameleers, M., & Schmuck, D. (2017). It's us against them: A comparative experiment on the effects of populist messages communicated via social media. *Information, Communication & Society*, 20(9), 1425–1444. doi:10.1080/1369118X.2017.1328523

Hameleers, M., Bos, L., Fawzi, N., Reinemann, C., Andreadis, I., Corbu, N., & Axelsson, S. (2018). Start spreading the news: A comparative experiment on the effects of populist communication on political engagement in sixteen European countries. *The International Journal of Press/Politics*, 23(4), 517–538. doi:10.1177/1940161218786786

Hasell, A., & Weeks, B. E. (2016). Partisan provocation: The role of partisan news use and emotional responses in political information sharing in social media. *Human Communication Research*, 42(4), 641–661. doi:10.1111/hcre.12092

Hasell, A. (2020). Shared emotion: The social amplification of partisan news on Twitter. *Digital Journalism*, 9, 1162–1183. doi:10.1080/21670811.2020.1831937

Heiss, R., Schmuck, D., & Matthes, J. (2019). What drives interaction in political actors' Facebook posts? Profile and content predictors of user engagement and political actors' reactions. *Information, Communication & Society*, 22(10), 1497–1513. doi:10.1080/1369118X.2018.1445273

Hoffman, L., & Rovine, M. J. (2007). Multilevel models for the experimental psychologist: Foundations and illustrative examples. *Behavior Research Methods*, 39(1), 101–117. doi:10.3758/BF03192848

Huddy, L., Feldman, S., & Cassese, E. (2007). On the distinct political effects of anxiety and anger. In R. Neuman, G. Marcus, A. Crigler, & M. MacKuen (Eds.), *The affect effect* (pp. 202–230). Chicago, IL: University of Chicago Press.

Ignazi, P. (2003). *Extreme right parties in Western Europe*. New York, NY: Oxford University Press.

Jacobs, K., Sandberg, L., & Spierings, N. (2020). Twitter and Facebook: Populists' double-barreled gun? *New Media & Society*, 22(4), 611–633. doi:10.1177/1461444819893991

Jenkins, L. (2018). Why do all our feelings about politics matter? *The British Journal of Politics and International Relations*, 20(1), 191–205. doi:10.1177/1369148117746917

John, N. A. (2013). The social logics of sharing. *The Communication Review*, 16(3), 113–131. doi:10.1080/10714421.2013.807119

Jost, P., Maurer, M., & Hassler, J. (2020). Populism fuels love and anger: The impact of message features on users' reactions on Facebook. *International Journal of Communication*, 14, 2081–2102.

Katz, J., Barris, M., & Jain, A. (2013). *The social media president: Barack Obama and the politics of digital engagement*. New York, NY: Palgrave Macmillan.

Krämer, B. (2014). Media populism: A conceptual clarification and some theses on its effects. *Communication Theory*, 24, 42–60. doi:10.1111/comt.12029

Larsson, A. O., & Moe, H. (2014). Triumph of the underdogs? Comparing Twitter use by political actors during two Norwegian election campaigns. *SAGE Open*, 4(4), 1–13. doi:10.1177/2158244014559015

Lazarus, R. (1991). *Emotion and adaptation*. New York, NY: Oxford University Press.

Lilleker, D. G., & Balaban, D. C. (2021). Populism on Facebook. In J. Haßler, M. Magin, U. Russmann, & V. Fenoll (Eds.), *Campaigning on Facebook in the 2019 European Parliament Election* (pp. 267–282). Cham, Switzerland: Palgrave Macmillan.

Marcus, G., & MacKuen, M. (1993). Anxiety, enthusiasm, and vote: The emotional underpinnings of learning and involvement during presidential campaigns. *American Political Science Review*, 87, 672–685. doi:10.2307/2938743

Marcus, G., Neuman, R., & MacKuen, M. (2000). *Affective intelligence and political judgment*. Chicago, IL: The University of Chicago Press.

Marcus, G., Neuman, R., MacKuen, M., Wolak, J., & Keele, L. (2006). The measure and mismeasure of emotion. In D. Redlawsk (Ed.), *Feeling Politics* (pp. 31–45). New York, NY: Palgrave Macmillan.

Marcus, G. E., Valentino, N., Vasilopoulos, P., & Foucault, M. (2019). Applying the theory of affective intelligence to support for authoritarian policies and parties. *Political Psychology*, 40, 109–139. doi:10.1111/pops.12571

Marlin, M. (2016). Concept of 'decentralization' and 'federalization' in Ukraine: Political signifiers or distinct constitutionalist approaches for devolutionary federalism? *Nationalism and Ethnic Politics*, 22(3), 278–299. doi:10.1080/13537113.2016.1203695

Marx, P. (2020). Anti-elite politics and emotional reactions to socio-economic problems: Experimental evidence on "pocketbook anger" from France, Germany, and the United States. *British Journal of Sociology*, 71, 608–624. doi:10.1111/1468-4446.12750

Mudde, C. (2002). *The ideology of the extreme right*. Manchester, UK: Manchester University Press.

Mullinix, K. J., Leeper, T. J., Druckman, J. N., & Freese, J. (2015). The generalizability of survey experiments. *Journal of Experimental Political Science*, 2(2), 109–138. doi:10.1017/XPS.2015.19

Namkoong, K., Fung, T., & Scheufele, D. A. (2012). The politics of emotion: News media attention, emotional responses, and participation during the 2004 U.S. presidential election. *Mass Communication and Society*, 15(1), 25–45. doi:10.1080/15205436.2011.563894

Norris, E.-D., Martinez-Vasquez, J., & Norregaard, J. (2000). *Making decentralization work: the case of Russia, Ukraine, and Kazakhstan* [Paper presentation]. International Monetary Fund Conference on Fiscal Decentralization, Washington, DC, USA

Onuch, O. (2015). EuroMaidan protests in Ukraine: Social media versus social networks. *Problems of Post-Communism*, 62(4), 217–235. doi:10.1080/10758216.2015.1037676

Pan, H., Liu, S., Miao, D., & Yuan, Y. (2018). Sample size determination for mediation analysis of longitudinal data. *BMC Medical Research Methodology*, 18(1), 1–11. doi:10.1186/s12874-018-0473-2

Quené, H., & van den Bergh, H. (2004). On multilevel modelling of data from repeated measures designs: A tutorial. *Speech Communication, 43*(1–2), 103–121. doi:10.1016/j.specom.2004.02.004

Rockwood, N., & Hayes, A. (2017). *MLmed: An SPSS macro for multilevel mediation and conditional process analysis.* Poster presentation. Boston, MA, USA: Association of Psychological Science Meeting.

Rojas, H., & Puig-i-Abril, E. (2009). Mobilizers mobilized: Information, expression, mobilization and participation in the digital age. *Journal of Computer-Mediated Communication, 14*(4), 902–927. doi:10.1111/j.1083-6101.2009.01475.x

Schmuck, D., & Matthes, J. (2017). Effects of economic and symbolic threat appeals in right-wing populist advertising on anti-immigrant attitudes: the impact of textual and visual appeals. *Political Communication, 34*(4), 607–626. doi:10.1080/10584609.2017.1316807

Smith, C. A., & Ellsworth, P. C. (1985). Patterns of cognitive appraisal in emotion. *Journal of Personality and Social Psychology, 48*(4), 813–838. doi:10.1037/0022-3514.48.4.813

Sterrett, D., Malato, D., Benz, J., Kantor, L., Tompson, T., Rosenstiel, T., & Loker, K. (2019). Who shared it? Deciding what news to trust on social media. *Digital Journalism, 7*(6), 783–801. doi:10.1080/21670811.2019.1623702

Tajfel, H. (1974). Social identity and intergroup behaviour. *Social Science Information, 13*(2), 65–93. doi:10.1177/053901847401300204

Tresch, A., Lefevere, J., & Walgrave, S. (2015). 'Steal me if you can!' The impact of campaign messages on associative issue ownership. *Party Politics, 21*(2), 198–208. doi:10.1177/1354068812472576

Valentino, N., Gregorowicz, K., & Groenendyk, E. (2009). Efficacy, emotions and the habit of participation. *Political Behavior, 31*(3), 307–330. doi:10.1007/s11109-008-9076-7

Valentino, N. A., Brader, T., Groenendyk, E. W., Gregorowicz, K., & Hutchings, V. L. (2011). Election night's alright for fighting: The role of emotions in political participation. *The Journal of Politics, 73*(1), 156–170. doi:10.1017/S0022381610000939

Valkenburg, P. M., & Peter, J. (2013). The differential susceptibility to media effects model. *Journal of Communication, 63*(2), 221–243. doi:10.1111/jcom.12024

Walgrave, S., & de Swert, K. (2004). The making of the (issues of) Vlaams Blok. *Political Communication, 21*(4), 479–500. doi:10.1080/10584600490522743

Wallace, C., & Latcheva, R. (2006). Economic transformation outside the law: Corruption, trust in public institutions and the informal economy in transition countries of Central and Eastern Europe. *Europe-Asia Studies, 58*(1), 81–102. doi:10.1080/09668130500401707

Widmann, T. (2021). How emotional are populists really? Factors explaining emotional appeals in the communication of political parties. *Political Psychology, 42*(1), 163–181. doi:10.1111/pops.12693

Wirz, D. (2018). Persuasion through emotion? An experimental test of the emotion-eliciting nature of populist communication. *International Journal of Communication, 12,* 1114–1138.

Wojcieszak, M., Bimber, B., Feldman, L., & Stroud, N. J. (2016). Partisan news and political participation: Exploring mediated relationships. *Political Communication, 33*(2), 241–260. doi:10.1080/10584609.2015.1051608

Zhang, Y., Wells, C., Wang, S., & Rohe, K. (2018). Attention and amplification in the hybrid media system: The composition and activity of Donald Trump's Twitter following during the 2016 presidential election. *New Media & Society, 20*(9), 3161–3182. doi:10.1177/1461444817744390

Online Appendix

Participant's use of Ukrainian and Russian language in everyday life

Index variable ($\alpha = .854$) comprised of three items, measuring what language respondents used (1) at home; (2) at school/work; (3) with friends; 1 corresponds to "always using Ukrainian," 2 to a "mixture of both languages," and 3 to "always using Russian" ($M = 1.6$, $SD = .73$).

Table 1A. (A) Geographical Distribution of Participants Home Regions Compared to Ukrainian Population (as of *November* 1, 2015 to match the timing of the study)

Region of Ukraine	Participants (% of the Sample)	Ukraine (% of the Population)
Cherkasy Oblast	3.00	2.75
Chernihiv Oblast	3.60	2.31
Chernivtsi Oblast	2.00	2.01
Crimea (Autonomous Republic)	2.30	4.33
Dnipropetrovsk Oblast	2.00	7.19
Donetsk Oblast	5.90	9.68
Ivano-Frankivsk Oblast	N/A	3.05
Kharkiv Oblast	1.70	6.00
Kherson Oblast	1.70	2.35
Khmelnitskyi Oblast	2.60	2.86
Kirovohrad Oblast	2.60	2.15
Kyiv (Municipality)	29.40	6.40
Kyiv Oblast	16.50	3.82
Luhansk Oblast	3.00	5.00
Lviv Oblast	8.90	5.60
Mykolaiv Oblast	1.30	2.56
Odessa Oblast	1.70	5.27
Poltava Oblast	3.60	3.18
Rivne Oblast	2.00	2.56
Sevastopol (Municipality)	.30	0.84
Sumy Oblast	2.60	2.46
Ternopil Oblast	3.30	2.35
Vinnytsia Oblast	5.60	3.54
Volyn Oblast	2.30	2.30
Zakarpattia Oblast	1.30	2.78
Zaporizhzhia Oblast	4.30	3.88
Zhytomyr Oblast	4.00	2.76

Source: State Statistic Service of Ukraine (http://www.ukrstat.gov.ua/).

Pretest results (N = 48)

Far-right posts

- Corruption (like $t(59) = 2.64$, $p < .05$; share $t(88) = 1.28$, $p > .05$; comment $t(94) = 1.39$, $p > .05$)
- Form of governance (like $t(83) = 1.51$, $p > .05$; share $t(64) = 1.81$, $p < .05$; comment $t(87) = 0.95$, $p > .05$)
- National language (like $t(60) = 3.28$, $p < .05$; share $t(54) = 2.72$, $p < .05$; comment $t(85) = 1.15$, $p > .05$)

Moderate posts

- Corruption (like $t(87) = 1.21$, $p < .05$; share $t(94) = 0.95$, $p < .05$; comment $t(93) = 0.62$, $p > .05$)
- Form of governance (like $t(94) = 0.06$, $p > .05$; share $t(94) = 0.29$, $p > .05$; comment $t(88) = 0.65$, $p < .05$)
- National language (like $t(48) = 0.33$, $p > .05$; share $t(92) = 0.38$, $p > .05$; comment $t(94) = 0.21$, $p > .05$)

Stimulus material in Ukrainian (original) and English (translated by the authors)

Far-right messages (assigned randomly, displayed in random order)

- *Corruption*

Всіх суддів позвільняти. Особливо Господарського суду – там найбільша корупція. І ніякої матеріальної винагороди. Конфіскація.

Fire all judges, especially in the Business Court – they have the largest corruption. There should be no financial damage recoup, only confiscation.

- *Future form of governance*

Не допустіть федералізацію України та сепаратизм на Донбасі.

Prevent federalization of Ukraine and separatism in Donbass.

- *Status of Russian language*:

Єдина державна мова – це аксіома, яка не може бути предметом політичних торгів

One state language is an axiom, which cannot be subject to political negotiations

Non-far-right messages (assigned randomly, displayed in random order):

- *Corruption*

Демонтувати статуї Леніна – мало Треба будувати справедливе гос-во без хабарництва, корупції, брехні, яке служить народу, а не владі

It is not enough to dismantle Lenin's statues – we need to build a just state without briberies, corruption, and lies that serves people and not officials

Table 2A. (A) Support for Far-right Parties among Study Participants, Ukrainian Youth, and Ukrainian Population

Far-right Party	Participants (% of the Sample)	Ukrainian Students (% of the Population)	Ukrainians (% of the Population)
Svoboda	5.00	2.60	4.71
Radykalna Partyja Oleha Lyashko	4.00	4.90	7.44
Pravy Sector	3.30	4.10	1.80

Sources: Central Election Committee of Ukraine (https://cvk.gov.ua/) and Analytical Center "Democracy Observation" (http://od.org.ua).

- *Future form of governance*

Питання федералізації слизьке і не однозначне. Але значну кількість прав і грошей потрібно передати на місця (як в тій же Польщі)

The question of federalization is dubious and ambiguous, but substantial number of rights and money has to be given to local governments (as in Poland)

- *Status of Russian language*

Чим менше російської мови у новій владі України тим менше буде територія майбутньої України. Беріть приклад з Канади.

The less Russian in new government of Ukraine, the less will be the territory of future Ukraine. Let's follow example of Canada

Donetsk don't tell: 'Hybrid war' in Ukraine and the limits of social media influence operations

Lennart Maschmeyer, Alexei Abrahams, Peter Pomerantsev, and Volodymyr Yermolenko

ABSTRACT
Many fear that social media enable more potent influence operations than traditional mass media. This belief is widely shared yet rarely tested. We challenge this emerging wisdom by comparing social media and television as vectors for influence operations targeting Ukraine. This article develops a theoretical framework based on media structure, showing how and why decentralized and centralized media offer distinct opportunities and challenges for conducting influence operations. This framework indicates a relative advantage for television in both dissemination and persuasiveness. We test this framework against the Russo-Ukrainian conflict (before the 2022 escalation), contributing new data from a national survey and a new dataset of Telegram activity. We identify fifteen disinformation narratives, and, using statistical analysis, examine correlations between media consumption, audience exposure to, and agreement with, narratives, and foreign policy preferences. To explore causal mechanisms, we follow up with content analysis. Findings strongly support our theoretical framework. While consuming some partisan social media channels is correlated with narrative exposure, there is no correlation with narrative agreement. Meanwhile, consumption of partisan television channels shows clear and consistent correlation. Finally, agreement with narratives also correlates with foreign policy preferences. However, and importantly, findings indicate the overall limitations of influence operations.

Many fear that information technology increases the potency of influence operations, posing a significant challenge to the liberal world order (Bennett & Livingston, 2018; Bisen, 2019; Deibert, 2020; Howard, 2020; Warner, 2019). Influence operations in general refer to intelligence operations that pursue active interference in an adversary's affairs (Callanan, 2009, p. 1), and specifically fears have centered on two instruments regularly used in such operations: propaganda and disinformation. Propaganda involves "the dissemination of information intended to manipulate perceptions in support of one's cause or to damage an adversary." (Lowenthal, 2009, p. 180). Disinformation is "non-attributed or falsely attributed communication, written or oral, containing intentionally false, incomplete, or misleading information (frequently combined with true information), which seeks to deceive, misinform, and/or mislead the target" (Shultz & Godson, 1984, p. 38).

These instruments produce political outcomes by influencing public opinion in a targeted state toward alignment with the interests of the sponsor, typically concerning foreign policy (Andrew & Mitrokhin, 1999, pp. 294–99; Pomerantsev & Weiss, 2014, p. 15). Emerging wisdom expects five key properties of social media to increase the effectiveness of influence operations: 1) openness, (2) anonymity, (3) customizability, (4) algorithmic favoring of polarizing content, and (5) automation.[1] Due to these characteristics, social media influence operations should both reach larger audiences and sway the opinions of a greater audience proportion.

These advantages remain hypothetical, however. Most existing research maps mechanisms and patterns in the dissemination of disinformation (Bradshaw, Howard, Kollanyi, & Neudert, 2020; Lazer et al., 2018; Linvill & Warren, 2020). In contrast to this "supply side" of disinformation, research on the demand side – and in particular, audience effects – is scarcer. Emerging experimental evidence indicates some audience effects (Bauer & von Hohenberg, 2020; Min & Luqiu, 2021;

Zimmermann & Kohring, 2020). Systematic evidence is lacking, however, and no studies have conducted a side-by-side comparison of different media platforms (Tsfati et al., 2020, p. 168). This paper contributes such a comparison, focusing on television and social media. We develop a theoretical framework linking media structure to distinct opportunities and challenges as vectors for influence operations and present new evidence from Ukraine – a crucial case with near-ideal conditions for effective influence operations. We argue emerging wisdom overestimates the opportunities social media offers while neglecting the challenges involved in implementing influence operations. Contrary to prevailing assumptions, we show that television, the archetypal 20th century mass medium, retains key advantages in content dissemination and persuasiveness.

To test this argument, the article examines how the secrecy, dissemination, and persuasiveness of influence operations via partisan social media channels compares to partisan television channels. This analysis contributes extensive new and original data. Specifically, we measure, across a wide range of media, the correlation between news consumption and exposure to disinformation narratives, the correlation between exposure and agreement with these narratives, as well as the correlation between narrative agreement and foreign policy preferences that align with the sponsor (Russia). We identify a set of 15 Russian-sponsored disinformation narratives and trace their dissemination, audience exposure to and agreement with these narratives across Ukraine's media system via a representative survey of 903 Ukrainians. We then focus the analysis a specific set of partisan television channels and Telegram channels known as major outlets for disinformation. To that end, we build a new dataset of messages posted on anonymous Telegram channels from July to October 2020.

Our findings show social media influence operations facilitate secrecy but struggle to disseminate content at scale. Partisan television channels reach a far wider audience than partisan social media. Survey data indicate partisan television audiences are not only exposed to a higher share of narratives but also agree with a much higher share of these narratives. Consumption of partisan television is most robustly correlated with exposure to, and agreement with, narratives. Conversely, and contrary to prevailing fears, consumption of partisan social media channels is neither statistically significantly correlated to audience agreement with, nor even to exposure to narratives. Only YouTube channels form a marked exception, yet considering the platform's centralized structure, this exception ultimately provides further support for the theory. In short, findings confirm television retains an advantage both in dissemination and persuasiveness. Hence, we conclude emerging wisdom errs in ascribing superior efficacy to social media influence operations. These findings indicate an urgent need to reassess prevailing fears of social media influence operations.

Influence operations, technology and media structure

Influence operations manipulate public opinion in a target state toward the interests of their sponsor, typically concerning foreign policy (Godson & Shultz, 1985, p. 36; Andrew, 2000, 631–32). Consequently, such operations matter in world politics because, provided they sway a sufficient proportion of citizens, they can affect both domestic and international political outcomes. Political scientists have traditionally dismissed the influence of public opinion on foreign policy, assuming the public is generally ill-informed and susceptible to elite cues (Almond, 1956; Axelrod, 1967). Yet recent work not only shows a clear influence of public opinion on foreign policy, but also a significant impact of mass media on public opinion (Soroka, 2003). These findings confirm the experience of former KGB disinformation operation Vladislav Bittman, who argued the rise of modern mass media, and especially television, increased the potency of influence operations by expanding the scale of the audience that can be reached (Bittman, 1985, p. 49).

Successful influence operations must fulfil three main conditions. First, they must produce narratives that effectively, and persuasively convey the intended message. Second, they must disseminate that message to a sufficiently large audience to affect national-level political decisions. Third, they must persuade a sufficient proportion of that audience. While mass media offer great opportunities for mass influence, achieving these conditions in practice has been difficult. Specifically, finding a way to manipulate foreign media outlets to produce and/or disseminate content aligned with the interests of the sponsor at sufficient scale to influence significant parts of a population while keeping this influence secret is extremely difficult (Bittman, 1985; Warner, 2019, p. 38).

Consider a television network, where both content production and dissemination is controlled by the station's management and employees. Infiltrating such a centralized organization is hard because it requires placing a human agent in a position capable of manipulating content production and dissemination. They require a cover identity passing the employer's scrutiny (Andrew, 2000, p. 613). Moreover, the agent must hide their identity while pushing out partisan content. Doing so is both challenging and involves significant risks of failure (Bittman, 1985). Consequently, traditional influence operations – like other types of covert operations – tended to be either too small to achieve an impact, or became too large to stay hidden.

Today, an emerging wisdom holds social media alleviate some of these challenges, rendering influence operations even more powerful. Specifically, five properties of social media are presumed to enable these advantages: *(1) openness, (2) anonymity, (3) customizability, (4) algorithmic favoring of polarizing content, and (5) automation.* Social media platforms offer unprecedented "openness." Anyone can open an account easily and for free (Reis, Correia, Murai, Veloso, & Benevenuto, 2019), facilitating the manipulation of narrative production and dissemination. Second, because few social media platforms have strong identity verification practices, operatives can easily obfuscate their identities, allowing them to create inauthentic accounts that look like real people, sharing news through peer groups (Bauer & von Hohenberg, 2020). Importantly, current research indicates social cues from peers shape citizen opinion as much, if not more, as elite cues (Kertzer & Zeitzoff, 2017). Inauthentic accounts that emulate peer cues thus plausibly increase persuasiveness. Third, influence operatives can tailor content to audiences at scale, facilitating both dissemination

and persuasiveness (Dunbar, 2021, p. 38). This ability reflects social media's "surveillance capital" business model, surveilling user behavior to model preferences and customize advertisements (Zuboff, 2015). This model also enables the fourth advantage: automated dissemination of polarizing content. To continuously surveil users, platforms must keep users persistently engaged. Users may choose what is *said*, but algorithms choose what is *read*. The more attention-grabbing the content, the greater user engagement tends to be. Hence, algorithms tend to promote polarizing and extreme content (Deibert, 2020, p. 135). Accordingly, there are signs of a fragmentation of the public sphere (Pariser, 2012; Pfetsch, 2018)— facilitating future influence operations targeting such fringe communities. Fifth, automation enables state actors to easily create thousands or even tens of thousands of accounts. These accounts can be centrally controlled with a computer program (a "bot" network) or managed by centrally commanded human users (a "sockpuppet" network). Such *inauthentic coordinated networks*, Owen Jones suggests, can substantively impact discourse (Jones, 2021). Ideally, they combine all of the advantages in production, dissemination, and persuasiveness.

These assumptions are now widely shared, yet rarely tested. While the impact of television on audience perception and policy preferences has long been empirically established (Behr & Iyengar, 1985, p. 39), the reach and effectiveness of social media continue to be primarily presumed rather than proven. A systematic comparison of media types and audience effects is lacking. Moreover, emerging wisdom focuses primarily on opportunities, neglecting the challenges involved in practice.

We argue that the prevailing focus on opportunities opened by technological change risks overshadowing the continuing salience of media structure as a determinant of the effectiveness of influence operations. Traditional mass media are centralized, meaning production and dissemination occur from one central hub. This centralized structure makes infiltration manipulation of these processes harder than in decentralized social media platforms where each node, i.e. user, can produce and disseminate content while emulating peers. However, once that hurdle has been overcome, centralized media – and we focus on television, the archetypical mass medium of the 20th century – provide significant advantages both in dissemination and persuasiveness.

In practice, social media's advantages in secrecy and persuasiveness primarily translate into efficacy increases at the *individual* level. The ability to hide content provenance that enables the emulation of peer cues provides a distinct advantage, and accordingly some see it as a defining feature of social media disinformation (Martin, Shapiro, & Nedashkovskaya, 2019, p. 2). Elevating this plausible capacity to persuade individuals to a national-level impact requires disseminating content at scale, however. And here centralized media has a key advantage since, contrary to prevailing expectations, scaling up social media operations involves significant efforts. Television stations have an established audience, and once an actor has found a way to manipulate the production and dissemination processes, the actor can reach that entire audience.

In contrast, freshly created social media accounts have no followers. Building up a following takes time and money, requiring users to game algorithms (Deibert, 2020, chap. 2). Meanwhile, efforts at automation have proven easily detectable (DFRLab, 2017). Creating credible accounts at sufficient numbers and with sufficient followers to achieve a national-level impact similarly takes significant efforts and time (Abrahams & Leber, 2021, p. 27). The same applies to content customization. Adjusting content to specific groups requires researching their needs and interests. Meanwhile, social media users cannot alter dissemination algorithms. Hence, dissemination depends on criteria set by algorithm designers, which are typically secret (Lustig et al., 2016). Customized content may thus fail to disseminate widely. Social media campaigns promise inauthentic networks of users to amplify content through sharing and automated dissemination, deceiving authentic users into believing epistemic communities with similar views exist (Martin, Shapiro, & Nedashkovskaya, 2019, p. 15). To achieve this, however, content must achieve sufficient user engagement to be prioritized by algorithms (Just & Latzer, 2017). Achieving these requirements is a non-trivial challenge – there is an entire industry devoted to it (Rival IQ, 2021) and in this attention economy sponsors of influence operations neither have a monopoly, nor superior knowledge of the underlying algorithms. Due to these challenges, social media influence operations are likely to be relatively small in scale and reach a correspondingly small audience. Within this small audience, the capacity to customize content individually and emulate peer cues may allow for higher persuasion rates individually compared to television that lacks both capacities.

Yet the centralized structure of television not only provides an advantage at disseminating content at scale to its entire audience, but also facilitates persuasiveness. In comparison to social media's emulation of peer cues and content customization, television offers a much cruder mechanism of shaping audience perception through repetition. Yet its efficacy is well-proven. Noelle-Neumann established that the more often people are exposed to television content the more they tend to believe it (Noelle-Neumann, 1993). Since content, once designed, can be repeated endlessly, doing so also requires less added efforts per repetition than social media operations, which required continued adjustments of content to game algorithms.

Finally, the same decentralized structure of social media that facilities anonymity also tends to undermines credibility, compared to centralized news outlets. Even when sponsors of social media influence operations manage to create accounts with large audiences, these lack the reputation and credibility of established television stations. Accordingly, survey data has consistently shown television to be perceived as more credible news sources than social media (Correspondent, Tom Knowles, Technology, 2023; Mehrabi, Hassan, Sham, & Sham Shahkat Ali, 2009; Salaudeen & Onyechi, 2020). Moreover, previous research indicates social media content is perceived as most credible when picked up by television news (Gearhart & Kang, 2014). This dynamic underlines that social media and traditional media do not exist in separate worlds, but interact both ways – the discussion picks up the implications in more detail. Consequently, influence operations through television are likely to both reach a larger audience *and* to sway the opinion of a larger share of its audience.

Hypotheses

Because we do not have access to the production processes via traditional media vis-à-vis social media themselves, we examine whether dissemination and persuasiveness of influence operations run through them correspond to the predictions of the theory. Since we focus on influence operations, rather than simply comparing what type of media people consume, we examine specific partisan channels on social and traditional media in Ukraine. We refer to these as partisan because previous research has shown them to be key vectors disseminating Russian-sponsored disinformation narratives – more on this in the methods section below. Accordingly, based on the theory developed above we formulate five main hypotheses.

H1: *The more people agree with narratives, the more likely their foreign policy preferences are to align with the sponsor's interests.*

As discussed, influence operations aim to manipulate public opinion, typically regarding foreign policy and we expect that the more often people are exposed to narratives, the more likely they are to be swayed by them – reflected in their foreign policy preferences.

H2: *Audiences of partisan television channels are more likely to be exposed to narratives than audiences of partisan social media channels.*

Due to the advantages of television in dissemination discussed above, we expect audiences of partisan television channels to be more likely to be exposed to these narratives than audiences of partisan social media channels.

H3: *Audiences of partisan television channels are more likely to agree with narratives than audiences of partisan social media channels.*

Due to the advantages of television in persuasiveness, we expect television audiences to be more likely to be swayed by narratives, and thus expect a greater correlation between exposure and agreement.

H4: *State sponsorship/content origin of influence operations via social media is less likely to be attributable than via television.*

The previous section that social media platforms facilitate anonymity, and identified significant challenges involved in keeping external manipulation of content production secret in television stations. Therefore, we expect the origins of social media influence operations to be less likely to become publicly known than for television stations.

H5: *Partisan television channels are likely to reach a larger audience than partisan social media channels.*

This hypothesis tests the expected dissemination advantage of television compared to social media.

Case study

To test this theory, we conduct a case study of the Russo-Ukrainian conflict since 2013. This conflict offers a most likely case for the expectation that social media increases the potency of influence operations for four main reasons. First, until the invasion this spring it has been the paradigmatic case of "hybrid war," meaning aggression short of open war empowered by new technology, and especially influence operations (Fitton, 2016). Second, Russia is widely perceived as a "master" of the latter (Hill, 2017; Chivvis, 2017). Finally, Ukraine's close cultural and linguistic proximity to Russia facilitates the deployment of effective narratives (Robbins, 2021). Fourth, social media have become the preferred news source for a majority of Ukrainians (Internews Ukraine, 2020).

Methodology

We employ mixed-methods, combining quantitative and content analysis to first verify which correlations predicted by our hypotheses are backed by the data before exploring potential causal explanations. We commence by identifying a set of 15 disinformation narratives attributed to based on media monitoring by [Internews Ukraine]. Its

"Open Source Communications Analytics and Research" project has identified a set of disinformation narratives from monitoring a wide set of Ukrainian media, including print and broadcast media, both traditional and social media. Consequently, we survey a random sample of 903 Ukrainians to track audience media consumption habits, exposure to narratives and agreement with the latter, as well as foreign policy preferences. We contracted the Kyiv International Institute for Sociology to carry out this survey.[2] Respondents were also asked how often they consumed 36 different media, including all relevant social media platforms (Twitter, Facebook, Vkontakte, WhatsApp, Telegram, Viber, YouTube), TV, newspaper, radio, etc. Additionally, they were asked how often they consumed specific TV channels (1 + 1, Україна, ICTV, СТБ, Інтер, 112 Україна, NewsOne, Прямий, П'ятий канал, Zik) and specific social media channels (Tiomnyi Rytsar, Legitimnyi, Rezident, and Joker on Telegram; Anatoliy and Olga Shariy, Klymenko Time, Strana.ua, Vitaliy Portnikov, Sergiy Ivanov, and Pavlo Kazarin on YouTube). Respondents were then asked how often they have encountered each of the 15 narratives (to test H2), and separately, how much they agree with each of them (to test H3). Additionally, the survey asked respondents whether or not they agreed with a series of statements about Ukrainian foreign policy (to test H1). Finally, we collected demographic and geographic data. See the Table 1 below for a full list of control variables.

We then ran a series of (*non-causal*) OLS regressions to calculate the residual correlation between key variables of interest after controlling for demographic and geographic covariates. The guiding intuition of our analysis was that while correlation does not imply causality, *lack of correlation implies lack of causality*. We chose OLS because it counts among the most transparent and best understood regression methods, maximizing the interpretability of our findings across disciplinary boundaries. However, we are aware in Political Science there is a preference for Logit regression for data involving binary indicator variables (such as the survey responses). Accordingly, we re-ran the entire set of regressions using Logit, which did not meaningfully alter results – see regression tables in online appendix, section 2 for reference. In this analysis, after controlling for demographic and geographic variation across rest whether the adoption of each of over a dozen foreign policy preferences, and agreement with each of 15 Russian narratives, correlates with frequent consumption of any of 36 traditional and social media channels.

Consequently, we traced the dissemination of narratives across social media and measure audience reach, building an original dataset of anonymous Telegram content. We include Telegram because emerging research identifies its anonymous channels as key outlets for disinformation (DFRLab, 2020; Osadchuk, 2020) In fact, an investigation by Ukrainian journalists warned of a "Russian invasion of the Ukrainian Telegram segment" because "anonymous channels have become a perfect tool for dissemination of Russian propaganda" (LIGA.net, 2020). A recent analysis by Texy.ua showed Telegram has become "the most popular social network in Ukraine and one of the most dangerous sources of Russian influence" (Drozdova, Dukach, & Kelm, 2022). Accordingly, we pick the five most popular anonymous channels identified in the sources just mentioned and build a dataset of all messages posted to them in the three months preceding the 2020 local elections (July – October 2020). We chose this timeframe since we would expect influence operations to be most active prior to elections. The resulting sample of 165 messages is hand-coded to identify mentions of narratives. We also track the audience size of each channel, as well as of individual messages (to test H5).

Finally, we compare these findings to three partisan TV channels ("112," "NewsOne" and "Zik"). These channels constitute the most important

Table 1. Control variables.

Controls (all binary indicators):	%
Ages 30–44	28.5
Ages 45–59	25.5
Ages 60+	28.0
Urban	66.3
Female	54.5
Married/dating	63.2
Postsecondary technical	55.6
Postsecondary academic	20.3
Employed	45.0
Household econ. status avg/above	43.2
Identify as Ukrainian	83.4
Identify as Russian	6.9

television channels known to disseminate disinformation narratives (Lennon, 2021; VoxUkraine, 2020). We track audience size (to test H5), but we were not able to conduct content analysis of the kind above. The reason is simple: there is no available data on content, and we lack the resources to watch and hand-code TV programming over months to generate such data.

Results

Disinformation narratives

From the [Internews Ukraine] media monitoring project, we identify fifteen distinct disinformation narratives (N1–15) pushed by partisan pundits and disseminated throughout different media. Their content is primarily anti-Western (11 out of 15) rather than pro-Russian (see below):

N1. *The medical reforms of Suprun [former Ukrainian health minister] are against Ukrainians.*

N2. *The Increase of gas prices is a genocide of Ukrainians.*

N3. *The EU uses Ukrainians for low-paid labor.*

N4. *The land reforms [in Ukraine] are driven by Western capitalists who want to buy all Ukrainian land.*

N5. *Ukraine is under external government by Western curators/creditors/"Sorosiata."*

N6. *Zelenskiy continues Poroshenko policies/is totally dependent on the West.*

N7. *Ukraine and Russia are equally responsible for the war in Donbas.*

N8. *The IMF has enslaved Ukraine for its natural resources.*

N9. *George Soros and the IMF want to exploit Ukrainian lands.*

N10. *EU integration has brought no benefits to Ukraine.*

N11. *Far-right movements/nationalists flourishing in Ukraine are a real political threat.*

N12. *The USA curates Ukrainian media/activists/politicians.*

N13. *Anti-corruption reforms are driven by Western capitalists to take over the Ukrainian economy.*

N14. *The West is as corrupt as Ukraine or more.*

N15. *The USA has deployed a network of bio labs in Ukraine.*

Survey findings

We analyzed survey results to test how foreign policy views, and agreement with/exposure to Russian narratives, correlated with media consumption habits, while controlling for demographic and geographic variation. Findings generally supported our hypotheses H1, H2 and H3.

First, survey results support the assumption that influence operations matter in international politics by influencing foreign policy preferences. To test this assumption, codified in H1, we compare the foreign policy preferences of those who agree with narratives versus those who do not. We binarize survey responses for the 15 Russian narratives into agree (1) and disagree (0), and likewise binarize responses for foreign policy preferences (Question 8 in the survey). We then regress the binary agreement variable of each foreign policy statement on the binary agreement variable for each Russian narrative, controlling for demographic and geographic covariates[3]:

$$agree_i = \beta_{fp} \cdot foreign\_policy\_preference_i + oblast_i + \beta \cdot \mathbf{X}_i + \varepsilon_i$$

Due to space constraints, we obviously cannot provide regression tables for each of the 120 regressions we ran, but we have provided a sample table in the online appendix, section 2 (as with all of the subsequent regressions). From each of the 120 regressions (15 narratives x 8 foreign policy preferences), we tally up the number of statistically positive, negative, or insignificant relationships, and tabulate them (see Table 2 below). Findings offer clear support for H1. It is evident that agreement with Russian narratives is correlated with foreign policy preferences that (1) favor alignment with Russia or no alignment at all and (2) disfavor alignment with the West.

Next, for each of the 15 Russian narratives, we tested how narrative exposure is correlated with narrative agreement (H2). If we were to find that exposure and agreement were negatively correlated, or not correlated at all, we could conclude immediately that exposure to Russian narratives is relatively harmless, and so Western fears over social media as a dangerous vector of Russian disinformation are overblown.

Table 2. Narrative agreement and foreign policy preferences[4].

Foreign policy preference	Narrative Correlation Positive correlation	Negative correlation	Insignificant correlation
Ukraine should remain non-aligned	15	0	0
Ukraine and Russia share common heritage	15	0	0
Ukraine should join customs union with Russia	15	0	0
Ukraine and Russian should be closer	15	0	0
Ukraine should join EU	0	12	3
Ukraine should be closer to EU	0	13	2
Ukraine should join NATO	0	14	1
Ukraine should be closer to USA	0	14	1

We regressed a binary indicator for agreement with each Russian narrative on a binary indicator for exposure to that narrative, plus the demographic and geographic controls[5]:

$$agree_i = \beta_{exposed} \cdot exposed_i + oblast_i + \beta \cdot \mathbf{X}_i + \varepsilon_i$$

The fourth column of Table 4 shows the coefficient of interest ($\beta_{exposed}$) for each regression. For all 15 regressions, the coefficients are positive and statistically significant, implying that exposure to narratives is positively correlated with agreement with narratives and thus supporting H2. This finding keeps alive the possibility that exposure causes agreement, but could just as well imply that Ukrainians predisposed to agree with Russian narratives actively seek out pro-Russian media, where they are subsequently exposed to the narratives (agreement causes exposure). Indeed, as columns 2 and 3 of Table 2 indicate, substantially more respondents agreed with the narratives than were ever exposed. In other words, many respondents had never heard these narratives before our survey, but immediately found them plausible. This suggests at the very least that Russian narratives resonate with Ukrainians' predispositions – a finding which complicates any broad claim that Russian influence operations (on social media or otherwise) dupe Ukrainians into changing their beliefs.

Agreement correlates with exposure, but how do agreement and exposure correlate with media consumption? 152 of our respondents (16.8%) reported little to no consumption of *any* of the 36 media we asked about, so we created a *media_consumption* binary variable that took the value 0 for these 152 respondents, and 1 for the rest. Table 3 below lists the results.

For each narrative, we regressed exposure on media consumption, then agreement on media consumption, again controlling for demographic and geographic dummies[6]:

$$agree_i = \beta_{media} \cdot media\_consumption_i + oblast_i + \beta \cdot \mathbf{X}_i + \varepsilon_i$$

$$exposed_i = \beta_{media} \cdot media\_consumption_i + oblast_i + \beta \cdot \mathbf{X}_i + \varepsilon_i$$

We present aggregate results of these 30 individual regressions in Table 4 below.

These findings suggest that those who consume some kind of media (social or otherwise) are more likely to be exposed to Russian narratives, but no more likely to agree with those narratives. By implication, there must be specific types of media, or specific channels, that predict agreement, while the rest do not. We now disaggregate media consumption to explore this, beginning by distinguishing audiences of social media versus television[7]:

Table 3. Narrative exposure and agreement.

Narrative	% exposed	% agree	coefficient*
N17	38.4	52.5	0.38***
N9	36.1	56.3	0.33***
N6	29.3	54.5	0.32***
N11	26.5	38.9	0.34***
N1	24	38.3	0.36***
N13	23.7	35.2	0.41***
N14	23.3	39.2	0.28***
N3	21.5	40.6	0.36***
N2	19.9	37.7	0.31***
N15	19.5	37.3	0.35***
N16	17.2	35.3	0.32***
N5	15.5	33.2	0.34***
N10	14.4	32.2	0.35***
N12	11.5	36.4	0.36***
N4	10.6	24.9	0.38***

Table 4. Media consumption and narratives.

	Exposure	Agreement	Disagreement
Media Consumption	9/15	0/15	2/15

$$agree_i = \beta_{media} \cdot media\_consumption_i + \beta_{TV}$$
$$\cdot TV\_consumption_i + \beta_{SM}$$
$$\cdot SM\_consumption_i + oblast_i + \beta \cdot \mathbf{X}_i + \varepsilon_i$$

$$exposed_i = \beta_{media} \cdot media\_consumption_i + \beta_{TV}$$
$$\cdot TV\_consumption_i + \beta_{SM}$$
$$\cdot SM\_consumption_i + oblast_i + \beta \cdot \mathbf{X}_i$$
$$+ \varepsilon_i$$

The dataset is well suited to this regression: 58% of respondents consume TV regularly, while 52% regularly consume social media, so there is healthy variation for both variables. Likewise, the overlap in these categories is healthy: among social media consumers, 40% do not consume TV; among TV consumers, 45% do not consume social media. Table 6 presents the aggregate results of these 30 regressions:

The findings in Table 5 that distinguishing by media type (social media versus TV) does not help predict narrative agreement. This finding contradicts any sweeping claim that social media is a more dangerous vector than TV, or vice versa. Evidently the consumption of neither medium, prima facie, is predictive of agreement with Russian narratives. But what if we narrow our focus to consumption of partisan social media and TV channels?

We re-run the regressions, this time including a consumption indicator for the five anonymous Telegram Channels and five YouTube channels mentioned above, and another indicator for consumption of the three television channels controlled by pro-Russian oligarch Viktor Medvedchuk.[8]

$$agree_i = \beta_{media} \cdot media\_consumption_i$$
$$+ \beta_{TV} \cdot TV\_consumption_i + \beta_{SM} \cdot SM\_consumption_i$$

Table 5. Media type and agreement.

	Exposure	Agreement	Disagreement
Media Consumption	1/15	0/15	2/15
TV	1/15	2/15	1/15
Social Media	0/15	1/15	0/15

Table 6. Partisan media and narratives.

	Exposure	Agreement	Disagreement
Partisan TV channels	10/15	14/15	0/15
Partisan SM channels	11/15	1/15	0/15
TV consumption	0/15	1/15	5/15
SM consumption	0/15	1/15	0/15
Media consumption	3/15	0/15	2/15

$$+ \beta_{medvechuk} \cdot medvechuk\_consumption_i$$
$$+ \beta_{SM\_partisan} \cdot SM\_partisan\_consumption_i$$
$$+ oblast_i + \beta \cdot \mathbf{X}_i + \varepsilon_i$$

$$exposed_i = \beta_{media} \cdot media\_consumption_i + \beta_{TV}$$
$$\cdot TV\_consumption_i + \beta_{SM}$$
$$\cdot SM\_consumption_i + \beta_{medvechuk}$$
$$\cdot medvechuk\_consumption_i$$
$$+ \beta_{SM\_partisan}$$
$$\cdot SM\_partisan\_consumption_i + oblast_i$$
$$+ \beta \cdot \mathbf{X}_i + \varepsilon_i$$

SM_partisan took the value 1 for 114 respondents (12.6%), a number well above the threshold for making credible statistical inference. Table 6 summarizes the findings.

Consistent with H2 and H3, we find that consumption of partisan TV and partisan social media are both highly predictive of exposure to Russian narratives, but only consumption of partisan TV predicts agreement with those narratives. Could it be, however, that the aggregation of partisan channels into a single binary indicator masks variation by platform? To address these, we further disaggregate our regression into separate indicators of Telegram and Telegram partisan consumption, and YouTube and YouTube partisan consumption:

$$agree_i = \beta_{media} \cdot media\_consumption_i + \beta_{TV} \cdot TV\_consumption_i$$
$$+ \beta_{SM} \cdot SM\_consumption_i + \beta_{medvechuk}$$
$$\cdot medvechuk\_consumption_i + \beta_{telegram}$$
$$\cdot telegram\_consumption_i + \beta_{telegram\_partisan}$$
$$\cdot telegram\_partisan\_consumption_i + \beta_{youtube}$$
$$\cdot youtube\_consumption_i + \beta_{youtube\_partisan}$$
$$\cdot youtube\_partisan\_consumption_i + \beta_{facebook}$$
$$\cdot facebook\_consumption_i + oblast_i + \beta \cdot \mathbf{X}_i + \varepsilon_i$$

$$exposed_i = \beta_{media} \cdot media\_consumption_i + \beta_{TV}$$
$$\cdot TV\_consumption_i + \beta_{SM} \cdot SM\_consumption_i$$
$$+ \beta_{medvechuk} \cdot medvechuk\_consumption_i + \beta_{telegram}$$
$$\cdot telegram\_consumption_i + \beta_{telegram\_partisan}$$
$$\cdot telegram\_partisan\_consumption_i + \beta_{youtube}$$
$$\cdot youtube\_consumption_i + \beta_{youtube\_partisan}$$
$$\cdot youtube\_partisan\_consumption_i + \beta_{facebook}$$
$$\cdot facebook\_consumption_i + oblast_i + \beta \cdot \mathbf{X}_i + \varepsilon_i$$

Table 7 shows that consumption of partisan TV channels is highly correlated with exposure to and agreement with Russian narratives. In contrast, consuming anonymous Telegram channels does not positively correlate with exposure or agreement, and indeed is mildly predictive of

Table 7. Partisan media and narratives (disaggregated).

	Exposure	Agreement	Disagreement
Partisan TV channels	11/15	14/15	0/15
Telegram (partisan)	0/15	0/15	2/15
Telegram (general)	0/15	0/15	2/15
Youtube (partisan)	10/15	0/15	1/15
Youtube (general)	1/15	0/15	1/15
Facebook (general)	0/15	0/15	5/15

Table 8. Telegram channel audience.

Channel	Subscribers
Legitimate	150,011
Resident	101,098
Dark Knight	72,594
Sorosiata	21,194
Joker	83,307
Total	**428,204**

disagreement. These results are broadly congruent with findings for Telegram in general. Audiences of partisan YouTube channels on the other hand exhibit a high rate of exposure to narratives (10 out of 15), and yet they do not show a corresponding rate of agreement (0 out of 15) – raising the possibility, for example, that these channels engage these narratives as a topic of conversation and then debunk or cast doubt upon them. Taken together, these findings run contrary to emergent wisdom that social media is a more effective vector of disinformation than television. While the findings are purely correlative, not causal, they suggest partisan television is if anything the more plausible vector.

Telegram

Anonymous Telegram channels are now widely held to be the most important medium for the dissemination of Russian-sponsored disinformation in Ukraine – yet evidence of Russian sponsorship remains scarce. Until today, only two of the five channels we examined ("The Legitimate" and "Resident") have been attributed to Russian intelligence by Ukraine's intelligence service (SBU Exposes Russian Agent Network, 2021). This ambiguity is in line with the expected ease of secrecy in social media influence operations, supporting H4. The limited reach of these channels, contrary to fears of a "Russian invasion," however, also confirms expectations, in support of H5. Overall, around 13% of survey respondents regularly use Telegram to get their news. However, the five anonymous channels reach a far smaller audience. See Table 8 below for subscriber numbers to the channels tracked in December 2020.

In total, they reach around 428k subscribers – or less than one percent of Ukraine's population of 44 million.

When tracing narrative dissemination through these channels, we found a surprisingly low percentage of coverage. As illustrated in Figure 1, only around 18% of the messages disseminated content aligned with the narratives tracked – surprising, considering these are purportedly key disinformation vectors. Further analysis shows that most content pushing narratives (51%) is concentrated within the channel with by far the lowest audience share, "Sorosiata" (17k subscribers). Figure 2 above shows the numbers of mentions per channel. It is especially surprising the two channels attributed to Russian intelligence show such low percentages (9% and 5%, respectively) of mentions. We do not have an immediate explanation, but this finding does correspond to our expectations concerning the challenges of sustained content dissemination and helps explain the lack of systematic correlation between consumption of these channels and narrative exposure and agreement.

Partisan television

The channels "112," "NewsOne" and 'Zik' counted among the most popular news sources for Ukrainians in 2020 with 1 m regular viewers (Television Industry Committee, 2021). Moreover, over 50% of Ukrainians get their news primarily

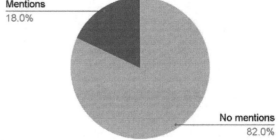

Figure 1. Aggregate mentions of narrative on tracked Telegram channels.

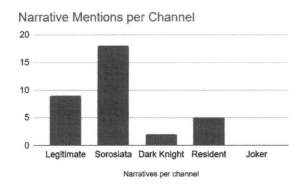

Figure 2. Narrative mentions per Telegram channel tracked.

from one of these three channels (National Council of Television and Radio Broadcasting of Ukraine, 2020). Their superior audience size compared to Telegram channels is in line with H5. In line with this finding, over 20% of respondents to our survey report watching one of these channels regularly. Meanwhile, these channels have a clear and publicly known link to Russia, supporting H1: All three are owned by the oligarch Viktor Medvedchuk, a close ally of Vladimir Putin (Miller, 2016).

Discussion

Findings strongly support our theory, confirming the political relevance of influence operations, television's advantages in dissemination and persuasion compared to social media, as well as the latter's edge in secrecy. Survey analysis showed a clear, statistically significant correlation between narrative exposure, agreement, and foreign policy preferences, in support of H1. These findings do not prove causation. However, the consistent correlation across narratives supports the assumption that influence operations can affect foreign policy preferences. If there was no correlation, the hypothesis would have to be rejected. The rates of statistically significant correlation between consumption of partisan television channels and exposure to narratives was also superior compared to partisan social media channels, supportive of H2. YouTube formed an exception. This exception, however, confirms two key predictions of our framework. YouTube is a centralized platform where videos, once uploaded, can be disseminated to a channel's entire audience, and repeatedly, without added costs. In this respect, it is similar to a traditional television station.

While the difference concerning exposure rates was overall relatively small, findings for narrative agreement were striking. Survey analysis showed a clear and statistically significant correlation between consumption of partisan television channels, exposure to, and agreement with, narratives. In contrast, social media consumption showed either no statistically significant correlation to agreement, or a *negative* correlation. Findings thus strongly support H3, in line with television's expected advantage in persuasion. In short, findings indicate consumption of partisan television channels significantly increases the likelihood audiences agree with narratives and hold corresponding foreign policy preferences, while no such correlation is evident among social media users. Moreover, the absence of any statistically significant correlation between exposure to narratives via YouTube and agreement with these narratives supports another key assumption of our framework: namely, the superior credibility and resulting persuasiveness of television stations compared to social media.

Although our findings do not prove causality, the consistent positive correlations pointed out above suggest a likely causal effect of consuming partisan television on audience foreign policy preferences. Future research is needed to establish the causal relationship. Even if there was a causal effect, however, it is important to consider its limited extent. Regressing foreign policy preference on media consumption shows, for example, that regular watchers of Medvedchuk-controlled TV are only 13% more likely to prefer Ukraine to pursue closer relations to Russia.[9] Accordingly, despite exposure over multiple years, Ukraine's foreign policy and public opinion have not shifted toward Russia's goals – that is, arguably, why Russia invaded in full force in 2022.

Even today, there is no evidence linking three of the five Telegram channels to Russian state-owned sources. In contrast, there is clear and tangible evidence linking the partisan television channels we focused on to the Kremlin since the owner is a close associate of Vladimir Putin. These findings support H4. As expected, Medvedchuk's TV channels also reach a larger audience than the partisan social media channels we examined, supporting H5.

Before moving on to implications, two alternate explanations and criticisms must be considered.

First, one potential rebuttal of our study would be that narratives themselves are irrelevant compared to techniques of amplification enabled by the structure of social media – foremost, the creation of botnets and what social media platforms call "coordinated inauthentic behavior." Yet there is no evidence of such patterns at scale in Ukraine (see online appendix, section 3), while we have shown a clear and measurable effect of narrative exposure on audience perception.

A second criticism would be that the causal mechanism behind the correlation between partisan television exposure and narrative agreement we observe is reversed: citizens select television channels based on their preferences. Our findings indicate this argument is plausible considering narrative agreement substantially outweighs exposure rates among survey respondents – roughly 17.8% of respondents had never/rarely heard narratives yet agreed with them. This finding implies these narratives resonate with the lived experience of many Ukrainians. Hence, it is plausible those Ukrainians gravitate toward consumption of (pro-Russian) media outlets that articulate what they already feel to be true. Even if that is the case, however, it does not explain the lack of the same selection effect and corresponding correlation for audiences of partisan social media channels – especially the two pro-Russian Telegram channels run by Russian military intelligence. Consequently, this reverse causal mechanism may be at play for some respondents concerning some narratives, yet this mechanism alone does not explain the far superior rates of exposure and agreement for television audiences vis-à-vis social media audiences.

Another potential criticism concerns our focus on Telegram, especially considering Facebook and YouTube both have far larger audiences than Telegram—31.8% of survey respondents regular use Facebook, and 30.7% YouTube. Hence, in theory they have a far larger reach and in an ideal world we would have conducted a detailed content analysis. However, in practice this has been impossible for similar reasons as for the partisan television channels discussed above. Content analysis of YouTube videos requires watching and coding by hand – and the six channels we tracked each upload at least 30-60 mins of video per day. Content analysis for all videos on the channels within the same period as for Telegram has simply been beyond our means. Meanwhile, on Facebook most narratives are shared via groups, many of which are invite-only, and more importantly, once they are known to be disinformation sources, Facebook deletes them (Reuters, 2020). We sent multiple requests to the anti-influence team at Facebook requesting access to their data, yet never received a response. Importantly, while we do not have content analysis, the survey analysis does include both Facebook and YouTube in measuring consumption, narrative exposure and agreement correlations. Finally, Twitter allows automated content analysis, yet it counts among the least relevant news sources in Ukraine. In fact, to make sure we are not missing anything, we built a dataset of tweets containing keywords related to the narratives we tracked during the same timeframe, which underlined the platform's irrelevance – instead producing some surprising linkages to American right-wing influencers. See the online appendix, section 3 for a detailed discussion.

Finally, there is the possibility television picks up and amplifies social media content. While we focus on direct control over content production, media organizations may pick up and disseminate narratives from other sources by themselves. This interaction is not only plausible, but has been documented by recent research. One study, for example, shows Fox News picking up and amplifying content from Russian state-controlled media (Gabbatt, 2022). Investigating such possible interactions between social media and traditional media by tracing the "genealogy" of narratives is a key topic deserving further research, especially considering it helps alleviate both media types relative disadvantages.

Conclusion

This article has argued that centralized media, and specifically television, retain important advantages over decentralized social media as vectors for influence operations. Evidence garnered from survey and content analysis provided strong support for our theory, showing partisan television channels to be far more influential than partisan social media channels in exposing audiences to disinformation narratives *and* indicating the former to be more effective in fostering audience agreement with narratives. Findings also supported the assumption that influence operations can shape foreign policy preferences, yet at the same time revealed their limited impact.

Two key implications for world politics follow. First, while we do not dismiss the potential effectiveness of social media in spreading disinformation, findings indicate it is important not to overestimate the threat. Conversely, it is important to consider the continued relevance, and possibly superior effectiveness, of traditional mass media as disinformation vectors. The Ukrainian government's ban imposed on the three partisan television channels we identified as major outlets for disinformation shortly after the conclusion of our study (unrelated to our efforts) provides added support for this conclusion (Office of the President of Ukraine, 2021).[10] So does other emerging research examining the impact of television on audiences (Carter & Carter, 2021).[11]

Second, apart from the relative effectiveness of different media platforms, our findings indicate the overall limitations of influence operations as instruments of power. Although we saw a positive correlation between exposure and agreement with narratives to foreign policy preferences favorable to Russia, there is no evidence indicating any measurable impact of sustained exposure to disinformation campaigns on Ukraine's foreign policy. Despite a barrage of disinformation targeting Ukrainian audiences over several years, Ukraine's has maintained its pro-EU and overall pro-Western course. Russia's invasion this year attests to the failure of its strategy of getting Ukraine to change course with measures short of war, in which disinformation has been a key element.

Finally, the limitations of the study must be considered. A single case limits generalizability. However, this conflict's characteristics as a crucial case do indicate global relevance of findings. Another caveat is the availability of traditional mass media vulnerable to compromise and co-optation as instruments of disinformation dissemination in Ukraine. Where such vulnerable media platforms are not available, the global reach of most social media platforms offers a key advantage. In other words, social media allows states to establish influence where traditional media is unavailable. Under what conditions this influence can achieve measurable impacts on foreign policy outcomes remains unclear, however. Importantly, even this paradigmatic case shows no significant impact on foreign policy.

Notes

1. To be discussed in detail in the next section.
2. See online appendix, section 1 for further details.
3. Note, as with all regressions in this paper, we do not ascribe a causal interpretation to the results.
4. Numbers were calculated by regressing an agreement binary (0=disagree, 1=agree) for each of the foreign policy preferences on an agreement binary for each of the Russian narratives, controlling for age, education, gender, marital status, employment status, ethnic identity, liberality, and oblast.
5. See online appendix, section 2 for a sample regression table.
6. See online appendix, section 2 for a sample regression table.
7. See online appendix, section 2 for a sample regression table.
8. See online appendix, section 2 for a sample regression table.
9. Statistically significant positive correlation, coefficient of 13.23.
10. Office of the President of Ukraine, "Ukraine's International Partners Support the Decision of the National Security and Defense Council to Impose Sanctions against a Number of TV Channels – President," Official website of the President of Ukraine, https://www.president.gov.ua/en/news/mizhnarodni-partneri-ukrayini-pidtrimuyut-rishennya-rnbo-pro-66377.
11. Carter and Carter, "Questioning More.."

Acknowledgement

The authors are grateful for constructive feedback on previous drafts of this article by Ron Deibert, Myriam Dunn-Cavelty, Rob Faris, Andrew Guess, Melissa Lee, Gabrielle Lim, Enzo Nussio, James Shires, Nina Silove, Andreas Wenger as well as the participants of the panel on "Influence Operations and Disinformation in the Digital Age" at ISA 2022, and the participants of the CSS Kolloqium in 2021. Their comments helped make this article stronger and clearer. Furthermore, the authors are indebted to Roman Kolodii and Mariya Green for their excellent research assistance.

Disclosure statement

No potential conflict of interest was reported by the author(s).

References

Abrahams, A., & Leber, A. (2021). Comparative approaches to mis/disinformation| electronic armies or cyber knights? The sources of pro-authoritarian discourse on middle east Twitter."|"Comparative approaches to mis/disinformation| Electronic armies or cyber knights? The sources of pro-authoritarian discourse on middle east Twitter. *International Journal of Communication*, 15(0), 27.

Almond, G. A. (1956). Public opinion and national security policy. *Public Opinion Quarterly*, 20(2), 371–378. doi:10.1086/266634

Andrew, C. M. (2000). *The Mitrokhin archive : The KGB in Europe and the West*. London: Allen Lane.

Andrew, C. M., & Mitrokhin, V. (1999). *The sword and the shield: The Mitrokhin archive and the secret history of the KGB* (1st ed.). New York: Basic Books.

Axelrod, R. (1967). THE structure of public opinion on policy issues. *Public Opinion Quarterly*, 31(1), 51–60. doi:10.1086/267481

Bauer, P. C., & von Hohenberg, B. C. (2020). Believing and sharing information by fake sources: An experiment. *Political Communication*, 0(0), 1–25. doi:10.1080/10584609.2020.1840462

Behr, R. L., & Iyengar, S. (1985). Television news, real-world cues, and changes in the public agenda. *Public Opinion Quarterly*, 49(1), 38–57. doi:10.1086/268900

Bennett, W. L., & Livingston, S. (2018). The disinformation order: Disruptive communication and the decline of democratic institutions. *European Journal of Communication*, 33(2), 122–139. doi:10.1177/0267323118760317

Bisen, A. (2019). *Disinformation is drowning democracy*. Foreign Policy (blog). https://foreignpolicy.com/2019/04/24/disinformation-is-drowning-democracy/ .

Bittman, L. (1985). *The KGB and soviet disinformation: An insider's view*. Washington: Pergamon-Brassey's.

Bradshaw, S., Howard, P. N., Kollanyi, B., & Neudert, L.M. (2020). Sourcing and automation of political news and information over social media in the United States, 2016-2018. *Political Communication*, 37(2), 173–193. doi:10.1080/10584609.2019.1663322

Callanan, J. (2009). *Covert action in the cold war: US policy, intelligence and CIA operations*. London ; New York: I.B. Tauris.

Carter, E. B., & Carter, B. L. (2021). Questioning more: RT, outward-facing propaganda, and the post-west world order. *Security Studies*, 0(0), 1–30. doi:10.1080/09636412.2021.1885730

Chivvis, C. S. (2017). *Understanding Russian 'hybrid warfare'*. RAND Corporation. https://www.rand.org/content/dam/rand/pubs/testimonies/CT400/CT468/RAND_CT468.pdf.

Correspondent, Tom Knowles, Technology. (2023, April 18). *Print and broadcast media more trusted than social*, sec. news. https://www.thetimes.co.uk/article/print-and-broadcast-media-more-trusted-than-social-2xp53mk05.

Deibert, R. J. (2020). *Reset: Reclaiming the internet for civil society*. Toronto, Canada: House of Anansi Press.

DFRLab. (2017). *#botspot: Twelve ways to spot a bot*. https://medium.com/dfrlab/botspot-twelve-ways-to-spot-a-bot-aedc7d9c110c.

DFRLab. (2020, February 24). *Anonymous Ukrainian telegram channels serve as gateways to fringe media - Atlantic council's DFRLab*. Atlantic Council (blog)https://www.atlanticcouncil.org/commentary/article/anonymous-ukrainian-telegram-channels-serve-as-gateways-to-fringe-media/

Drozdova, Y., Dukach, Y., & Kelm, N. (2022). *Telegram occupation. How Russia wanted to breed a media monster, but ended up with a paper tiger*. Texty.ua. https://texty.org.ua/projects/108161/telegram-occupation-how-russia-wanted-breed-media-monster-ended-paper-tiger/.

Dunbar, R. I. M. (2021). Do online social media cut through the constraints that limit the size of offline social networks? *Royal Society Open Science*, 3(1), 150292. doi:10.1098/rsos.150292

Fitton, O. (2016). Cyber operations and gray zones: Challenges for NATO. *Connections*, 15(2), 109–119. doi:10.11610/Connections.15.2.08

Gabbatt, A. (2022, February 26). *Tucker Carlson leads rightwing charge to blame everyone but Putin*. The Guardian, sec. Media. https://www.theguardian.com/media/2022/feb/25/tucker-carlson-fox-news-russia-putin.

Gearhart, S., & Kang, S. (2014). Social media in television news: The effects of Twitter and Facebook comments on journalism. *Electronic News*, 8(4), 243–259. doi:10.1177/1931243114567565

Godson, R., & Shultz, R. (1985). Soviet active measures: Distinctions and definitions. *Defense Analysis*, 1(2), 101–110. doi:10.1080/07430178508405191

Hill, T. M. (2017, November 21). *Is the U.S. serious about countering Russia's information war on democracies?* Brookings (blog). https://www.brookings.edu/blog/order-from-chaos/2017/11/21/is-the-u-s-serious-about-countering-russias-information-war-on-democracies/ .

Howard, P. N. (2020). *Lie machines: How to save democracy from troll armies, deceitful robots, junk news operations, and political operatives*. New Haven: Yale University Press.

Internews Ukraine. (2020). *USAID-internews 2020 media consumption survey*. https://internews.in.ua/wp-content/uploads/2018/09/2018-MediaConsumSurvey_eng_FIN.pdf.

Jones, M. O. (2021). *Digital authoritarianism in the Middle East: Deception, disinformation and social media*. London: S.l.: Hurst & Company.

Just, N., & Latzer, M. (2017). Governance by algorithms: Reality construction by algorithmic selection on the internet. *Media, Culture & Society, 39*(2), 238–258. doi:10.1177/0163443716643157

Kertzer, J. D., & Zeitzoff, T. (2017). A bottom-up theory of public opinion about foreign policy. *American Journal of Political Science, 61*(3), 543–558. doi:10.1111/ajps.12314

Lazer, D. M. J., Baum, M. A., Benkler, Y., Berinsky, A. J., Greenhill, K. M., Menczer, F., Metzger, M. J., Nyhan B., Pennycook G., Rothschild D., Schudson M. (2018). The science of fake news. *Science, 359*(6380), 1094–1096. doi:10.1126/science.aao2998

Lennon, O. (2021). *Kennan cable no. 45: Six reasons the 'opposition platform' Won in Eastern Ukraine*. 45. Kennan Cable. Wilson Center. https://www.wilsoncenter.org/publication/kennan-cable-no-45-six-reasons-the-opposition-platform-won-eastern-ukraine .

LIGA.net. (2020). *Telegram. How the anonymous empire of Pavel Durov works*. https://project.liga.net/projects/durov_telegram_eng/.

Linvill, D. L., & Warren, P. L. (2020). Troll factories: Manufacturing specialized disinformation on Twitter. *Political Communication, 37*(4), 447–467. doi:10.1080/10584609.2020.1718257

Lowenthal, M. M. (2009). *Intelligence: From secrets to policy* (4th ed.). Washington, D.C: CQ Press.

Lustig, C., Pine, K., Nardi, B., Irani, L., Kyung Lee, M., Nafus, D., & Sandvig, C. (2016). Algorithmic authority: The ethics, politics, and economics of algorithms that interpret, decide, and manage. *Proceedings of the 2016 CHI Conference Extended Abstracts on Human Factors in Computing Systems* (pp. 1057–1062). CHI EA '16. New York, NY, USA: Association for Computing Machinery. doi: 10.1145/2851581.2886426.

Martin, D. A., Shapiro, J. A., & Nedashkovskaya, M. (2019). Recent trends in online foreign influence efforts. *Journal of Information Warfare, 18*(3), 15–48.

Mehrabi, D., Hassan, M., Sham, M., & Sham Shahkat Ali, M. (2009, November). News media credibility of the internet and television. *European Journal of Social Sciences, 11*(1).

Miller, C. (2016). *Behind the scenes in Ukraine, ties to Putin help power broker pull strings*. RadioFreeEurope/RadioLiberty. https://www.rferl.org/a/ukraine-medvedchuk-putin-prince-darkness-gray-cardinal/27943679.html.

Min, B., & Luqiu, L. R. (2021). How propaganda techniques leverage their advantages: A cross-national study of the effects of Chinese international propaganda on the U.S. and South Korean audiences. *Political Communication, 38*(3), 305–325. doi:10.1080/10584609.2020.1763524

National Council of Television and Radio Broadcasting of Ukraine. (2020, January 24). *Рейтинги Телеканалів Серед Користувачів IPTV/OTT у III Кварталі 2019 Року*. Національна Рада України з Питань Телебачення і Радіомовлення. https://www.nrada.gov.ua/rejtyngy-telekanaliv-sered-korystuvachiv-iptv-ott-u-iii-kvartali-2019-roku/.

Noelle-Neumann, E. (1993). *The spiral of silence: Public opinion–our social skin*. Chicago: University of Chicago Press.

Office of the President of Ukraine. (2021, February 5). *Ukraine's international partners support the decision of the national security and defense council to impose sanctions against a number of TV channels - President*. Official Website of the President of Ukraine. https://www.president.gov.ua/en/news/mizhnarodni-partneri-ukrayini-pidtrimuyut-rishennya-rnbo-pro-66377.

Osadchuk, R. (2020, September 1). *How Pro-Kremlin telegram channels influence Ukrainian parliamentary decisions*. Medium (blog). https://medium.com/dfrlab/how-pro-kremlin-telegram-channels-influence-ukrainian-parliamentary-decisions-791ac939cdd.

Pariser, E. (2012). *The filter bubble: How the new personalized web is changing what we read and how we think* (Reprint ed.). London: Penguin Books.

Pfetsch, B. (2018). Dissonant and disconnected public spheres as challenge for political communication research. *Javnost - the Public, 25*(1–2), 59–65. doi:10.1080/13183222.2018.1423942

Pomerantsev, P., & Weiss, M. (2014). *The menace of unreality: How the Kremlin weaponizes information, culture and money*. The Interpreter & Institute of Modern Russia. http://www.interpretermag.com/wp-content/uploads/2014/11/The_Menace_of_Unreality_Final.pdf.

Reis, J. C. S., Correia, A., Murai, F., Veloso, A., & Benevenuto, F. (2019). Supervised learning for fake news detection. *IEEE Intelligent Systems, 34*(2), 76–81. doi:10.1109/MIS.2019.2899143

Reuters. (2020, February 12). *Facebook says it dismantles Russian intelligence operation targeting Ukraine*. sec. Media and Telecoms. https://www.reuters.com/article/us-russia-facebook-idUSKBN2061NC

Rival IQ. (2021). *2021 Social media industry benchmark report*. https://www.rivaliq.com/blog/social-media-industry-benchmark-report/.

Robbins, J. (2021). *Countering Russian disinformation*. Center for Strategic and International Studies. https://www.csis.org/blogs/post-soviet-post/countering-russian-disinformation.

Salaudeen, M. A., & Onyechi, N. (2020). Digital media vs mainstream media: Exploring the influences of media exposure and information preference as correlates of media credibility. Edited by Martina Topic. *Cogent Arts & Humanities*, *7*(1), 1837461. 10.1080/23311983.2020.1837461

SBU Exposes Russian Agent Network. (2021, February 1). SSU. https://ssu.gov.ua/en/novyny/sbu-vykryla-ahenturnu-merezhu-spetssluzhb-rf-yaka-destabilizuvala-sytuatsiiu-v-ukraini-cherez-telegramkanaly.

Shultz, R. H., & Godson, R. (1984). *Dezinformatsia: Active measures in soviet strategy*. Washington: Pergamon-Brassey's.

Soroka, S. N. (2003). Media, public opinion, and foreign policy. *Harvard International Journal of Press/politics*, *8*(1), 27–48. doi:10.1177/1081180X02238783

Television Industry Committee. (2021, March 29). *Top-channels TB*. TB. http://tampanel.com.ua/en/rubrics/canals/ .

Tsfati, Y., Boomgaarden, H. G., Strömbäck, J., Vliegenthart, R., Damstra, A., & Lindgren, E. (2020). Causes and consequences of mainstream media dissemination of fake news: Literature review and synthesis. *Annals of the International Communication Association*, *44*(2), 157–173. doi:10.1080/23808985.2020.1759443

VoxUkraine. (2020, March 23). *Smells like Medvedchuk, Kremlin Propaganda and Soviet Union*. VoxUkraine (blog). https://voxukraine.org/en/smells-like-medvedchuk-kremlin-propaganda-and-soviet-union/.

Warner, M. (2019). A matter of trust: Covert action reconsidered. *Studies in Intelligence*, *63*, 4. https://www.cia.gov/library/center-for-the-study-of-intelligence/csi-publications/csi-studies/studies/vol-63-no-4/pdfs/Covert-Action-Reconsidered.pdf

Zimmermann, F., & Kohring, M. (2020). Mistrust, disinforming news, and vote choice: A panel survey on the origins and consequences of believing disinformation in the 2017 German parliamentary election. *Political Communication*, *37*(2), 215–237. doi:10.1080/10584609.2019.1686095

Zuboff, S. (2015). Big other: Surveillance capitalism and the prospects of an information civilization. *Journal of Information Technology; Basingstoke*, *30*(1), 75–89. doi:10.1057/jit.2015.5

Index

Note: Figures are indicated by *italics*. Tables are indicated by **bold**. Endnotes are indicated by the page number followed by 'n' and the endnote number e.g., 20n1 refers to endnote 1 on page 20.

Abrahams, A. 139
Adamczewska, K. 61
Ahmed, S. 95
Albrecht, E. 110, 117
Alexander, N. 110, 118
audience logic journalists: Albania and Kosovo 77, 81, 84, 85, 87 coding categories 81–2; content analysis 81; data contradict theoretical predictions 87; democratic value, audience engagement 77–8; digital media transformations 77; election coverage, Facebook 84–6; election news coverage 80–1, 88; election news production **80**; election reporting 78–9; Facebook engagement 82–4, **83**, **84**, 86; Facebook's news feed algorithm 76, 88; in-depth interviews 82; market logic 87; negativity 79; news gap 76; personalization 79; social media engagement 77; social media gap 87; socio-political context 87

Bailard, C. S. 14, 21, 22
Bene, M. 26
Bennett, W. L. 119n5
Bergmann, Z. 110
Bonacci, D. 65
Bordewijk, J. L. 62
Bossetta, M. 9

Camaj, L. 76
Castro Herrero, L. 95
Čejková, L. 92
Çela, E. 76
central and eastern Europe (CEE): climate change-oriented movement 4; democracy Index rankings **2**; democracy scores **3**; democratic market economies 1; EU's approach 3; international literature countries 4; market economies 1; media logic/audience logic theoretical approaches 4; pandemic challenges 2; populist politicians 1; sharp digital divides 1; Ukrainian/Russian language, participant use 137–8
Ceron, A. 26
Cho, J. 95
Choi, Y. J. 95
Christian-conservative ideology 117, 118
climate change-oriented movement, Czechia/Hungary: conservative green politics 118; Czech Republic 9, 15; FFF 108; public sphere 118
conservative green politics 118
Court of Justice of the European Union (CJEU) 43

democracy: illiberal populism 10; index ranking **2**; liberal 3, 11; positive effects 14; quality 11, 14; satisfaction 15; scores, changes **3**; SNS users 10, 12, *13*; VDEM indices 10
democratic backsliding 43
dissemination algorithms 77, 139, 141–3
Doroshenko, L. 122

e-expression 107
Eigmüller, M. 43
electoral democracy 3, 16
Ennser-Jedenastik, L. 26
Erbe, J. 45, 46
Esser, F. 95
Europeanization *see* print media

Facebook: 3, 4, 12, 26, 28, 32, 38
far-right messages, emotions: anger/anxiety 125–6; ANOVA models **129**; anti-elitism 124; anti-system 123; emotions, issue **132**; enthusiasm 125–6, 132; expressive activities 123, 124–5; expressive activities, issues **130**; go viral, social media 133; interaction effect **131**; media gate-keepers 122; message amplification, social media 122; message-issue interaction effect 127–9; message-type effect 124; multilevel mediation model **130**; nationalism 123; political engagement 122; populist parties 124; post-Euromaidan Ukraine 126–7; psychological mechanism 122; results 129–33; social media amplification activities 123; social media communication 132
Fridays for Future's (FFF) 108

general council of the judiciary (CGPJ) 44

Hiaeshutter-Rice, D. 30
Hrbková, L. 92
Huttunen, J. 110, 117
hybrid war, Ukraine: archetypical 20th century mass medium 140; dissemination of disinformation 139; influence operations 139; partisan television 148–9, 151; Russo-Ukrainian conflict 143, *144*; social and traditional media 143; social media accounts 142; surveillance capital 141; Telegram 148; 903 Ukrainians, survey 140

information and communication technology (ICT) 11

Jackson, D. 26
Jensen, K. B. 72n2
journalists/politicians communication strategy: analyzed social networks 68, **68**; CEE countries, social media 64–6; election campaigns 61; hidden relationship 61; information flow model 62–3, **62**; methods 66–8; network 69; parliamentary election, Poland 66, 72n5; passive strategy 61; patterns of information flow 69, *69*, 70; political posts, Twitter/Facebook 67; reaction/conversation pattern **70**; SNA 68, 71; social media 63–4, 71; traditional media 61
judicial reforms 44
Jurišić, J. 65

Kaushik, K. 43
Kerum, H. 95

Kingdon, J. W. 46
Koopmans, R. 45, 46

Lee, J. H. 95
Lee, S. 95
liberal democracy: 11, 16, 22, 122, 123
Lilleker, D. 26
López-Rabadán, P. 72n3

Macková, A. 92
Maschmeyer, L. 139
Matthes, C.-Y. 47
Mazák, J. 12
McDowall, A. 110, 118
McMillan, S. J. 72n2
Mellado, C. 72n3
mirror holding 14, 15, 21, 22
Mishler, W. 14
mixed-effect models 133n2
Molyneux, L. 64
Mourão, R. R. 64

Neag, A. 107
negative messages, Facebook: amplification strategy 27–9; coded posts **31**; communication channels 26; communication strategies 38; data/analysis 31–2; distribution of posts *33*; electoral campaigning 26; electoral communication 27; European elections 39; increasing voter's search 26; median post shares *33, 34, 37*; negative/positive statements, posts 32–4; party characteristics 27, 29–30, 34–7; political choices 26; sample/data collection 30–1; Twitter/Instagram 39; type of election 38
Novotná, M. 92
Nuernbergk, C. 64

online media 13, 47, 51, 61, 64
Ossewaarde, R 110

partisan-based affective polarization: affective political polarization 93; context-based differences 93; Czechia 94, 102; disagreement/negativity, SNS 95–6, 102, 103; high-choice media environment 97–8; higher political interest 97–8; individual media practices 93; methodology 98–9; political antagonism 93, 101, 102; regression analysis, results 99–101, **100**; selective avoidance/attitudinal homogeneity, SNS 94, 96–7; SNS 92; partisan television channels 140, 143, 149, 151
Petray, T. 110, 118
Placek, M. 9, 22
political campaigning *see* negative campaigning, Facebook
Pomerantsev, P. 139
print media: cross-national/cross-media research design 47–8; data collection/operationalization 48–9; EU actors 52, 54; Germany 48; hybrid media system 46–7, 54; IoJ value 43, 49, 52, 53; legacy/social media *49*; Europeanization levels, Germany/Poland/Spain *49*; offline media 44; political agenda-setting 46–7; robust justice system 43; social media 51–2; traditional media 49–51; Twitter 53; value conflicts/media debates 44–6

Rafaeli, S. 62
Rainie, L. 99
Rega, R. 64
restricted maximum likelihood estimation (REML) 129, 133n2
Rexha, G. 76

Rojas, H. 95
Rose, R. 14
Rosenfeldová, J. 107

Smith, A. 99
social networking sites (SNS) 92; Bailard's theory 14; control variables 17; country democracy rating 16; Czechia 92; data/methods 15; democracy rating 18; democracy satisfaction 15–16; democratic backsliding 10–11, 16; democratic conditions, changing 9; five-year change, democracy rating 20, 21, 20; ICT 11; internet access, CEE 11, 11–12; one-year change, democracy rating 18, 19, 19; online media/political attitudes 12–13; populism, and support 10–11; pro-democratic movements 22; quality of democracy 20; social media use 16; social media/democracy interactions 17; VDEM 10; window opening/mirror holding functions 14, 15, 21, 22
social media: case study 143; control variables **144**; disinformation 139, 145; emerging wisdom 139; foreign policy **146**, 149, 151; hypothesis 142–3, 149; media type and agreement **147**; methodology 144–5; narrative agreement/foreign policy preferences 146; narrative exposure and agreement **146**; partisan media/narratives **147**, **148**; partisan television channels 140, 148–50; survey results 145–8; technology/media structure 140–2; Telegram 148, **148**, 149, 150; tracked Telegram channel *148, 149*; Ukraine, new evidence 140
Steppat, D. 95
Stetka, V. 12
Surowiec, P. 12

Telegram channels 140, 147, 148, **148**, **149**, 150
television 94, 140
Treaty of the European Union (TEU) 43
Tu, F. 122

United Nations World Development Indicators (WDI) 10

Vaccari, C. 96
Valeriani, A. 96
van Kaam, B. 62
Vancsó, A. 107
Vesnic-Alujevic, L. 65
Vochocová, L. 107

Wallaschek, S. 43
Weeks, B. 30
window opening 14, 15, 21, 22

Yamamoto, M. 95
Yermolenko, V. 139
youth activists: childism approach 107–10; digital technologies 107; direct environmental protection 113–14; e-expression 107; exclusion strategies *112*; FFF 108, 118, 119; labeling strategies 112; labelling 115–17; leftists/liberals 115–17; methodology 111–12; negative portrayal, media 110–11; online spaces 107; plant trees 113; political action 113; political-discursive inclusion 107; politically active 114–15; role-based exclusion 117; social movements 107; sustainable lifestyle frame 117; traditional parliamentary systems 107; truancy frame 117; value-based exclusion 117
YouTube 140, 144, 147, 149, 150

Zaller, J. 14